ALSO BY JULIAN BARNES

England, England

Cross Channel

Letters from London

The Porcupine

Talking It Over

A History of the World in 10½ Chapters

Staring at the Sun

Flaubert's Parrot

Before She Met Me

Metroland

Love, etc.

Something to Declare

JULIAN BARNES

Something to Declare

Essays on France

Alfred A. Knopf   *New York*   2002

THIS IS A BORZOI BOOK
PUBLISHED BY ALFRED A. KNOPF

www.aaknopf.com

Originally published in Great Britain by Picador, London.

Knopf, Borzoi Books, and the colophon are registered
trademarks of Random House, Inc.

ISBN: 0-375-41513-0
LCCN: 2002109567

Manufactured in the United States of America
First American Edition

A. L. B.

1909–1992

K. M. B.

1915–1997

Contents

Contents

Illustrations

Preface

I first went to France in the summer of 1959 at the age of thirteen. My pre-adolescence had been car-free and island-bound; now there stood in front of our house a gun-metal-grey Triumph Mayflower, bought secondhand, suddenly affordable thanks to a £200 grant from Great Aunt Edie. It struck me then—as any car would have done—as deeply handsome, if perhaps a little too boxy and sharp-edged for true elegance; last year, in a poll of British autophiles, it was voted one of the ten ugliest cars ever built. Registration plate RTW1, red leather upholstery, walnut dashboard, no radio, and a blue metal RAC badge on the front. (The RAC man, portly and moustachioed, with heavy patched boots and a subservient manner, had arrived to enrol us. His first, preposterous question to my father—"Now, sir, how many cars have you got?"—passed into quiet family myth.) That cars were intended not just for safe commuting but also for perilous voyage was endorsed by the Triumph's subtitle, and further by its illustrative hubcaps: at their centre was an emblematic boss depicting, in blue and red enamel, a Mercator projection of the globe.

Our first expedition was from suburban Middlesex to provincial France. At Newhaven we watched nervously as the Mayflower was slung by crane with routine insouciance over our heads and down into the ferry's hold. The metal RAC badge at the front was now matched by a metal GB plate at the rear. My mother drove; my father map-read and performed emergency hand-signals; my brother and I sat in the back and worried. Over the next few summers we would loop our way through different regions of France, mostly avoiding large cities and always avoiding Paris. We would visit châteaux and churches, grottoes and museums, inducing in me a lifelong phobia for the guided tour. I was the official photographer, first in black-and-white (home processed), later in colour transparency. My parents tended to feature only when the view-finder's vista seemed dull; then, remembering the dictates of *Amateur Photographer*, I would summon them to provide "foreground interest." We picnicked at lunchtime and towards five o'clock would start looking for a small hotel; the red Michelin was our missal. In those days, as soon as you left the Channel ports behind, the roads were empty of non-French cars; when you saw another GB coming in your direction, you would wave (though never, in our family, hoot).

That first, monstrous expedition into the exotic was a gentle tour of Normandy. From Dieppe we drove to Cany-Barville, of which I remember only two things: a vast and watery soup pullulating with some non-British grain or pulse; and being sent out on my first foreign morning for the newspaper. Which one did they want? Oh, just get the local one, my father replied unhelpfully. I had the normal adolescent's self-consciousness—that's to say, one that weighs like a stone-filled rucksack and feels of a different order from everyone else's. It was a heroic journey across the street and towards the shop, imperilled at every step by garlic-chewing low-lifes who drank red wine for breakfast and cut their bread—and youngsters' throats—with pocket knives. *"Le journal de la région,"* I repeated mantrically to myself, *"Le journal de la région, le journal de la région."* I no longer remember if I even uttered the words, or just flung my coins at some nicotined child-molester with a cry of "Keep the change." All I remember is the purity of my fear, the absoluteness of my embarrassment, and the lack of vivid praise from my parents on my safe return.

From Cany-Barville to Thury-Harcourt: did all French villages have such solemn hyphenation? None of that Something-upon-Whatsit, Thingummy-in-the-Tum-Tum. Cany-Barville, Thury-Harcourt: this was different, grave. Thereafter, my memories become slighter, more banal; perhaps not even memories, but half-forgotten impressions revived by photographs. A brown-beamed coaching inn, a rough-fleeced donkey in a rough-grassed park, my first squat French château with pepperpot towers (Combourg), my first soaring ditto (Josselin). Then first viewings of Chartres, the Bayeux Tapestry, and Chateaubriand's aqueous tomb. On the tranquil roads we mingled with traffic of lustrous oddity. French cars were very unMayflowery: curved in the weirdest places, coloured according to a different palette, and often formidably eccentric—witness the Panhard. They had corrugated butchers' vans, Deux Chevaux with canvas stacker seats, Maigret Citroëns, and later the otherworldly DS, whose initials punned on divinity.

And then there was the formidable eccentricity of the food. Their butter was wanly unsalted, blood came out of their meat, and they would put anything, absolutely anything, into soup. They grew perfectly edible tomatoes and then doused them in foul vinaigrette; ditto lettuce, ditto carrots, ditto beetroot. Normally you could detect that foul vinaigrette had been slimed over the salad; but sometimes they fooled you by slurping it into the bottom of the bowl, so that when with hopeful heart you lifted a leaf from the top . . . Bread was good (but see butter); chips were good (but see meat); vegetables were unpredictable. What were those things that weren't proper runner beans but round, fat, overcooked, and—cold! There was pâté: forget it, anything could have gone into that; though not as anything as the anything that went into their gristly, warty *saucissons,* assembled from the disposings of an axe murderer. There was cheese. No, there were thousands of cheeses, and I would eat only one of them—Gruyère. Fruit was reliable—not much they could do to ruin that; indeed, they grew very large and juicy red apples you could positively look forward to. They liked onions far too much. They brushed their teeth with garlic paste. They camouflaged quite edible meat and fish with sauces of dubious origin and name. Then there was wine, which bore a close resemblance to vinaigrette; and coffee, which I hated. Occasionally there would be a noxious, unassessable dish which explained all too well what you found and smelt behind the teak-stained door of *les waters*, where gigantic feet in knobbed porcelain awaited you, followed by a gigantic flush which drenched your turn-ups.

Where does your love of France come from, Monsieur Barnes? Oh, I reply, both my parents taught French; I went to France with them on holiday; I read French at school and university; I taught for a year at a Catholic school in Rennes (where my gastronomic conservatism was unpicked); my favourite writer is Flaubert; many of my intellectual reference points are French; and so on. It does the job as an answer; but it's an untruthfully smooth narrative. Those early holidays were filled with anxiety (would anyone understand a word I said? would my father get ratty in the heat? would we fail to find a hotel room with twin beds, since my brother, no doubt for good reason, declined to bunk down with me?). Later, in the long silent quarrel and *faux* existentialism of late adolescence, I took against my parents' values and therefore against their love of France. At university I gave up languages for philosophy, found myself ill-equipped for it, and returned reluctantly to French. In my twenties, other countries appealed more. It was only in my thirties that I started seeing France again with non-filial, non-academic eyes.

Doubtless there was an element of cultural snobbery in my initial preference for things Gallic: their Romantics seemed more romantic than ours, their Decadents more decadent, their Moderns more modern. Rimbaud versus Swinburne was simply no contest; Voltaire seemed just smarter than Dr. Johnson. Some of these early judgements were correct: it wasn't hard—or wrong—to prefer French cinema of the Sixties to ours. And culture maintained my relationship with France in those years of separation: books, art, song, films, sport. Later, when I began returning to France regularly, it was often to the kind of France—provincial, villagey, under-populated—that my parents preferred. My automatic images of "being in France" are initially pictorial: quiet canals lined with trees as regular as comb-teeth; a hunched bridge across shallow, pebbly water; dormant vines resting their flayed arms on taut wires; a scatter of fowl panicking on a dung-strewn back road; morning mist shifting like dry ice around a fat hayrick. And when my images stop being pastoral, they do not change much in key: not to Paris or the larger cities or some yelping exhibitionist beach, but to quiet working villages with rusting café tables, lunchtime torpor, pollarded plane-trees, the dusty thud of boules, and an all-purpose *épicerie;* here a house-wall still bears a faded DUBO, DUBON, DUBONNET and a war memorial lists the brutal necropolis of 1914–18. Not much agri-business here; not much rural unemployment visible. Where are your stroppy farmers and your goitered drunks? Don't forget that the mayor's wife writes poison pen letters, and there was a nasty unsolved murder down by the picturesquely disused *lavoir.* Fill in, beneath those pollarded trees, the chaotically parked cars, the patient Malian with his blanketful of bangles, the back-blast of a thunderous lorry; erase the *épicerie* and replace it with the out-of-town supermarket. Yes, but I like most of that too.

Is my view of France partial? Certainly. Knowing a second country means choosing what you want from it, finding antitheses to your normal, English, urban life; discarding the sense of responsibility you feel about your own country, giving yourself a rest from the bilious emotions stirred by your own public representatives. My partial France is provincial in topography and contrarian in spirit; a France of the regions rather than the centre, of José Bové rather than sleek-suited Eurocrat, of Cathar martyr rather than papal legate. The cultural period I am constantly drawn back to is roughly 1850–1925, from the culmination of Realism to the fission of Modernism: a wondrous stretch not just for French culture but also for French cultural hospitality. It still seems miraculous that a well-connected Parisian could, within the space of fifteen years, have examined the still-wet *Demoiselles d'Avignon,* attended the première of *The Rite of Spring,* and bought a first edition of *Ulysses,* all without having to catch the Métro, let alone a steamer.

Central for me in the development of the modern sensibility

is the figure of Gustave Flaubert. "I wish he'd *shut up* about Flaubert," Kingsley Amis, with pop-eyed truculence, once complained to a friend of mine. Fat chance: Flaubert, the writer's writer *par excellence,* the saint and martyr of literature, the perfector of realism, the creator of the modern novel with *Madame Bovary,* and then, a quarter of a century later, the assistant creator of the modernist novel with *Bouvard et Pécuchet.* According to Cyril Connolly, *Bouvard et Pécuchet* was Joyce's favourite novel (Richard Ellmann thought this probable, if lacking documentary proof). Not Shutting Up About Flaubert—see the second half of this book—remains a necessary pleasure. When the *Times Literary Supplement* sent me the fourth volume of his *Correspondance* for review in 1998, the semi-satirical comp-slip tucked into the book read, "Could we have a million words, please (by April 13, if possible)?"

In *Bouvard et Pécuchet* there is a scene in which the two antiheroes visit Fécamp. They walk along the shoreline, and Pécuchet, who has temporarily turned geologist, speculates on the consequences of an earthquake beneath the English Channel. The water, he explains to his friend, would rush out into the Atlantic, the coastlines would begin to totter, and then the two land-masses would shuffle across and reunite after all these millennia. Bouvard, terrified by the prospect, runs away—as much, you might conclude, at the notion of the British coming any nearer as at the catastrophe itself.

Despite our membership in the European Union, despite the Channel Tunnel's visual abolition of water and cliff, some of my compatriots still exhibit a Bouvardian alarm at having the French as neighbours, let alone closer ones. Francophobia remains our first form of Europhobia, though not of xenophobia (ethnic minorities have edged out the French in that regard). The French are genuinely puzzled by the bile of our tabloid press, shocked that a country known for phlegm and decorous manners can also deal in such jeering contempt. It's not really you, I try to explain; it's just that you are more than yourselves, you have become the symbol of all that is foreign; everything, not just Frenchness, begins at Calais. Whereas you may look across your different frontiers and be offered a choice of four great civilizations, we in our offshore islands are surrounded by you on one side and fish on the other three. No wonder we feel about you more strongly, more obsessingly—whether as Francophile or Francophobe—than you feel about us.

Each time I give this explanation, I am less convinced by my words. Yes, they're sort of true; but it's also the case that the French are so . . . well, French, and therefore designed by God to seem as provokingly dissimilar from the British as possible. Catholic, Cartesian, Mediterranean; Machiavellian in politics, Jesuitical in argument, Casanovan in sex; relaxed about pleasure, and treating the arts as central to life, rather than some add-on, like a set of alloy wheels. What assemblage could be better targeted to enrage the puritanical lager-lunkhead blessed and prodded by our tabloid press, or even some posher patriots? When Salman Rushdie received his *fatwa,* British Airways refused to let him fly with them. Air France, asked their position, replied: "We respect the French custom regarding the rights of man, which means that we transport passengers without discrimination. If Mr. Rushdie wished to travel with Air France, he would not be refused." It was an enraging piece of one-upmanship, morally superior, flourishing *les droits de l'homme* in our faces (as if the French had invented them!), and above all, *right.* In public life, the French are just as hypocritical as we are; the difference would seem to be that their hypocrisy pays lip-service to idealism, whereas ours pays lip-service to pragmatism.

Such differences ought to survive in the name of biodiversity. We are losing human languages almost as fast as we are losing animal species; we are also losing something much less quantifiable, human difference. "Oh, but surely, Monsieur Barnes, you are still quite entirely British, and I am no less *Franche, hein?*" Yes—that's to say, no. I may and do seem very British to a French interlocutor, and s/he thoroughly French to me. But I am less British than my father, and he less than my grandfather. So what, Monsieur Barnes?

Your grandfather, you tell me, went abroad only once in his life, to France for the First World War; your father was engaged in the second. Surely a bit of globalization and European homogenization is a small price to pay for the fact that you managed to dodge the third? Isn't the last half-century of European peace something to celebrate? And here you are, complaining that French shopkeepers no longer take four-hour lunch-breaks, and what's that High Street store doing just down the road from the Beaubourg?

Yes—that's to say, no. The European Union seems nowadays to be less about friendly difference than about centralization of power and commercial harmonization: in other words, creating an ever-bigger pool of docile consumers for transnational corporations. When the British were enthusiastically helping the Americans to bomb Serbia, one of the slimiest arguments around was: "This proves the European project has an ethical as well as an economic dimension." (Well, don't forget all those rebuilding contracts after the war . . .) In its imperial days, Britain was a great standardizer and centralizer; now it likes to present itself as a bulwark against over-zealous federalism. To the European eye, this is no more than self-interested idling. So what's your position, Monsieur Barnes? Europhile but Bureausceptic, internationalist but culturally protectionist, liberal-left, green. Not many votes there, *mon ami.* My brother is a philosophical anarchist with an ambition "not to live anywhere." My mother described herself as true blue. My father was taciturn with liberal tendencies. Some political biodiversity there, at least.

In 1997 I went to France with my parents for the last time. For once I was taking them, rather than the other way round. My mother had died a few months previously, my father in 1992, and I was transporting their ashes towards a final scattering on the Côte Atlantique. We took the Eurostar, familiar to me, but a first time for them. I had the necessary "out-of-England" certificate for my mother, but had failed to get one for my father, so watched the x-ray machine at Waterloo Station with a certain apprehension. In a holdall, beneath a couple of shirts, my father was in the traditional oak casket, my mother in a heavy-duty plastic screw-top jar. I was doing the first leg to Paris; my niece would transport them to the Indre, then my brother and his wife would take them on westwards.

In my Paris hotel room I switched my parents to a plastic shoulder-bag from a London clothes shop (it had at least a French name: *Les Deux Zèbres*). I tested for weight: heavy still, but the bag seemed solid. My niece lived up in the 18e. When I got to her apartment block, the entryphone had broken down; I was let in, but unable to receive directions to the apartment. Inside was a gloomy, half-lit hallway. My parents were pulling at my shoulder. I groped for names on the first couple of doors: both were blank. There was a prevailing smell of boiled cabbage from the crepuscular stairwell. I realized that I would have to trudge round every floor scouring every door for my niece's name. At this moment the lanyard on my shoulder-bag ripped through the plastic, and I dropped my parents. They hit the concrete floor so noisily that I was sure one if not both of their containers must have split open. I imagined myself hand-scooping the ashes back in. I imagined some neighbour's poked face, and my scrabbling explanation, *"Er, voici ma mère, et, er, ici, c'est mon père."*

It was, as I failed to realize at the time, a small Flaubertian moment. In 1846 the novelist helped bury his younger sister Caroline. The gravediggers at the Cimetière Monumental in Rouen had made the hole too narrow. After shaking and pulling at the coffin, after attacking it with spades and crowbars, they resorted to stamping on it "just above Caroline's head" to force it down. Flaubert described all this in a letter to his friend Maxime Du Camp: "I was as tearless as a tombstone, but seething with anger. I wanted to tell you this, thinking that it would give you pleasure. You are sufficiently intelligent, and love me enough, to understand that word 'pleasure,' which would make a bourgeois laugh."

JULIAN BARNES
August 2001

(1)

An Englishman Abroad

A typical Ultimate Peasant

In the spring of 1998 I was on a walking holiday in the Vercors, south of Grenoble. On a perfect May morning, two of us were traversing a high upland plateau just below the snowline. Turf impeccable enough to re-lay fairways at Augusta was crossed by thin, pure streams; here, in boastful profusion—Nature showing what it can do when left alone—were a billion gentians, edelweiss, dwarf narcissi, buttercups, and orchids; once or twice, against the melting snow, we glimpsed what was probably a small fox, depending on how big marmots grow. A padlocked shack denoted a provisional human presence in what was otherwise a swathe of changeless France. In the late afternoon we descended into a small village, some forty buildings jammed between two hills. As the grass track gave way to semi-asphalt, we encountered another item from changeless France: a peasant pasturing his goats on the public hedgeside. He was ancient, rubicund, and toothless, accompanied by a psychotically hostile dog of mixed ancestry, and as he told us the long story of his rheumatism he would, as punctuation, give the nearest goat a dust-raising thwack with his stick.

The village was as you might expect: a church, a desiccated water fountain, a former school still bearing a faded RF on its forehead, a boulangerie open one hour a day, an auberge, two walkers' hostels. Some of the houses had been freshly made over, with parchment stone and custard mortar; others were *in restauro*. Over dinner we asked Madame how many *indigènes* still lived in the village. Just the one, she replied: the peasant whom we had met. He may look eighty, she said, but was only about sixty—"And yet he lives a very *bio,* a very *écolo,* life." We agreed that you could have too much *bio* and *écolo* in your life. Was drink the cause of his seeming dilapidation? No, not this one: it was his cousin, the village's penultimate peasant, who used to drink. Or at least he did until the day he went down the mountain to vote, and someone in a café told him he didn't look too well. They took him to the hospital for observation, he couldn't drink for eight days, and promptly died.

The surviving Ultimate Peasant followed a rigidly structured life: he rose at five, and went up the mountain to collect dead wood for a fire ritually lit at five in the evening, every day, regardless of season or weather. He lived with and off his goats; he had a certain amount of money, but didn't spend anything. He had never married. "I suppose he could get a Russian," said Madame. There is still a bachelors' fête not too far away, where women traditionally came for husbands. Years ago they would be Portuguese or Spanish; nowadays they are Polish or Russian. But this solution is improbable. In the meantime, everyone in the village does errands for the Ultimate One ("It took him fifteen years to say Thank You"). He doesn't drive and—according to the incomers— couldn't live through the winter without their help. At some point he, the last *indigène,* will die, and then this village, which seemed on first acquaintance so authentic, will become completely false— or, if you prefer, will finish reinventing itself for the modern world. It will be sustained by tourism rather than agriculture; be reliant on cars and out-of-town shopping; and be virtually uninhabited in winter. A seasonal village, repeating from time to time a few of the communal acts which its originators and their successors performed out of necessity and belief and habit.

La France profonde has disappeared within our century; or at least is now graspable only in tainted form. Edith Wharton saw this about to happen as she roared through France with Henry James at her side. "The trivial motorist," as she described herself, was to prove the forerunner of other destructive agents: war, peace, communications technology, mass tourism, the industrialization of agriculture, the unfettered free market, Americanization, Eurification, greed, short-termism, complacent ahistoricism.

The old nation-states of Europe are gradually being homogenized into herdable groups of international consumers separated only by language. Is this a fair—or, at least, the only—price to pay for the avoidance of those recidivist spasms of continent-wide warfare which marked our previous history? Perhaps. Would the Ultimate Peasant prefer to start his life now, with an easier workload, social benefits, subventions from Brussels, satellite porn, and an off-road vehicle? Perhaps. But both the lowering of ambition among the European leadership and the lowering of distinctiveness among the European populations have to be noted. We give character to our own particular region of dullness by certain totemic cults and, where necessary, by the invention of tradition. The French are as good at this as anybody; and the Francophile's dismay at such permitted dilution of the Gallic essence is the greater because the French have always made the largest claims, both for themselves and for Europe.

The historian Richard Cobb first went to France in 1935, to a Paris which still (just) contained Edith Wharton, though what fascinated him was popular life rather than literary pilgrimage: the street vendors and flame-swallowers, the strolling musicians and prostitutes, the manacled strong men enjoying *"droit de pavé* on the immensely wide pavement"; the world of obscure bars and tiny, four-table restaurants; the exuberance, volubility, and cheerful anarchy of the daily scene; and behind it all, that enviable ease with pleasure which so attracts the repressed English. He delighted in the pungent Métro and the convivial *plate-forme d'autobus* (a Cobb leitmotif, along with leprous Utrillo walls and the *faux manoir normand*), while asserting, and proving, that a city could only be truly known if explored on foot.

He acquired what he called a "second identity," didn't regret the partial loss of Englishness, and loved being asked if he was Belgian (though this is normally a somewhat poisoned compliment from the French to the Francophone). He had either one French wife (if you believe the index to *Paris and Elsewhere*) or two (if you follow the logic of his widely divergent descriptions of what might theoretically be the same woman), and then an English one; children, too, it seems. Before, and perhaps in between, he acquired a connoisseur's knowledge of prostitution: "Most Paris brothels tended to look like public lavatories—English ones, not French ones." Cobb's life became so French that French things started happening to him: he used to visit Gaby la Landaise, a prostitute from Dax, every payday for a year (I think we are in the late Forties or early Fifties), until the Friday he learned that she had just put a revolver in her mouth and shot herself, "in one of the sparse bedrooms on the fifth floor, No. 78." Another small case for Maigret. Meanwhile, the history Cobb was absorbed in became as French as his identity. Not only was it all about France, specifically the Revolution, specifically its later stages, but it was written and published in French: his first book in English didn't appear until he was fifty-two.

Cobb's France is not that of the traditional English Francophile, who tends to prefer the south, the countryside, the sun, the deceptively original village; who likes things as different from England as possible. Cobb preferred cities (indeed, he scarcely seems to notice the pastoral); he loved the north, which included Belgium; when he went south at all, it was to great centres like Lyon or Marseilles. He was addicted to walking, but walking in cities; it's not clear whether he ever drove; certainly he favoured public transport, with its opportunities for eavesdropping and casual observation. He was in no way a snob—a spell in the British army, he claimed, had divested him of class—except in the sense that he tended not to give the middle and upper classes the benefit of the doubt. (History, you could say, had already given them that.) He preferred *les petites gens* both in his life and in his writing: small tradespeople, working folk, servants, laundresses, wigmakers' assistants, cardsharps, water-carriers, prostitutes, idlers, semi-criminals; his closest French friend was both a deserter and a thief.

Though a democrat in his social tastes, he saw enough of the

French Communist Party to distrust generalized belief systems; he had no appetite for eating off those comradely plates which, as the food disappeared, slowly disclosed Picasso's benign icon of Stalin. He was, by his own description, "a very lonely person"; he was also, by his own evidence, social and convivial, a welcoming fellow drinker. A paradoxical man, then, a solitary with frequent companions; also a paradoxical historian, since in his life he clearly needed order and ritual to keep chaos and brutality at bay, yet he spent his career with one of the most disorderly and violent periods in France's history.

Cobb's social writing is personal and impressionistic, while his history is archival and fanatically detailed. Yet both depend upon the same principles and focus: a very English taste for the particular and the local, coupled with a disregard for theory, scheme, and overarching structure, for century-hopping generalization, let alone "models." In the middle of a characteristically enormous sentence about the problem, after five years of Revolutionary upheaval, of establishing anyone's true identity, especially at the lowest levels of society, Cobb refers to "the historian like the police and other repressive authorities before him." Cobb was fond of this comparison in its benign form: the historian as a detective who takes his time, never rushes to conclusions, learns the geography of the crime, walks the streets, takes a pastis, sniffs the air, asks seemingly irrelevant questions. The trope is also reversible: thus Inspector Maigret, for Cobb, is "a historian of habit, of the *déjà vu* . . . a historian of the unpredictable . . . a historian of class"; he may be limitingly unaware of change but is vividly alert to "habit, routine, assumption, banality, everydayness, seasonability, popular conservatism." This is the historian/detective as virtuous investigator; but Cobb's seemingly throwaway allusion to "other repressive authorities" (the slight looseness of the grammar allows for ambiguity) alerts us also to the down-side of the historian's search for clarity and certitude: the ordering and ordering-about of humanity, the rigid classification, the distant decision-making, the unpersoning, the disappearing, the use of the convenient oubliette.

Cobb was a "historian of individuality" in both senses of the phrase. For him, history "has never been an intellectual debate"; it doesn't start from an argument or a theory. With a robust and deliberately offensive pragmatism, he insisted that "I do not know what history is about, nor what social function it serves. I have never given the matter a thought." He prefers to begin from the opposite end, with a specific person in a specific place at a specific time. Having pounded the streets himself, Cobb was imaginatively alive to the effect of urban geography on the possibilities of historical event: how the river brings news as well as logs; how bridges funnel a population across a city, making identity checks, arrest, and even murder that much more feasible. His exposition of the effect of geography and administrative boundary on the development of Lyon—its buildings taller, its streets darker, its society more perpendicular, its network of passageways more conducive to crime and escape—is Cobb at his most masterly.

It is at street level, too, that Cobb seeks his historical personnel. The proclaimers of Revolution interest him less than the zealous butcher, sceptical baker, and befuddled candlestick-maker low down in the chain of command. In a key statement of intent, Cobb distinguishes his line of approach to revolutionary élites from that of Albert Soboul:

> He does name the militants, but he does not give them the benefit of a personality. The result is that we can see how they operated, but we gain virtually no impression of what they were like, whether they were sincere or time-wasters, whether they were out for publicity or for the fruits of office, whether they had sound sense or were crackpots. We just have to accept that they were militants and that something, whether ambition or sincerity, distinguished them from the general mass of their neighbours.

Cobb understood that many individuals—even seeming idealists—join movements for mixed motives, but that the movements themselves like to pretend, as their adherents sup from Stalin plates, that motives are unfailingly pure; he also knew that individuals will retrospectively purify their motives if and when a movement becomes successful. Cobb is against complete motive—an individual with a complete motive is probably a "crackpot" of one sort or another (not that such crackpots do not have their influence on history)—just as he is against complete solutions. Whether a revolution is examined from the ground up, or from theory down, there will always be "mystery and accident" at or close to the heart of it. He is also—as a Maigretian—a believer in "routine, assumption, banality." To study the moment of revolutionary violence is necessary; but Cobb never forgets that such moments are rare in a human life, as they are rare in human history. The fear, the anticipation, and the memory of violence may be pervasive, but the moment itself is surrounded and given context by a lifetime of work, love, mourning, illness, shopping, play, boredom, and so on.

Cobb's ground-up individualism and tireless archive-truffling helped protect him from the sin of hindsight. Of course, history is by its nature an act of hindsight, of understanding, or understanding better, what was understood less well at the time, or of understanding again what has been temporarily forgotten. But the writing of history is always vulnerable to the contaminated now, to the knowledge of what has occurred between there and here. The Commune knew the Revolution but the Revolution couldn't imagine the Commune. This is obvious, but temptingly forgettable. Further, the Revolution may by its example and declarations have been partly responsible for a subsequent society in which the poor and disadvantaged were treated less badly; but the historian must discover and insist that during the Revolution itself the poor lived as poorly as they ever had, while the repressive Royalist legislation aimed at controlling them was not only not repealed, but vigorously enforced by their new masters. All that the common people got from the Revolution, in Cobb's view, was a brief glimpse of power—power never again experienced, for all the plausible hypocrisies of later forms of government.

Cobb's history is archival, discursive, buttonholing, undogmatic, imaginatively sympathetic, incomplete, droll; sometimes chaotic, often manic, always pungently detailed. In *Classical Education* (1985) he describes watching a cinema newsreel about the assassination in Marseilles of King Alexander of Yugoslavia: "there was even a shot of the King, through the open rear door of the car—I think it was a Panhard-Levassor—lying on the floor." "I think it was a Panhard-Levassor": it is in such tangy asides— usually between dashes; he puts much, even semi-colons, inside his dashes—that the charm of Cobb's writing lies. His sentences, as miniatures of his overall narrative manner, often just grow and grow; though it is a Byronic rather than a Proustian extension, one of spurts and dashes, furiously alive, furiously observing. The historian as novelist? Up to a point. In *Paris and Elsewhere* Cobb proposes "the framework of a novel that has not been written and that I will not be likely to write." It is set in Ixelles, one of the independent municipalities of Greater Brussels, between the mid-Forties and mid-Fifties. Cobb evokes with care and vigour the townscape and its socially stratified populace; he describes the inhabitants' various itineraries and jots down decorative street scenes; he remembers the changing quality of the light; he hints at death and murder and transformation. But he's right: he wouldn't ever have written this novel. The historian, especially of the Cobbian kind, is a sort of novelist, but one who instead of inventing plot and character is obliged to discover them; who instead of setting characters in motion against one another with some foreknowledge of their natures and destinies tries to guess at what often incoherent characters were up to amid a distraction of lies and suppressions. This may well be the harder kind of work, especially when the sought plot proves nugatory, fragmented, trampled into indetectability by previous searchers; or, when found, is unpleasing to the reader or even to the historian himself.

David Gilmour sees Cobb's career in terms of a curve, beginning with a long obscurity, as the provincial academic explored and relished his second identity. He attained general recognition only in the mid-Seventies, following his appointment as Professor of

Modern History at Oxford. During this period France gave him the *Légion d'honneur;* literary editors sought his prose, and the radio his voice; one year he was a "controversial" chairman of the Booker Prize. (He was controversial mainly for remarking in his judicial speech that he'd never read Proust, an admission some thought a joke, and others deliberately pseudo-philistine. In fact, Proust wasn't his period, and Proust's personnel were hardly *petites gens.* It is the typical, conventional, popular novelist, the scourer of the streets and celebrator of the ordinary, who is of most use to such a historian. Cobb's taste was thus for Simenon, Pagnol, Cendrars, Queneau, René Fallet, Sue, MacOrlan, and Restif de la Bretonne.) Then, from the mid-Eighties, the curve descended, in a return to comparative obscurity, but now accompanied by illness and unhappiness. By the time of Cobb's death in 1996 the only historical work of his available in English was *The People's Armies*—ironically a translation by another hand.

This is sad, but not entirely a surprise. Cobb never wrote a big, popular book, not least because he never lowered his sights or tour-guided his terrain. He sought to convey his fascination, but never tried to ingratiate himself with the casual reader:

> First of all, then, we have to deal with the *sans-culotte* as such—that is to say, with a person not as he was, let us say, in 1792, or as he would have become in 1795 or in 1796, but as he was for a brief period from 1793 to 1794. For the life and death of the *sans-culotte* can be circumscribed within a period running more or less from April 1793 to April 1794, allowing for a possible overlap up to Thermidor year II or even to Brumaire year III. It would be stretching the species too far to describe, as a Norwegian historian has done . . . [etc.]

Cobb knew that the truth lay in the detail, and the detail meant complication, elaboration, doubt. He would never have made a TV don. As a reviewer he was famous in literary editors' offices for the unanswered telephone and the unguessable delivery date: his copy, typewritten to the very edge of innumerable small index cards, would arrive when it chose to arrive—always brilliant, always vastly over length, always uncuttable. The wise editor would sit tight, knowing that when the elusive text did finally turn up it would surely make a lead review. In a way, these semi-public years of Cobb's were the untypical ones. He was the sort of historian who inspired other historians, who taught by example, who was a quiet cult. Becoming a foppish opinion-monger, goosing the tabloid readers of Middle England, hoovering up the three-book advance: this was never his world. He would rather have another three a.m. calvados and watch the Rouen fishmongresses gut the night's catch by kerosene lamp.

There *is* a line of disenchantment and melancholy running through Cobb's life and work. But it is not about himself; it is about France. It may be that other countries, like politicians, are there to disappoint us; and that those who take a second identity are more vulnerable to such disappointment. Your *alter* country is all that your first was not; commitment to it involves idealism, love, sentimentality, and a certain selective vision. Over the years, however, you may discover that the alluring differences only half-conceal grinding similarities (the snootiness of élites, the complacency of the bourgeoisie, the conservatism of the proletariat); you may also start noticing aspects of that otherness which you dislike, or which seem aimed at destroying what initially drew you to the country. Where now are the idling Rouen trolleybus with its pole unhooked, the jolly shop-window mime artists, the companionable sadsacks in all-night bars? Items of old France are still there, in places; the four-table family restaurant can yet be found, though with greater difficulty. But your love has become vulnerable, nostalgia threatens to become corrosive, and a moment of terminal fracture beckons. All of this happened to Cobb.

He was always a good hater, of course. *His* France—urban, northern, provincial, pedestrian, noisy, unpuritanical, festive—was in contrast to, and predicated upon, another France: bureaucratic, official, suburban, safe, rule-crazy, scared. Cobb had bright scorn for: the Bordelais, the police, bossy women behind *guichets*, Victor Hugo ("France's National Bore"), Sartre, Le Corbusier ("the Swiss *démolomane*," "the implacable Helvetian"), Jean-Luc Godard (another implacable Helvetian), Baron Haussmann ("the Alsatian Attila"), the Boulevard Saint-Michel—indeed, the whole of the Latin Quarter—Georges Pompidou (a "visionary vandal" worse than Haussmann), pedestrian precincts, and the scrubbed petrification of buildings restored for people to look at rather than live in.

Just as he was a historian of individuality, Cobb was a believer in the individualistic city, one marked by variousness and the human scale: different people leading different lives in different yet neighbouring streets. In his lifetime he saw the heart of Brussels wrecked, and parts of Paris go, especially the Marais and the *Six-ième*. He watched the French capital become increasingly a single-class city, in a process of social cleansing promoted by money, municipal vanity, and museumification.

This may seem exaggerated. Paris has probably suffered less than many other Western European cities; while the lover of rural France has watched even starker transformations than the lover of urban France.* But each later generation draws a new base line, and finds it hard to imagine what has already been lost. The defining France Cobb first encountered in 1935 would have been closer to Edith Wharton's France of thirty years earlier than to De Gaulle's and Pompidou's of thirty years later. The Fifth Republic was at least as effective (being more sly, and acting with more general consent) as Louis XIV or the Revolution in the continuing drive to centralize, standardize, and domesticate the nation. This smug postwar expansionism provoked one of Cobb's most splenetic denunciations, of the:

---

*That story of the mildly peaky peasant killed by alcohol deprivation and modern medicine is widely told; it has become an enduring and necessary Rural Myth.

ten years of Gaullist paternalism and political anaesthesia and exclusive concern for the material comforts of an unquestioning and vulgar pursuit of the new car, the TV, holidays in more and more exotic surroundings, early marriage, a family of manageable size, and the youthful climb up the technocratic ladder, as people, on the road to material success and managerial position, moved further and further out of the city, to live in pseudo-rural "neighbourhood" estates: riding, swimming-pool, tennis, park, children's playground, patio, whisky, invitations to young married colleagues in the same income group, a limited infidelity (in the same income group), talk of the next car and the next holiday, rapid trips abroad for the firm (discreet infidelity, limited to the Common Market zone), masculinity and violence expressed in terms of horsepower and speed of driving.

It all got worse (it always does); indeed, it reached a poignant climax in 1989, when Cobb was so disgusted by the Bicentennial celebrations that the Revolution's great historian resolved never to write about France again. This was a sad, love-lost, and possibly naïve decision. Renan said that "getting its history wrong is part of being a nation," and a nation rarely gets its history as wrong as when congratulating itself on a famous yet intensely contradictory event. Cobb might have known this. But it is a measure of the largeness and precision of his love for the country that it could in the end so disappoint him.

(2)

Spending Their Deaths
on Holiday

Three beers, one ashtray, three singers: *(l. to r.)*
Jacques Brel, Léo Ferré, Georges Brassens

Don't talk to me about Janis Joplin, Jim Morrison, Brian Jones, Jimi Hendrix, that lost Beach Boy, or any of the lesser pop-rock deaths. I get no necrothrill from a drug overdose, a stoned slump into the void glorified as "life at the edge," an episode of melodramatic self-indulgence inflated into the greatest loss to the musical world since the early death of Schubert. No: the three deaths I prefer to hymn are sourly ordinary, dragging hospital terminations of the kind more likely to await the rest of us: heart disease, cancer, cancer. Boris Vian on 23 June 1959, Jacques Brel on 9 October 1978, and finally Georges Brassens on 29 October 1981 at 23:15 precisely. That was the moment at which French song—Francophone song, to be exact, since Brel was Belgian—died for me; or at least stopped being interesting.

I spent the academic year of 1966–7 teaching as a *lecteur d'anglais* (the slightly posher term for *assistant*) at the Collège Saint-Martin in Rennes. My task was to instruct my pupils in "English conversation and English civilization," which in effect meant devising various strategies to keep them quiet and avoid the glowering irruption into the classroom of the *surveillant général*, an ex–Algerian War veteran who terrified me even more than he did the boys. Some of my pupils, by means of diligently failing the *baccalauréat* and being sent back to retake it, were almost the same age as me, and certainly more sophisticated. I'm not sure how reliably English civilization was depicted in our conversations—I remember being grilled about London night-clubs (I bluffed tremendously) and London girls (ditto); though I would become more plausibly authoritative on the key cultural question of that time, whether or not the Beatles would break up. More benefit probably flowed in the opposite direction. Living among priests I became familiar with the kindlier side of the Catholic religion; eating at the school I found that roast beef came in other hues than field-marshal grey; and in my solitude I was enriched and consoled by the discovery of French song.

For about two-thirds of that year the top of the French hit-parade was squatted on by "A Whiter Shade of Pale," that haunting confection from Procul Harum. But the singers who roared from my squeaky French player with a stylus-weight of about two kilos were all local: Brassens and Brel, Vian and Reggiani; high-boho Léo Ferré, pointedly *engagé* Jean Ferrat, soufflée-voiced Ingénieur des Ponts et Chaussées Guy Béart, lugubrious Anne Vanderlove, bouncy Georges Chelon, yearning Barbara, chubbily smutty Pierre Perret, winsome Anne Sylvestre, and promising Rennes-born débutant Jacques Bertin. I gave a polite nod to earlier generations (Piaf, Trenet, Rossi), a shrug to the international cabaret artists (Aznavour, Distel, the ear-cupping Bécaud), a pained smile to that Hayley Mills of *chanson*, Françoise Hardy, and a sneer to the home-grown *yéyé*-mongers, Hallyday, Claude François and Eddy Mitchell. ("Clo-Clo" had at least kept his own name. Mitchell began life as the priestly sounding Claude Moine, Hallyday as the distinctly unrockerish Jean-Philippe Smet. On the other hand, "Clo-Clo" made up for this with a spectacularly unstylish death, involving the bath, electricity and, it was rumoured, a minority sexual practice.)

Procul Harum's line-up changed even before their song became a hit, and its less than cogent words were penned by Nobody Remembers Whom. Most of the singers I admired, by contrast, were individualists who wrote or co-wrote their own stuff; while some owned the whole aesthetic means of production and were badged with the lordly initials "ACI"—*auteur-compositeur-interprète*. The three who have accompanied me most down the years, their poppy, fizzing vinyl surfaces finally traded up to CD, are Boris

Vian, Jacques Brel, and Georges Brassens. All three had emerged during the early Fifties, when they were first recorded by Jacques Canetti, brother of the Nobel-winning Elias. Vian, wry and urbane, sang at the world with a cutting edge of sardonic disbelief. Brel, urgent and impassioned, sang at the world as if it could have sense shaken into it by music, could be saved from its follies and brutalities by his vocal embrace. Brassens, intimate and formal, sang at the world as if it were an old lover whose ways are teasingly familiar and from whom not too much is expected. Vian died at thirty-nine; Brel at forty-nine; Brassens, in a final act of non-conformity, just managed to stagger past fifty-nine.

Many of the singers I listened to expressed a vibrant anti-clericalism; but the indulgent Père Fleury in the next cell to mine only complained at the volume of secular ranting when he was in the middle of confessing a pupil. Most of the Fathers treated my atheism—like my nationality, my long hair, and my austerity in the face of wine—as something basically odd but tolerable. Père Marais, one of the more ironical and inflammatory priests (who fondly remembered London bus-conductors shortening "Thank you" to "Kew") used to apostrophize me with an amused eye: "You just wait for the next world, you civilians, then we clergy will show you who's going to be saved. You may have the upper hand now but later on you're really going to be in the shit." Père de Goësbriand, from an aristocratic Breton family, who was much teased for having been shot in the left buttock during the war ("Running away, Hubert?" "We were surrounded!"), overheard me arguing one day with Père Marais, and afterwards voiced his anxiety: if I hadn't been baptized, he pointed out, then I had no soul and hadn't a prayer of getting to Heaven. He was much pre-occupied with this final destination; on another occasion, he told me with a confidential wink, "Of course, you don't think I'd put up with all this if there wasn't Heaven in it for me at the end, do you?"

The physics teacher, Père Daumer, a fleshy, hip-heavy, hairless man who was never out of his cassock (his nickname among the pupils was "The Third Sex") also displayed moral concern for me.

After I had been in residence a few weeks, he took me aside and explained that some of the words I was hearing over meals at my end of the refectory table were vulgar and not repeatable in polite conversation.* I, in return, worried about Père Daumer, who despite a severe conservatism in religious matters was a devotee of films on television, and was thus obliged to wade through a lot of soul-tarnishing stuff: Godard's *A bout de souffle* had aroused his particular disapproval. However, such was his cinematic passion that he would doggedly stay in the fag-fogged TV room until the credits. Then he would rise and pronounce judgement before going off to bed. "Not worth the trouble" was a favourite verdict. Once, to my delight, he gave some piece of sinful froth the full treatment. "Lacking both interest *and* morality," he remarked, doffing his little square black cap at me. "Bonsoir, Monsieur Barnes."

There was considerable doctrinal disagreement in this house of Eudistes. Not from Père Calvard, an ardent Breton patriot who managed to combine Druidism and Catholicism with no ideological difficulty; nor from the football-mad Père Le Mauff, who would briskly assert, "Metaphysics is rubbish" before going off to tend his hive of bees, his broken-winged buzzard, his month-old fox-cub. The dispute was the sempiternal one between Ancients and Moderns, and embraced teaching methods as much as beliefs. Père Tupin, a young firebrand who believed in "dialogue" with pupils, and would even discuss masturbation with them, had recently got into trouble with the authorities for taking the words of a pop song as text for his sermon. (He got into trouble with me over this too, since to my amazement he hadn't chosen Brel or Brassens but a piece of dreck warbled by someone like Sylvie Vartan.) Presiding over these theologically sultry days at the College was Père Denis,

---

*When Paul Valéry met the correct English poet W. E. Henley in 1896, he was shocked to find the Englishman expressed himself with much idiomatic and perfectly accented obscenity. It turned out that Henley had learnt French from Rimbaud and Verlaine.

a Père Supérieur renowned for his fair-minded timidity, his desire to approve of most things he set eyes on, and a certain tentativeness in conversation. Père Marais used to recall at frequent intervals— and always with undiminished glee—an outing with the Père Supérieur and one of my predecessors as *lecteur d'anglais*. At one point they had passed a dog. "Tell me, Monsieur Smith," the Superior had asked with an exact but hesitant civility. "Do you have dogs in England?"

I like to remember that Boris Vian was one of the amplified voices with which I used to blast Père Fleury (who dodged behind trees when he saw a nun approaching, and who also rolled the fattest gaspers I have ever seen, each requiring two full cigarette papers). But this must be a false memory. Vian's fame as an interpreter didn't really begin until 1979, twenty years after his death, when Philips released a commemorative LP. In 1966–7 he was mainly known through the voices of others: Serge Reggiani had begun his career performing Vian's work; Peter, Paul and Mary made a transatlantic campus heart-plucker out of "The Deserter"; and Jean Ferrat had offered up his smokey-jazz homage "Boris." Vian was remembered instead as everything except an interpreter: song-writer, poet, novelist, playwright, translator, actor, jazz trumpeter, pataphysician. He was the most cosmopolitan of my top three; his photo-biography begins with him standing, aged twelve, behind a chubby adolescent in long shorts and a criss-cross sweater who turns out to be the fourteen-year-old Yehudi Menuhin; later we see him with his arm round Miles Davis, chatting to Ellington, meeting Erroll Garner at Orly airport in 1957; here he is on the beach at Antibes and Saint Tropez, behind the wheel of his Aston Martin, his Morgan, his 1911 Brazier; on film he lurks in the shadows with Jeanne Moreau in the Vadim version of *Les Liaisons dangereuses*. He wrote songs with Aznavourian profligacy: over 700 of them, some jazz-influenced, some in the style of *rock humoristique* that he pioneered with Henri Salvador. Despite "Le Déserteur," he didn't write "protest songs" so much as songs of satirical provocation, anarchic moralities like "Le Petit com-

merce," which laments the plight of an arms salesman so successful that all his clients kill one another off and reduce him to penury.
In his lifetime Vian wasn't held to be a convincing interpreter of
his own work, but the 1979 Philips disc gives the lie to this: his
ironic, whippy-tongued delivery was the apt match for his sly and
worldly songs.

So Vian was necessarily for later. In 1966–7 it was Jacques Brel
who spoke most directly, publicly, and intimately to the twenty-
year-old I then was. While British rockers strutted their pit-bull
masculinity, Brel sang of sexual hurt and romantic humiliation;
while Distel smarmed on about *luuurv*, Brel exalted *la tendresse*.
In other moods he gleefully spanked the bourgeoisie, lobbed
grenades at the military, wrangled doggedly with God, and sang
about death with a vibrant terror which seemed to replicate
my own. Yet even when he agreed with you, he saw further. You
think "Les Bourgeois" is just a rousing war-cry— *"C'est comme les
cochons / Plus ça devient vieux, plus ça devient bête"* ("They're like
pigs / The older they get, the stupider")—but it turns out in its
final verse to be a sager comment on the whole inevitable process of *embourgeoisement*, with youthful mockers transformed into
middle-aged mockees. It was Brel's mixture of satire, wisdom, and
heart that did for me: alongside the snarl and the lush contempt was
a bursting emotionalism, a celebration of love as *la tendre guerre*,
an aching sympathy for the weak, the lost, the *amputés de coeur*.
This Belgian came out of a cold, flat, wet country, yet sang with
such heat; he hurled himself with dangerous directness at his audience, not caring whose toes he stepped on, acting and clowning,
playing drunks and simpletons, even doing sheep-noises, but
bundling you up in that rich gargly tonsilly voice and whirling you
round in his thrilling taunts and joyous dreams.

Today he is dead—buried at Altuona a few metres away from
Gauguin—and his musical remains sit on the shelf in a cube of ten
CDs: smaller than the box you'd get someone's ashes in. Playing
through this whole *oeuvre* again, I am struck by how long it took
him (compared to Brassens, say) to find his true musical identity.

His early songs are weakened by sentimentality and preachiness: not for nothing was he teased as "l'Abbé Brel." (He had had a late-adolescent brush with muscular Christianity, and we should always beware the lapsed evangelist.) He strains for poeticality, has a taste for moody townscapes, and offers a routine view of girls and love which often has a drab tang of misogyny (it's hard to think of a more charm-free description of an ex-lover than the phrase *"matériel déclassé"* from "La Haine"). The moral thumpiness is heightened by the use of organ and backing choir, not to mention the spoken *ex cathedra* pronouncement. A typical song of this early period is "Prière païenne," a pious attempt to convince the Virgin Mary that carnal love is pretty much a metaphorical equivalent of spiritual love. Mary, if listening, might have given a sceptical pout.

Once Brel has wriggled free of these beginnings and sorted out his orchestration (high whiney strings like the complaining *vent du nord*, snarly brass, whizzy accordion), he drove his way to a short yet wonderfully rich creative peak, lasting from about 1961 to 1967. He sang of the north, of getting drunk (in the north), of sexual betrayal (and getting drunk, as a result, in the north), of being widowed (and discovering, on the day of the funeral, that you have been sexually betrayed, and therefore getting drunk—probably in the north—as a result). He sang exactly of childhood's yearnings, of the pursuit and loss of *le Far-West*. He sang what must be the only song in general currency inspired by the queue for a military brothel. He sang ragingly of "adult" foolishness— *"Il nous fallut bien du talent / Pour être vieux sans être adultes"* ("It really took a deal of skill / To get to be old without getting to be adult")— and mockingly of the old man's death he was never to know. He sang funeral laments for his friends ("Jojo," "Fernand") which now have to double in our listening as elegies for him too. In his maturity he could still be merely contrary (as in the puckishly anti-ruralist "Les Moutons"); but it is his understanding of the complication and weak starting-point of most human dealings that gives his work its strength and continuing life. *"On se croit mèche, on n'est que suif*" (We think we are the wick, but we are only the tallow). We dream of going to sea—and end up as captain of a breakwater. Logically, the source of all this imperfection must be imperfect Himself:

> *Moi, si j'étais le bon Dieu*
> *Je crois que je serais pas fier*
> *Je sais, on fait ce qu'on peut,*
> *Mais y a la manière.* *

"Lacking both interest *and* morality," Père Daumer would doubtless have said, doffing his black cap.

While I was in France Brel made his sole appearance in Britain (Brassens visited us just once as well); and in 1967 came the announcement—far more catastrophic than any Beatles break-up—that he was retiring, or at least abandoning his *tours de chant*. Unlike those indefatigable retirees whose valedictory appearances are an annual event on several continents, Brel said he would give up, and then just did. His energy went instead into films and musicals, travel, and his new Polynesian life. Though he was to record a final album a decade later, his public recitals were over. But first he came to Rennes.

I knew nothing about him except that he was Belgian, slim, dark, and horse-toothed; that he smoked like a Frenchman and knew how to pilot light aircraft. Most of this information was drawn from the sumptuous folding album covers of Disques Barclay. I didn't want to know more either. The songs were the man; any biography was unimportant, reductive. Who cared if there was a real Marieke or Mathilde or Madeleine behind "Marieke" and "Mathilde" and "Madeleine"? When Olivier Todd's posthumous *Jacques Brel: Une Vie* came out, I duly read it, and was duly disappointed: not by the discovery that Brel was a good bit more

---

*"And if I were God / I don't think I'd be too proud / I know, you can only do what you can / But it's the way you do it that counts."

imperfect than his songs, but by a biographer who had begun in sympathy and ended in nagging disapproval, his enthusiasm for the work diminished by his knowledge of the man. It was little compensation to make the occasional *trouvaille:* for instance, that "La Valse à mille temps" had its moment of origin when Brel was driving towards Tangier from the mountains, and discovered in the rhythm of the road's innumerable bends the surging acceleration of a waltz.

It was a hot evening, even hotter up in the gallery. The show began at about ten with Brel's regular warm-up act, a black American group called the Delta Rhythm Boys, who were doubtless very good but seemed to me interminable. I was sleepy and hungry by the time—nearing midnight—that Brel came on stage, yet all was instantly forgiven. A minimal band (piano, drums, bass, accordion) and no fancy lighting or presentation. After the first song, he took off his jacket *("Ça chauffe, hein?")*. The audience never once clapped in self-applauding recognition at the start of a song; even the intros had become precious. Of course, I knew most of the songs already from disc, so the words came from within me as well as from the stage, in that haunting stereo of memory and the real moment. Down there, on that familiar equine face, the sweat famously poured: Brel was said to lose 800g during a recital. He hurtled straight from one song into the next, without a pause, without any colluding chat, for an hour, then brusquely stopped. And that was it—no encores, no showbiz, no lachrymose farewell. He left us without ceremony.

Brel had the romantic presence, the newsworthy life, the concentrated burst of albums. Brassens had a bearish reputation, was publicly reticent, and assembled his work slowly but persistently over thirty years, with a quiet tenacity appropriate to the son and grandson of stonemasons. He was more classical in style than Brel, and more literary (he had even tried to write fiction). He looked and sounded like a sage from a hill-village, but in fact had never lived in the country and said he would be a naturalized Parisian if such a thing were possible. He sang with a growling, chestnut voice, with a rolling Provençal *r*, with a crisp, humorous delivery. For all the jollity and disruptiveness of his texts, his sound always remained austere. His maximum orchestration consisted of a second guitar and a double bass, both as discreet as the confessional. There is a moment in "La Non-demande en mariage" when the bass—after fifteen years of chuntering away quietly in the background—comes loping in with a loud and insistently held contribution. It registers seismically with the listener.

The Brassens canon, as it struck successive generations from the Fifties onwards, was warming and freeing. He was an anarchist: not so much a political one (though he had been a member of the Fédération d'Anarchistes at the end of the war), still less a hippified one, but a genuine and unpretentious free spirit. He was a man of the people, though not a man of the crowd, and his songs display an even-handed disdain for all organizers of society regardless of political persuasion. He mistrusted the group, believing that as soon as there are more than four of you, you become a *bande de cons* ("Le Pluriel"); he detested all uniforms "except that of the postman"; and seems to have had a sociopathic hatred for station-masters. Like Vian and Brel he wrote anti-militaristic songs, but his hatred of war did not find predictable expression: see, for instance, his jaunty consumers' report on the subject—*"Moi, mon colon, cell' que j'préfère / C'est la guerr' de quatorz'-dix-huit!"* ("My real favourite, Colonel / Is Nineteen Fourteen-Eighteen.") His unpolite mockery of most sensible preconceptions about life was the more bracing—if initially puzzling—for being allied to a code of charity, pleasure, and humour.

He celebrated the downtrodden: cowards, pimps, gravediggers, tarts with ordinary hearts, women with huge arses, traitors, shaven-headed collaborationists, and older women. As I get older myself I increasingly treasure his line from "Saturne"—*"Et la petite pisseuse d'en face / Peut bien aller se rhabiller"* ("And the little brat opposite / Can go and put her clothes back on"). He was on the side of the solitary pyromaniac against the combined forces of the *sapeurs pompiers;* he saluted the man who had burgled his house (arguing that since the burglar got what he wanted, and he, Brassens, had derived a song from the incident, then the two of them were quits). He praised cats, pipes, male comradeship, and the artichoke-hearted woman who gives everyone a leaf. He execrated judges, gendarmes, right-thinking people, and the callously principled. Yet his tenderness could be robust, and enemies were not always forgiven. In the mid-Sixties, Brassens visibly lost weight, shrinking from an ursine presence towards comparative gauntness. Journalists informed their readers that the great singer had cancer. Their speculations were true; but though true, none the less intrusive. Brassens responded with "Le Bulletin de santé," in which he admits that he has indeed left the ranks of the obese, but not for the reasons some impute. No—*non, non, non, trois fois non*—what has caused him to lose so much weight is not illness but the fact that he has spent a vast amount of time and energy fucking journalists' wives. Not the most delicate riposte, perhaps, but the provocation was hardly delicate either. And just to emphasize the aggressive corporeality of the matter, Brassens filches Mallarmé's line *"Je suis hanté: l'Azur, l'Azur, l'Azur, l'Azur!"* and depoeticizes it into *"Je suis hanté: le rut, le rut, le rut, le rut!"* (haunted not by a blue sky, but by sex).

In "Le Mauvais sujet repenti," one of his earliest songs (1953), Brassens takes on the voice of a pimp (or at least a semi-pro) to discuss the training-up of a débutante tart's sexual gift:

> *L'avait l'don, c'est vrai, j'en conviens,*
> *L'avait le génie,*
> *Mais, sans technique, un don n'est rien*
> *Qu'un' sal' manie . . .*

Without technique, a gift—even one amounting to genius—is no more than a filthy habit.* Despite—or perhaps because of—

---

*A note on the social penetration of Brassens's work. Three decades and more later, Jacques Fouroux was preparing the French rugby team to face the New his restricted range of possible sound, Brassens throughout his career was constantly elaborating his technique, inventing, tautening, broadening: across three decades his ballads get grander, his melodies denser, his repeat-schemes more intricate.

Thematically, his songs complicate too, as his understanding of the world complicates. In his early work, sex is a jolly and frequently satirical business, in which adultery is an act of cheerful revenge, escaped gorillas have their way with robed judges, and genial fetishists are obsessed with the bellybuttons of policemen's wives. In maturity, Brassens is more likely to hymn the Penelope who strays, the adulterer who can only perform if he really likes the husband he's cuckolding, and the poignant position ("Ma Maîtresse, La Traîtresse") of the lover who feels betrayed when his mistress chooses to sleep with her husband. The singer is also quite happy to insult the Frenchman's self-image as a lover whose silky skills unfailingly provoke ecstasy: "Ninety-five per cent," the song of that title maintains, is the percentage of women who are faking it. But then Brassens never pleased by seeking to please. Another statistic: in 1977 a survey found that 64.7 per cent of the nation would like to be in his skin because for them he represented The Happy Man. Asked to comment, he replied, *"Ah, les cons . . ."*

The Collège Saint-Martin at Rennes was where I saw my first dead body: that of Père Roussel, a young priest who had succumbed in his twenties to some ungodly disease. He was laid out in a vestibule off the entrance hall to the main building, and boys were encouraged to visit him and pray for his soul. I drew the line at this, though I gazed through the windowed doors at the pallid, bespectacled figure lying on his back.

Upstairs I listened to Brel satirically discussing his own death in "Tango Funèbre" and in "Le Moribond":

Zealanders in the ritual encounter between flair and structured method. The coach reminded his men that, "to quote Brassens, *le talent sans technique n'est qu'une sale manie.*"

Et je veux qu'on rie
Je veux qu'on danse
Je veux qu'on s'amuse comme des fous
Je veux qu'on rie
Je veux qu'on danse
Quand c'est qu'on me mettra dans mon trou*

As for Brassens, the album that he brought out during my year in Rennes—*Georges Brassens IX*—began with an enormous departure for this established master of the two-, three-, or if you were very lucky four-minute ballad. "Supplique pour être enterré sur la plage de Sète" ("Petition to Be Buried on the Beach at Sète") weighs in at a marathon seven minutes and eighteen seconds. It is a grand, lilting, jocular codicil to his earlier testamentary songs, and contains specific instruction for the disposal of his body. He wants it transported *"dans un sleeping du Paris-Mediterranée"* to the "minuscule" station at Sète (where the station-master would probably have the delicacy to give himself the day off), and thence to the beach for burial. The eternal *estivant* is to lie in the sun between sky and sea, spending his death on holiday. He hopes that girls will undress behind his tomb; perhaps one of them will even stretch out on the sand in the shadow of his cross—thus affording his spirit *"un petit bonheur posthume."* And just as Brel in Altuona was to have Gauguin for company, at Sète Brassens would be close to Paul Valéry, delineator and occupant of *Le Cimetière marin*. The singer, a humble troubadour beside the great poet, would at least be able to congratulate himself that *"Mon cimetière soit plus marin que le sien"* ("My graveyard is nearer the sea than his").

In the event, he didn't quite make the beach. Instead, on the first weekend of November 1981, he was added to the family vault in the Corniche cemetery: this despite complaining in the "Supplique" that the vault was already stuffed to bursting point and he

---

*"I want you to laugh / I want you to dance / I want you to have a bloody good time . . . when they put me into my hole."

didn't want to be reduced to shouting "Move along inside there please"— *"Place aux jeunes en quelque sorte."* (The sea is barely visible from here, and his grave after all less *"marin"* than Valéry's.) The ending of his life contained the symmetry he desired and feared: born in Sète in 1921, the naturalized Parisian returned to die there sixty years later. In that shortened span he never travelled well himself, being allergic to aeroplanes and abroad; while his songs, with their compacted, allusive, slangy texts and spare music, have travelled less successfully than those of Brel. But he was France's greatest and wisest singer, and we should visit him— spending his death on holiday—in whatever way we can.

(3)

The Promises of Their Ordination

Jean Seberg kisses Jean-Paul Belmondo
to advertise *A bout de souffle*

Near the start of Truffaut's *Tirez sur le pianiste* there is a deft moment of authorial cheek. Charlie (Charles Aznavour) returns from the piano bar to his rented room and climbs wearily into bed, cuddling an ashtray the size of a salad bowl. Clarisse (Michèle Mercier), the jolly tart who lives next door, sidles in with an offer. Charlie says he lacks the money; she offers him credit; he declines. None the less she stays, undresses, climbs into bed beside him, and sits, her breasts fully visible, talking about a movie she's just seen. He interrupts her: "In the cinema, it's always like *this*,"—and he pulls the bedclothes up around her into a parody of the starlet-sitting-respectably-up-in-bed shot. It is lightly done, and fits the jokey, tumbling relationship between Charlie and Clarisse. Still, it has its echo. *In the cinema, it's always like this:* but it isn't like this in life, and from now on it won't be like this in the cinema either.

My movie education began in Paris during the early Sixties, when the *nouvelle vague* was still a surfer's paradise. Godard's *A bout de souffle*, with a script by Truffaut, seemed the ultimate modern film: brave, nose-thumbing, hip, stylish, sexy, anti-authoritarian, above all true to the jagged inconsequentiality and moral vacuum of life as Godard and I (plus Truffaut and a few more initiates) perceived it to be. Like *Tirez sur le pianiste* it thrilled to loucheness and the rough touch of urban contemporaneity: "The Underpass in Modern French Film" is a thesis waiting to be written. If the theme of both films was Man on the Run, the technique was Camera on the Run: the lens probed and wandered, scuttled and hopped. Godard and Truffaut were exultantly picking apart the grammar of film and risking new combinations; together they were seeing afresh both life and the possibilities of art, in a joyful collaborative rivalry reminiscent of, well, Braque and Picasso perhaps.

Watching *A bout de souffle* again after a gap of more than twenty years, my first reaction was to lament the way things seem unquenchably novel when you are eighteen because of an unawareness of context and prehistory. In the present case: tone from American film noir, moral stance from *L'Etranger* (much watered), pretentiousness and fake *aperçus* from avant-garde café life. Today the shooting of the policeman in the opening minutes no longer seems to me a moment of liberating, audacious anarchy, but a calculated ploy by both anti-hero and director/writer (kill a cop to give your film a gallon of plot-gas). What still grips, however, is the panache of Godard's direction. Here is someone in immediate control of the medium, confident enough to try anything (how long can that sequence of Belmondo and Seberg not going to bed together possibly last? Well, about as long as the parallel sequence in *Tirez sur le pianiste* where Thérésa confesses her "vileness" with the impresario). The zest, the cockiness, the sheer ardour of filmmaking remain as infectious as ever, and almost cover up the melancholy truth: that *A bout de souffle* is a tremendous display of style balancing on a minimum of content. The closeness of Truffaut and Godard at the time of these two films was deceptive. *A bout de souffle* still looks more accomplished than *Tirez sur le pianiste*. But Truffaut was just trying on the bell-bottoms; Godard was laying in a lifetime's supply.

The *nouvelle vague* was a revolt against *le cinéma de papa*, but it was less a matter of mass parricide than of selective culling. The wisest innovators know—or at least find out—that the history of art may appear linear and progressive but is in fact circular, cross-referential, and back-tracking. The practitioners of the *nouvelle vague* were immersed (some, like Truffaut, as critics) in what had preceded them. This was perhaps the only artistic revolution that began in a museum (the Cinémathèque), and in their films the revolutionaries acknowledged with many a wink and nod their favoured masters: thus in *La Nuit américaine* the film crew set off for a location shoot down the Rue Jean Vigo. Such hat-tipping was returned: Jean Renoir (Truffaut's French hero as opposed to his American hero, Hitchcock) slyly dedicated *My Life and Films* to "those film-makers who are known to the public as the 'New Wave' and whose preoccupations are also mine." The *nouvelle vague* was denunciatory and iconoclastic in manner; but while knocking the heads off a few statues it none the less carried on building the cathedral. It developed and promoted the *auteur* theory, while also retrospectively applying it to American *cinéastes* like Howard Hawks; it loosened the financial garrotte with which film backer had long held film maker; it confirmed a move away from studio shooting to a sort of *plein-airisme;* and it turned its back on the established star system, while inevitably producing stars of its own, some of whom duly behaved with traditional megalomania.

By 1982 Truffaut could take a historial view of the *Cahiers du cinéma* row of the 1950s. He told the American critic Jim Paris that he still looked out for examples of *le cinéma de papa* when they came around again on television. He always hoped for a "pleasant surprise." But the distinguished film maker of fifty found that his objections remained the same as those of the feisty young critic: "These relate mainly to the representation of love, the female characters, the anti-bourgeois *statements,* the absence of children and above all the falseness of the dialogue." He concluded:

> The revolt, to use a very grand word, of *Cahiers du cinéma* was more moral than aesthetic. What we were arguing for was an *equality* of observation on the part of the artist *vis-à-vis* his characters instead of a distribution of sympathy and antipathy which in most cases betrayed the servility of artists with regard to the stars of their films and, on the other hand, their demagoguery with regard to the public.

To each his own revolt: for Godard it was chiefly aesthetic and political, for Truffaut financial and moral. "Why don't you make political films?" the tiresome German fan demands of the film director Ferrand (played by Truffaut himself) in *La Nuit améri-caine*. "Why don't you make erotic films?" Ferrand doesn't reply; he is too busy getting on with the job. And in Truffaut's case, too, the main answer must come from a body of work whose character was settled early, and more by cinematic instinct than ideological decision. "A film-maker shows what his career will be in his first 150 feet of film," Truffaut wrote of Jean Vigo. Apply this test to his own first feature, *Les Mistons*, and what sort of film maker do we discover? One attracted to the love story that ends badly, and with a singular empathy for the child on the nervous edge of ado-lescence; one with a taste for cinematic quotation, borrowed gags, and surprise cameo moments, plus a reliance on the literary device of voice-over narration; a storyteller imbued with charm, lyricism, *aigre-doux* humour, and a predilection for sunlit woodlands. (Is there a danger of sentimentality? Perhaps. But we might recall Alain-Fournier's reply to this charge: "Sentimentality is when it doesn't come off—when it does, you get a true expression of life's sorrow.") And if we look behind the film, we discover an equally vital element: *Les Mistons* was largely financed by Truf-faut's wife. This is a key lesson of the *nouvelle vague*, and one on which Truffaut and Godard could agree: that in an essentially col-laborative medium, collaboration with the wrong money destroys individualism.

"When I was a child . . . I hated my family, I was bored by my family." The young Truffaut dropped out of school at fourteen, and diversified into petty theft and minor vagabondage. When he stole a typewriter, his father committed him to a psychiatric "observation centre." (A few years previously, Godard had stolen from Swiss Television, and been put in a mental hospital by his father.) Truffaut next joined the army, only to spend his time there in a constant state of near desertion. These experiences fed directly into the Antoine Doinel cycle of films, with the febrile, burning-eyed Jean-Pierre Léaud as Truffaut's half-lost, half-damaged alter ego. This rich theme of fractured childhood and the search for a salvaging parent figure climaxes in Truffaut's painful and pessimistic masterpiece, *L'Enfant sauvage*, the tale of Victor, the Wild Boy of Aveyron, and Dr. Itard, his potential saviour. But while Truffaut's own story was that of a wild boy tamed and helped by a surrogate father (the film critic André Bazin), one finally consoled and fulfilled by learning to speak the language of film, *L'Enfant sauvage* is a bleak example of the story not working out. For all Itard's patience, inventiveness, and occasional exasperated toughness, small breakthroughs fail to lead to larger ones. Victor cannot finally be helped, the damage being too great for more than superficial remedy; he manages to pick up a few words and a few tricks, but fails to master language in such a way as to bring true communication and possible consolation.

Truffaut was lucky to find the right language himself. He was, in the phrase he applied to Vigo, "a spectator who fell in love with films." At fifteen he founded a *ciné-club*, at eighteen he started as a film critic. His life thereafter was utterly in and of the cinema, that place of light and warmth as rain and darkness descend outside. He was writer, director, actor, co-producer, critic, historian, interviewer, and activist. "Films are smoother than life," Truffaut explains to Léaud on celluloid in *La Nuit américaine*. "For people like you and me, our happiness lies in films." His private life also unreeled much within the surrogate family of the cinema: he married the daughter of a leading French distributor and producer; many of his affairs were with actresses.

"Films resemble the people who make them," he wrote. In his published letters, as in his films, Truffaut is genial, accessible, humorous, and melancholy. He is affectionate, playful, stylish; not averse to luxury ("Better to weep in a Jaguar than in the Métro"); instinctive rather than intellectual, an autodidact with some of that breed's hectoring propensities. He is wary of theory, just as he is wary of those who claim to love humanity in the abstract; he prefers the specific instance and the particular individual. The only shocking thing to emerge from his letters is that he was a small man who had a fetishistic collection of Eiffel Towers. And the only strikingly unFrench thing is a complete lack of interest in food. Lapsing for a moment into theory, he comes up with a surprising, and surprisingly pat, reason: "Bruno Bettelheim explains that, with food, one has the same relationship as with one's mother, and I really believe that that's the case with me. The fact remains that an hour after a meal I am incapable of saying what I ate." In his letters Truffaut's mother is as scarce as a menu: she pops up only to comment acerbically that *La Peau douce* is "a little less vulgar" than *Jules et Jim.*

"Good films are ones that are made in ordinary rooms, with one's backside on a chair." And the professional problems that beset Truffaut were also ordinary: the *nouvelle vague* could not vaporize the old frustrations. There was the slipperiness of finance; the moaning of writers whose work has been adapted and therefore traduced (Maurice Pons disapproved of Bernadette's bicycle in *Les Mistons,* while David Goodis liked *Tirez sur le pianiste* much less when he saw it with subtitles: his ignorance of French had previously allowed him to believe that the film was being more faithful to his book); the uppitiness of some actors; the cecity of critics; and the inaccurate praise of fans (Truffaut once met some Alabaman film buffs who congratulated him on a hit-parade of movies, none of which he had actually made).

Truffaut's evident lovability and his professional cheerfulness enclosed an undertow of gloom—he made *Jules et Jim* "under the impression that it's going to be amusing and discovering as I go along that the only thing that saves it is its melancholy"—while his affability often gave away to touchiness. "Every artist," he wrote in 1965, "must dream of reaching . . . the point at which 'opinions' [about his or her work] are meaningless"; but like most artists Truffaut never recognized that he'd reached the point, and to the end of his life was writing letters of rebuke and correction to journalists who misrepresented him. This lack of final confidence might also explain the diligence with which he encouraged Truf-

faut Studies wherever they appeared. Alternative explanations
would include natural courtesy and natural ambition. There is also
a toughness and aggression that stayed with him long after his
rumbustious critical apprenticeship. When an agent tried to push
an actress on to him, he replied: "If I may judge from your letter,
from the way it is typed and laid out, and the condition in which
it arrived, complete with documents, I should say that Mademoiselle X might best be offered the role of an illiterate slut." When
hustled for his signature on a petition, he did more than merely
decline:

Dear Madame,
  Since you charmingly insist that I add my signature to the
list of those who have signed the Manifesto for Survival, I find
myself obliged, other than by silent abstention, to inform you of
my disagreement with its text which is, in my opinion, completely
woolly, vague and insipid and bristling with too many capital
letters.

Truffaut's taste for literary abuse is most fully deployed in his
1973 exchange with Godard over *La Nuit américaine*. It consists,
in fact, of a single letter from Godard and a single reply from
Truffaut, but even so strolls into any future anthology of artistic
quarrels. "Yesterday I saw *La Nuit américaine*," Godard begins.
"Probably no one else will call you a liar, so I will." Truffaut is "a
liar" because of the absence of "criticism" in the film, because he
fails to tell the truth about film-making, its processes, personnel,
and off-screen entanglements. "Liar, because the shot of you and
Jacqueline Bisset the other evening at Chez Francis [a Paris restau-
rant] is not in your film, and one can't help wondering why the
director is the only one who doesn't screw in *La Nuit américaine*."
If Godard were to make a comparable movie, it would include
such truths as "how the old man from Publidécor paints Maria
Schneider's backside in *Last Tango*, how Rassam's switchboard
operator telephones and how Malle's accountant balances the

books." Having established Truffaut's bad faith and his own moral superiority, Godard then seeks to touch his former friend and collaborator for money. It is, after all, because Truffaut's films—and those of Malle and Rassam—are so expensive that there isn't enough cash around to fund Godard's latest. So why doesn't Truffaut come in as co-producer: "for 10 million? for 5 million? Considering *La Nuit américaine,* you ought to help me, so that the public doesn't get the idea we all make films like you."

Godard's sovereign scorn can hardly be untainted by envy. Since 1959 moviegoers had, on the one hand, been arguing the various merits of *Les 400 Coups, Jules et Jim, L'Enfant sauvage,* and *La Nuit américaine* (backed up by *Tirez sur le pianiste, La Peau douce,* and *Fahrenheit 451*), while on the other hand they had observed the grim decline of the maker of *A bout de souffle* into smug sloganeering. Happily, Truffaut does not allow his greater success to prevent a precise and ferocious settling of accounts. His six-page letter is the more violent for having been bottled up so long: Truffaut had not previously replied to Godard's sneers. Now he does. Godard thinks the truth should be told about the cinema and sex?

> You cast Catherine Ribeiro, whom I had sent to you, in *Les Carabiniers,* and then threw yourself on her the way Chaplin throws himself on his secretary in *The Great Dictator* (it wasn't I who made the comparison) . . . With every shot of X—in *Week-End* it was as though you were tipping a wink at your pals: this whore wants to make a film with me, take a good look at how I treat her: there are whores and there are poetic young women.

Funding difficulties?

> I need have no worries on your account, in Paris there are still enough wealthy young men, with a chip on their shoulder because they had their first car at 18, who will be delighted to pay their dues by announcing: "I'm the producer of Godard's next film."

Bad faith?

> I've felt nothing but contempt for you [since 1968]—as when I
> saw the scene in *Vent d'est* showing how to make a Molotov cock-
> tail and, a year later, you got cold feet the first time you were
> asked to distribute *La Cause du peuple* [Sartre's newspaper] in the
> street. The notion that all men are equal is theoretical with you,
> it isn't deeply felt, which is why you have never succeeded in
> loving anyone or helping anyone, other than by shoving a few
> banknotes at them.

Godard is not just a liar, but a phony, a poseur, an élitist, a narcis-
sist, "a piece of shit on a pedestal," an assiduous cultivator of his
own subversive image. He treats individuals disdainfully while
fawning before an abstract concept of "the masses." Even his mili-
tancy is false:

> You need to play a role and the role needs to be a prestigious one;
> I've always had the impression that real militants are like cleaning
> women, doing a thankless, daily but necessary job. But you,
> you're the Ursula Andress of militancy, you make a brief appear-
> ance, just enough time for the cameras to flash, you make two or
> three duly startling remarks and then you disappear again, trail-
> ing clouds of self-serving mystery.

This thorough trashing of Godard's character and by extension his
work ("Films resemble the people who make them") ends with a
well-aimed quote from Bernanos: "If I had, like you, failed to keep
the promises of my ordination, I would prefer it to have been for
a woman's love rather than for what you call your intellectual
development."

The spectacle is exciting, the more so if we declare our man the
winner; but finally depressing. Co-ordinees and collaborators in
their youth, Truffaut and Godard have now diverged totally. Their
quarrel is also part of the old one between head and heart, the aes-

thetic and the moral, theory and individualism; the strategy of offence versus the strategy of charm. Whereas Truffaut was good at customer relations, being civil and helpful to those genuinely interested in his work, Godard was famously cavalier and confrontational, offering contempt as proof of integrity. Invited to London some years ago to lecture at the National Film Theatre, he accepted, then changed his mind at the last minute and sent a jaunty telegram:

IF I AM NOT THERE TAKE ANYONE IN THE STREET THE POOREST IF POSSIBLE GIVE HIM THE HUNDRED POUNDS AND TALK WITH HIM OF IMAGES AND SOUNDS AND YOU WILL LEARN FROM HIM MUCH MORE THAN FROM ME BECAUSE IT IS THE POOR PEOPLE WHO ARE REALLY INVENTING THE LANGUAGE STOP YOUR ANONYMOUS GODARD.

When this message was read out to the expectant crowd, many applauded, either from sycophancy or aesthetic agreement. One dissident stood up and shouted, understandably if perhaps too all-encompassingly, "Sod the Frogs!"

On 21 October 1984, Truffaut died from a brain tumour. His last published letter (of January 1984) was characteristic:

On 12 September last, I was operated on for an aneurism of the brain, but film criticism was *20 years ahead* of conventional medicine, since, when my 2nd film, *Tirez sur le pianiste*, came out, it declared that such a film could only have been made by someone whose brain wasn't functioning normally!

Godard's introduction to these letters ends with a posturing flourish that would not have surprised Truffaut: "François is perhaps dead. I am perhaps alive. But then, is there a difference?" Another error of category from Jean-Luc. There is a difference, sad and enormous, not least for those of us who now feel cheated out of the remainder of the Truffaut canon. Godard, ever-radical, went to direct a European commercial for Nike.

(4)

The Land Without
Brussels Sprouts

MINESTRA DI POMIDORO (Tomato Soup)

Melt 1½ lb. of chopped and skinned tomatoes in olive oil; add a clove of garlic and some fresh parsley or basil or marjoram. Cook for 5 minutes, then add a pint of meat or chicken stock, salt and pepper, and a pinch of sugar. Cook for 5 minutes more only.

By this method the flavour of the tomatoes is retained, and the soup tastes very fresh.

A simple recipe

In 1959, Evelyn Waugh revised *Brideshead Revisited* for a collected edition. Fourteen years on from first publication, he admitted that the novel had a number of "grosser passages" which required modification. These had been provoked by the conditions of wartime composition:

> It was a bleak period of present privation and threatening disaster—the period of soya beans and Basic English—and in consequence the book is infused with a kind of gluttony, for food and wine, for the splendours of the recent past, and for rhetorical and ornamental language, which now with a full stomach I find distasteful.

Nor did this "bleak period" end in 1945. Austerity and rationing continued under the peacetime Labour Government, which Waugh biliously characterized as "the Cripps-Attlee terror" but many thought a rare reforming administration. "I suppose you will not come back to this country," he wrote to the Paris-based Nancy Mitford in July 1946. "You are very wise. The food gets drearier and drearier." An elderly friend of mine recently confirmed this observation. "We ate better during the war than after it," he recalled. Rationing was prolonged until 1954, while exchange-control regulations restricted foreign travel except for those with money in their shoes.

Yet *Brideshead*'s initial success was partly due to its very gluttony of prose and content; while the overhang of austerity helped further exoticize the work of voluptuaries such as Lawrence Durrell and Cyril Connolly. Elizabeth David, a young upper-middle-class Englishwoman, had spent the war in Egypt working for the Admiralty and the Ministry of Information, and had known Durrell in his Alexandrian period. Back in Britain during the harsh winter of 1946–7, she found herself in a Ross-on-Wye hotel where the food was "produced with a kind of bleak triumph which amounted almost to a hatred of humanity and humanity's needs." In response, she started jotting down what was as much a series of aromatic memories as useful advice for embattled British housewives. One such memory was a recipe for stuffing and roasting a whole sheep. At the time, the meat ration consisted of a pound per person per week. It was partly the surreal implausibility of the dish which persuaded the publisher's reader to recommend the work.

A Book of Mediterranean Food came out in 1950. Forty-two years later, when she died, Elizabeth David—by now "E.D." even to those who had never met her—was routinely farewelled as the doyenne of food writers; the most important influence on the British kitchen since Mrs. Beeton; the woman who brought the aromatic south to our dank and foggy islands. The legend went like this: poor benighted Brits, mired in snoek and Spam, believing olive oil was something you bought at the chemist's to dewax ears, were hauled into culinary awareness by E. David, whereupon they all started growing their own basil and baking their own bread. In some respects, this legend is accurate. A painter friend, now in his sixties, recalls his mother saying, "Eating for me is like cleaning my teeth"; he now cooks to a standard that E.D. would herself approve. Her writing could be immediately inspiring: my wife recalls reading an E.D. article about breadmaking and setting off at once to scour west London for live yeast. She made her acolytic bread for several months until a gas bill suggested the down-side to home baking for the single person.

At the same time, the story is, of course, more complicated. Just as there was little stuffing of whole sheep in 1950s Britain, so a lot of E.D.'s lauded ingredients were unobtainable to the point of myth. Early readers of Elizabeth David were inevitably indulging in a little light gastroporn. If male adolescents of the time consumed girlie magazines while waiting for the real thing, British domestic cooks had a few panting years to endure before the garlic and basil became available and olive oil was liberated from the chemist's. Between 1950 and 1960, Mrs. David published five classic guides to Mediterranean, Italian, French Country, French Provincial, and Summer cooking; yet her influence didn't really begin to take hold until the Sixties and Seventies. And while her books sold more than a million copies over the years, her sales penetration wasn't necessarily all that broad. People who know about Elizabeth David tend to own four or five of her books, so we might be talking of two hundred thousand households, perhaps fewer. She was much acknowledged in the breach, and her secondary influence was probably greater than her primary one. For instance, she constantly urged the necessity and virtue of using the correct equipment and proper serving dishes, opening her own shop in Chelsea to this purpose: but it was the entrepreneur and style commissar Terence Conran who popularized her ideas.

Another reason for this secondary influence was her absolute refusal to be a public figure. She received many honours, both in Britain and France, but her form of communication was the written word. She belonged much more to the prewar world of Norman Douglas (writer and gastronome, early friend and influence) than to the postwar television world of the personality chef and the décor huckster. Her first and only public interview occurred on television in 1989, when she was seventy-five. It was a coup for the production company, rather like netting J. D. Salinger or Thomas Pynchon; but the result was awkward and at times pitiable. Evelyn Waugh was also spiritually pre-television, but his occasional appearances were compelling, not least for the evident contempt with which he regarded this infantile medium. E.D. had some of the same cornered-badger prickliness, but asserted herself by evasion, leaving long silences, giving two-word answers, and evincing far less interest in the process, the medium, and the question than in the stuffed courgette in front of her on the plate.

She could be formidable and dismissive in person, permanently banishing those who offended or failed her; and she is often formidable in the text. She writes like a writer—that's to say, as one addressing an equal—rather than as an indulgent instructress jollying along any passing five-thumbed débutant. She is not complicit with other people's ignorance. Reading her, you have a strong sense of a person whose cardinal principles were truth and pleasure. This does not make for an easy relationship with those who take truthfulness to be a sign of hauteur and pleasure, a sibling of self-indulgence.

One of the ironies of E.D.'s career was that by the time she was acknowledged as a defining cultural influence she had stopped writing the kind of books which had made her one. Her work had become more scholarly and less frequent; over the last three decades of her life she produced just three grave volumes on bread, spices, and ice. A broader irony was that she encouraged more and more Britons to seek out good food in France (as being the nearest part of the Mediterranean basin) at a time when its national cuisine was passing through one of its worst crises in centuries.

I first noticed that something was up—or potentially up—in about 1980. I was having dinner near the station at Brive-la-Gaillarde. The restaurant, used by commercial travellers and those about to put their car on the overnight motorail to Boulogne, was small and unpretentious; there might have been a timid domestic murderer at the next table, but only Richard Cobb would have spotted him. You can guess the culinary plot: red check tablecloth, *plateau de crudités*, steak with thin-cut jaundiced *frites*, local cheese, then a choice of fruit or *crème caramel*. A bottle of red opened and left on the table. The kind of friendly, reliable place that leaves no special memory. This one did. I was sitting there in genial anticipation of my final French meal of the trip when something awful happened: they brought me an *amuse-gueule*.

Nowadays this wouldn't even provoke a pause in the conversation. Then it made my spirits sink. You think this is what you ought to do? You think people will have a lower opinion of you if you fail to offer a dinky *je ne sais quoi* in a flaky-pastry whatsit? My doomy response may have been excessive but was not, in retrospect, inaccurate. The French, for all their reputation as anarchic individualists and committed regionalists, have also been ruthless centralizers and dogged followers of fashion. One minute it's the *amuse-gueule*, next it'll be plates the size of birdbaths, followed by an outbreak of courgette circles topped with hillocks of fake caviare, and before you know where you are the chef at the humble Restaurant de la Gare will be shaking your hand, bugging you for praise, and trying to sell you raspberry vinegar and his book of gastro-wisdom on the way out.

Naturally, I blamed—and continued to blame—*nouvelle cuisine*, its oppressive orthodoxy, and the craven implementation of its supposed principles by chefs whose talents lie elsewhere. (I also blame the languid, preening prose of its long-time propagandists at Gault-Millau. Try this for the opening line of a restaurant write-up: "Artists often feel, at a certain moment in their lives, the need once more to hear the world begin to shake.") Elizabeth David, of course, saw further. There is nothing wrong, or odd—or, for that matter, *nouvelle*—about *nouvelle cuisine*. The first quotation in the *Oxford English Dictionary* may date only from 1975, but the phrase and the concept both go back to the mid-eighteenth century. As E.D. pointed out, "*Nouvelle cuisine* then, as now, meant lighter food, less of it, costing more." Then as now, new meant healthier and more delicate; then as now, the wiser of the *nouvellistes* admitted that their innovations only worked because they were based on the sound foundation of traditional methods. Like the *nouvelle vague*, twentieth-century *nouvelle cuisine* was a noisy, useful, publicity-driven revolt: one against *le cinéma de papa*, the other against *la cuisine de maman*. Both resulted in a temporary forgetting of just exactly what Maman and Papa did; also, and of how ineluctable genetic inheritance is. Just as Truffaut revered Jean Renoir, Bocuse acknowledged that most of his recipes were adaptations of Alfred Guérot, "one of the great chefs, the most comprehensive chefs of the first half of this century."

This doesn't mean that damage hasn't been done. Anyone who's eaten through the last few decades in France knows that at the day-to-day level the quality of restaurant cooking has fallen, that pretentious and theoretical food goes largely unpunished, and that generally you will eat better in Italy. Elizabeth David knew better, though, than to blame it all on *nouvelle cuisine*. For her, the decline had already set in by the mid-Sixties. In 1980 she recorded "the melancholy fact that during these [last] fifteen years I have eaten far worse meals, and more expensively—a bad meal is always expensive—than I would have believed possible in any civilized country." It was partly culinary fashion, but more importantly a loss of technique in the kitchen and changing social habits. Nowadays there are fewer native French in the dining-rooms, and many more uncomplaining foreigners. Employment law has also affected things: the "35-hours" rule may protect sweated labour in a fast-food outlet, but has harmed the small family restaurant.

Four years after E.D.'s death, a group of friends and followers put together a best-of volume, barded with tributes and homages. The oddest comment in the whole book came from Sir Terence Conran, who during that 1989 TV programme had proclaimed, "She writes really beautifully." After her death, he seems to have changed his mind, snootily referring to "a style that was a curious hybrid of the enthusiastic schoolmistress and the dowager duchess." Sir Terence—whose Habitat stores E.D. referred to as "Tattycat"—is not a persuasive authority: the prose of his own four-paragraph tribute is both slovenly and egotistical, as studded with "I" as a ham with cloves. E.D. wrote as she cooked: with simplicity, purity, colour, self-effacing authority, and a respect for tradition.

Her instructions are laconic, even impressionistic; they imply a reader-cook skilled in the basics and prepared to vary and improvise according to time and market supply. Most people aren't like this, of course. Many of us cook with a kind of anxious pedantry, convinced that if the exact wording, and the exact spirit behind that wording, isn't followed, then our guests will throw up first their hands and then their stomachs. E.D. herself was not unaware of failure: "In cooking, the possibility of muffing a dish is always with us. Nobody can eliminate that." But some food writers know better how to predict (often literal) sticking points, and how to mitigate the guilt and self-loathing of failure.

And it's not just the full muff one fears. When you succeed with a dish described by other writers, you feel you have made that dish; when you succeed with E.D., you feel—and this is doubtless an unfair, chippy response to her Olympian standing— that you have made "an E.D. dish," one, moreover, that she herself would have made just a little bit better. Half-competent amateurs quickly learn not to cook from volumes with full-page gastroporn pix, because their own culinary productions can never attain such lustre. Fortunately, Elizabeth David's books were illustrated with mere black-and-white drawings; but her prose nevertheless predicts a similar gap between her fragrant concoction and your burnt offering.

It is the touch of unthinking imprecision which is so unnerving. The other week, for instance, I had a go at something which looks pretty unmuffable. Page 47, Minestra di Pomidoro, from her *Italian Food* (chosen by Waugh as his Book of the Year in 1954). The recipe consists of three sentences of instruction, followed by three of commentary. Its underlying premise is that you must cook the soup for no longer than ten minutes to ensure that all the initial freshness of the tomatoes is retained. With a confidence verging on the fullish I assembled the necessaries, including homemade chicken stock and fresh basil from the greenhouse.

E.D.'s first sentence reads like this: "Melt 1½ lbs (675g) of chopped and skinned tomatoes in olive oil; add a clove of garlic and some fresh parsley or basil or marjoram." Simple? Listen: nothing is simple to the Anxious Pedant. The restaurateur Prue Leith once watched a wretched cookery-school pupil (male, of course) deconstruct the following first line of a recipe: "Separate the eggs." For a thoughtful while he pondered the two eggs placed in front of him, before carefully moving one a few inches to his left and the other a few inches to his right. Satisfied, he went on to the second line of instruction. I feel for this bonehead. And if he is reading this I'm sure he will sympathize with the glossological fever that the first line of Minestra di Pomidoro provoked. The initial problem areas were: (1) "Chopped": no indication of size of desired dice. (2) "Skinned": does this naturally imply "deseeded" or did the recipe date from pre-deseeding days? (3) "Olive oil": how much exactly; or even approximately? (4) "A clove of garlic": three possible interpretations: (a) popped in whole (unlikely); (b) crushed juicily with the garlic crusher (but would she approve of such an instrument—lots of them don't, do they?);* (c) finely chopped. (5) "Parsley or basil or marjoram": well, which is best, and what difference does it make? She can't be expecting us to exercise our free will, can she?

All this is a normal, indeed ritual, part of cooking, it seems to me. I duly argued myself to various conclusions. (Recipes that blandly lay down probable timings for preparation and cooking should also, if they are being honest, add extra minutes for paralysing fits of indecision.) The tomatoes were chopped, and the oil sizzling, when my understanding thumped belatedly against the first word of the recipe: "Melt." How could I have missed it until now? *Melt? Melt a tomato?* Even a chopped one? The implausibility of the verb froze me. Perhaps if you're south of Naples, and beneath the intense noonday sun your fingers have just that moment eased from the plant something that is less a tomato than a warm scarlet deliquescence waiting to happen; then, perhaps, the thing might melt under your spatula. But would these muscular cubettes I was now easing into the oil ever do such a thing? I found myself, as the Anxious Pedant frequently does, caught between

*She didn't. Two of the things she always refused to stock at the Elizabeth David shop were the wall-mounted knife-sharpener and the garlic press.

two incompatibilities. On the one hand, I believed, or wanted to believe, that with a few encouraging prods the tomatoes would, by a culinary process hitherto unknown to me but promised by my trustworthy tutress, suddenly melt; at the same time, I was pursued by the sane fear that cooking the surly chunks any longer in the oil and thus adding to the over-all ten-minute time limit would make them lose their freshness and vitiate the whole point of the recipe. For several fretful minutes I waited for the miracle "melt." Then, with a cookish oath, I seized the potato masher and mashed the shit out of them, hurriedly washed up the guilty instrument, and continued to the next stage of the recipe. The soup did, in the end, taste wonderful—even if not quite as wonderful as if E.D. had made it.

Could it be that Elizabeth David was too good a writer to be a food writer? Or is this just special pleading by one who needs constant textual hand-holding? Probably. E.D. cites a recipe of the French gastrotechnologist Edouard de Pomiane as "the best kind of cookery writing," by which she means something that is "courageous, courteous, adult." Further, "It is creative in the true sense of that ill-used word, creative because it invites the reader to use his own critical and inventive faculties, sends him out to make discoveries, form his own opinions, observe things for himself, instead of slavishly accepting what the books tell him." E.D. herself could not be better described than as "courageous, courteous, adult." Perhaps her ellipses are in fact sly encouragements to adulthood. Perhaps my frenzied use of the potato masher was, in its small and shameful way, creative?

Elizabeth David stood for: excellence of ingredients, simplicity of preparation, respect for tradition and for region. She stood against: fuss, overdecoration, pretentiousness; "heaps of vegetables" and "food tormented into irrelevant shapes": the castellated radish, the limply supportive lettuce leaf, the worm-cast of potato salad. She was wary of three-star restaurants and ambivalent about *nouvelle cuisine*. She sang of the Mediterranean but was also learned about British food. Her approach is always unsnobbish, even if snobberies attach to some of her followers. She could be scholarly about the history of sardine canning, and equally precise about "the sound of air gruesomely whistling through sheeps' lungs frying in oil." She described the state of the British bread industry with a fury worthy of Evelyn Waugh, but, instead of Wavianly bemoaning the equivalent of the Cripps-Attlee terror and retreating into the brandy balloon, she told people how to go about making proper bread themselves, and so helped kick-start the British bread revival.

E.D. was a liberator; perhaps it is not absurd to compare her effect on a certain sector of tired, hungry, impoverished Fifties Britain with Kinsey's effect on America. Perhaps she knew even more than he: that pine nuts, basil, and garlic are more certain providers of pleasure than unreliable human flesh. She became famous, revered and fetishized within her own culture, to the point where one instinctively searches for the *but*. Asking around among foodies, I turned up a few small buts, or semi-buts: that all food writing is evolutionary, not revolutionary; that other, forgotten figures were aware of the South at the same time; that her influence is narrower than supporters claim, or hope; that the over-all effect of her work has been to persuade Britain away from its authentic culinary roots, resulting in the geographical anomaly of the Birmingham housewife proudly serving up a Provençal dinner. "To put it crudely," an ex-restaurant critic suggested to me, "where are the recipes for Brussels sprouts?" Where, indeed; and that is part of the point. In *French Provincial Cooking* Elizabeth David quoted Ford Madox Ford, fellow-Mediterraneanist and enthusiastic home cook, on one of the prime virtues of Provence: "There there is no more any evil, for there the apple will not flourish and the Brussels sprout will not grow at all."*

These buts and semi-buts would have been irrelevant to those who assembled in February of 1994 for the sale of E.D.'s kitchen

---

*Sprouts were an *idée fixe* for Ford: "Any alienist will tell you that the first thing he does with a homicidal maniac after he gets him into an asylum is to deliver, with immense purges, his stomach from bull-beef and Brussels Sprouts."

remnants. I went along one viewing afternoon, intending to return for the sale, but was unnerved by the atmosphere, a smellable mix of melancholy, hysteria, and acquisitiveness. The melancholy came not so much from the hovering fact of Mrs. David's death two years previously as from the pathetic nature of most items: chipped jugs, two-legged colanders, battered sieves, stained cookbooks, bashed-up wooden spoons. Apart from a Welsh dresser and the large table at which E.D. had both cooked and written (bought by Prue Leith for eleven hundred pounds), it was—objectively— junk. As one of her nephews tactlessly admitted, "The best has been creamed off. It's gone to family and friends. These are the dregs." But these resonant dregs had been touched by the radioactive hand of Mrs. David, and the auction raised £49,000, three times the Phillips estimate. Francis Wheen, the biographer of Karl Marx, spent £220 of his capital on three cheesegraters, two paperbacks, and a nutmeg grater—the last item still containing a talismanically half-used nutmeg.

In 1976, when Elizabeth David collected her O.B.E., the Queen asked her what she did. "Write cookery books, Ma'am." To which the Queen responded, "How useful." It isn't known if the monarch then rushed—or sent—out for potted basil, extra-virgin olive oil, live yeast, and the right sort of bread crock. But for once she spoke for her nation. E.D. was, and after her death continues to be, very useful. It isn't always the correct accolade for a prose writer, but on this occasion it is.

(5)

Tour de France 1907

The Pont du Gard: "a little stupid,"
according to Henry James

The first *Michelin Guide to France*—limp-bound, pocket-sized, and, of course, red—came out in 1900. "The appearance of this work," its foreword pomped, "coincides with that of the new century, and the one will last as long as the other. The art of motoring has just been born; it will develop with each year, and the tyre will develop with it, since the tyre is the essential organ without which the car cannot travel." The years between 1900 and 1914 were a blessed age for motorists (and, no doubt, for tyre-developers): a time at which—for those who could afford it—technology seemed to have advanced the possibilities of pleasure with no apparent drawback. "In those days," Ford Madox Ford recalled, "the automobile was a rapturous novelty, and when we had any buckshee money at all it went on hiring cars." Henry James declared that "the motor is a magical marvel," and there can have been few more attractive countries in which to turn loose its magic than what he called "this large smooth old France."

Edith Wharton—like Ford, like Conrad, like Kipling—took to motoring with a passion. The rapturous novelty was modern yet also cleverly historical: for Wharton it restored "the romance of travel," offering the "recovered pleasures" experienced by "our posting grandparents." What had destroyed these pleasures were the iron routes and timetables of the railway; now the motorist was freed from such dependency, and could enjoy a sharp sense of increased individual liberty. As the *Baedeker Guide to Southern France* of 1907—the year in which she undertook the second of her three "motor-flights"—candidly put it: "Motoring enjoys an enormous vogue in France, principally owing to the absence of police-restrictions and to the excellent roads." From the opposite end of the century, when Europe's autoroutes are clogged with freight, and individual vehicular liberty often consists of no more than the right to be by yourself in a traffic jam, it's easy to imagine, and to envy vividly, our own motoring grandparents.

Edith Wharton was quite unconcerned about all mechanical aspects of the magical marvel; but she grasped clearly what Percy Lubbock called "the opportunity of its power." As he put it, she "remained an example to all for the intelligence with which she worked the capacity of her slave. It played an honourable, never obtrusive or assertive part in innumerable excursions"—in England, France, Italy, and the States. It also brought unexpected creative benefits. In her autobiography *A Backward Glance*, Wharton describes her early American motoring adventures, and how "one would set out on a ten-mile run with more apprehension than would now attend a journey across Africa." Gradually, she began to make longer and longer sorties into the remote blue hills of Massachusetts and New Hampshire, "discovering derelict villages with Georgian churches and balustraded house-fronts, exploring slumbrous mountain valleys, and coming back, weary but laden with a new harvest of beauty." Laden sometimes with more than this: for it was the suddenly possible exploration of these "villages still bedrowsed in a decaying rural existence," filled with "sad slow-speaking people," that provoked her bleak masterpiece *Ethan Frome*, as well as its warmer pendant *Summer*.

In this American phase Edith Wharton and her husband Teddy got through numerous motors: "selling, buying and exchanging went on continually, though without appreciably better results." The three journeys she described in *A Motor-Flight Through France* were all undertaken in the same secondhand 15hp Panhard bought by Teddy in London. Literary—and perhaps automobilistic—decorum prevented her giving us details of punctures, oil-changes, and breakdowns; social decorum from giving us details of fellow passengers. Also textually suppressed was the level of domestic support on these motor-flights: half a dozen servants went ahead by train or van and prepared for the subsequent arrival of the principals. Writing from the Grand Hotel in Pau while Teddy Wharton was laid up with bronchitis, Henry James alluded to this aspect of their travels in a typical parenthetical curlicue: "My hosts are full of amenity, sympathy, appreciation, etc., (as well as of wondrous other servanted and avant-courier'd arts of travel)."

The first flight, a two-week run from Boulogne down to Clermont-Ferrand and back to Paris, took place in May 1906 with Edith's brother Harry Jones for company; the second, a big circle of the south-west, the Pyrenees, and the Rhône Valley, occupied just over three weeks of March–April 1907, with Henry James as fellow passenger; for the third, a quick dash into Picardy over the Whitsun weekend in 1907, Edith and Teddy were unaccompanied. Their regular chauffeur was Charles Cook, a man of "native Yankee saneness and intelligence," according to James. Wharton wrote up the flights for the *Atlantic Monthly,* and published them in book form in 1908.

It would be a misapprehension to assume that James—elderly, distinguished, yet not rich—was the guest of the younger and much richer Whartons. In fact, he paid his own way, and the hotels de luxe which his hosts automatically patronized put him to financial strain. As he admitted in another letter from Pau, he was living "an expensive fairy-tale," learning once again how it was always "one's rich friends who cost one." He realized with some apprehension that by the end of the trip there would be six servants, plus chauffeur Cook, to tip. James evidently forbore to mention such embarrassments to the Whartons, although Edith would certainly have had a general awareness of his financially subservient state. Percy Lubbock tells a story of the two writers taking a drive in Edith Wharton's latest brand-new motor—bought, she just happens to mention, with the proceeds of her last novel. "With the proceeds of *my* last novel," James replies meditatively, "I purchased a small go-cart, or hand-barrow, on which my guests' luggage is wheeled from the station to my house. With the proceeds of my next novel I shall have it painted."

The early motorist had to be an adventurous stoic. The 1900 *Michelin Guide,* alongside various remedies for mechanical ills, lists its special formula for "driver's eye-lotion" (450g infusion of coca leaves, 25g cherry-laurel water, 15g biborate of soda). Wharton's very first motoring experience—a thrilling hundred-mile round trip from Rome to the Villa Caparola in 1903—left her with two afflictions: acute motor-fever and acute laryngitis, the latter keeping her in bed for several days. On subsequent expeditions she was obliged, even in the hottest weather, to take the precaution of being "swaddled in a stifling hood with a mica window, till some benefactor of the race invented the windscreen and made motoring an unmixed joy." The Wharton windscreen appears to have arrived between the first and second motor-flights. For the 1906 trip they went unscreened and were pursued by rain: "It has been a cold, dark dreary spring in Europe, owing to Vesuvius they say." But we know that at some point before departure for the south Teddy Wharton personally made modifications to the car, closing in the body, installing interior electric light, and adding "every known accessorie and comfort."

It was Henry James who proposed himself as companion on the second and longest of these motor-flights. When he heard about the previous year's trip—and in particular about the visit to George Sand's house at Nohant—he reacted with theatrical yet real jealousy. He had, he wrote to Edith, "a strange telepathic intuition. A few days after you sloped off to France I said to myself suddenly: 'They're on their way to Nohant, d—n them! They're going there—they *are* there!' " Such envy is understandable: during his younger days in Paris, James had met Flaubert, Gautier, and Maupassant, each of whom had described to him the Second Empire's most famous literary pilgrimage—then made by train and diligence—to visit *la mère Sand.* Now, writing from the Reform Club in November 1906, James begs Wharton to recount

"Your adventure and impressions of Nohant—as to which I burn and yearn for fond particulars. Perhaps if you have the proper Vehicle of Passion—as I make no doubt—you will be going there once more—in which case *do* take me!" This request accounts for the only narrative duplication in *A Motor-Flight;* though on the second visit to Nohant James's presence helped gain them access to the interior of the house.

On 20 March 1907 the Whartons and James, with Cook at the wheel, set off from Paris in the Vehicle of Passion. This was James's generic sobriquet for the Wharton motor; individual engines had their particular nicknames, such as "the Chariot of Fire," "Alfred de Musset," "George" (after Sand), and "Hortense" (after the erotic novelist Hortense Allart). The journey must have had an extra edge of shading for James, because exactly a quarter of a century earlier, in 1882, he had himself made *A Little Tour in France,* also published in periodical then hard-bound form. Many of the places he visited then he was to revisit with the Whartons, especially on the southern section: Angoûleme, Bordeaux, Toulouse, Carcassonne, Nîmes, Avignon, Bourg-en-Bresse, and Dijon. Leon Edel characterizes his Tour as "neat, well-placed, inexpensive"; now he was involved in the whirl and luxury of the Whartons'. His had been a typically nineteenth-century journey: by train and horse to squalid inn. Now the Vehicle of Passion sped them to a hotel which would be rejected if it failed to reach Edith's high expectations. Sometimes a whole town was judged unfit for Whartonian overnighting. Sometimes a whole region: in central France, she notes, "one is often doomed to pine" for "digestible food and clean beds." James, with more tolerance, or resignation, had previously identified "that familiar and intermittent hospitality which a few weeks spent in the French provinces teaches you to regard as the highest attainable form of accommodation."

Motoring now permitted the fastidious to indulge a certain topographical snobbery. There was no need to approach a town through the "mean purlieus" of the railway station, the "area of ugliness and desolation created by the railway itself"; your first impression of a place could once again—as for your posting grandparents—be "romantic or stately." This cocooning effect extended beyond the mere avoidance of marshalling yards: speed, the motor, chosen *compagnons de voyage,* and avant-courier'd servants all minimized the kind of chance human contact thrown up by earlier, slower, solitary travelling. Wharton's book chronicles peasant faces glimpsed in doorways and the flushed servant at the auberge, but it's significant that the two largest human presences in her text were already long dead: George Sand and Madame de Sévigné.

James's *Little Tour* is inclined to make us nostalgic for that era of leisurely, meticulous yet also somewhat lazy travel, our guide a highly sophisticated man taking his sensibility, like some great dog, for a walk. *A Motor-Flight* is the work of a genuine modern tourist. Someone with just as much art and sensibility as James, but closer to us; someone facing—and choosing to face—a hastier flurry of sense impressions, a quicker mental satiety; someone also whose presence and activities, unlike those of the solitary ruin-bibber, are going to change the land under inspection. "The demands of motoring are introducing modern plumbing and Maple furniture into the uttermost parts of France," Wharton acknowledges. Those romantic old inns, where it is "charming to breakfast, if precarious to sleep," are already doomed.

Although Wharton offers herself as "the trivial motorist, the mere snarer of haphazard impressions," we should not be misled by this self-presentation as an aesthetic amateur. The French cathedrals were for her vivid embodiments of architectural principles long understood and digested, rather than (as for the true trivial motorist) a puzzle of intersecting elements for which the guidebook must supply the crossword solution. When she discusses the "hale durability" of the Romanesque, laments that France "has never wholly understood the use of brick," drops an aside about what English Gothic lost by committing itself to the square east end; when she disentangles the Crusader church at Neuvy-Saint-

Sépulcre, luxuriates in the façade of Reims cathedral, wittily casti-
gates the "hairless pink monster" at Albi; when she decries the
work of Viollet-le-Duc without being so doctrinaire as to ignore
his occasional coups; when she praises the benign neglect of buildings, which allows them to show their "scars and hues of age"
rather than appearing as spruce old ladies; when she invokes the
aesthetic centrality of the Italian hill-town whose architecture
embellishes and completes the contours of the landscape—on such
occasions we attend to an authority, not to a mere motorist.

At the same time—and this is part of what makes her close to
us—she is not content to treat the successive edifices before her
like some version of wine-tasting, an occasion for fine minds with
fine purses to display their fine discriminations. What does it, can
it, should it mean for a person of a later, swifter civilization to
examine these remnants of an earlier, slower yet surer civilization?
Can we view them imaginatively, or only solipsistically? What sort
of pleasure, what rousing to reverence can we legitimately expect?
She addresses such questions at the start of the book, at Amiens,
and returns to them near its close, at Reims. She was skilled at
focusing them because—like James—she was aware of coming
from "a land which has undertaken to get on without a past,"
whose citizen-tourists at large in Europe were inclined to treat the
architectural expression of vast historical forces as a mere aesthetic
diversion. This approach is even commoner nowadays, and we
should all be rebuked and enlightened by Wharton's example.

She is, indeed, that rare and oxymoronic thing, the wise tourist;
one eager to give an account of "what he sees, and *feels beneath the
thing seen*" (the italics, as well as the masculine pronoun, are hers).
She has great powers of mental comparison: leaving Beauvais, she
finds that she has not really quitted it because she is still—and her
phrase is scentedly Jamesian—"imprisoned in that tremendous
memory." She treasures buildings that carry the imagination back
in a direct flight, to a time when "piety still walked with art."
Tourism for her is thus not passive but constructive, re-creative.

There is a completeness as well as a wisdom to her: she moves easily between landscape, architecture, and humanity, treating them as overlapping rather than self-contained areas of study; she can do that hardest of art-critical jobs, which is to make tapestries sound interesting; and just when you think she might be coasting she will be startlingly evocative. The carved mermaids on the choir-stalls of Saint Savin leap out at us as "creatures of bale and beauty, who seem to have brought from across the Alps their pagan eyes and sidelong Lombard smile"; the Pyrenees, when viewed from the taming distance of the terrace at Pau, are "subjected to a kind of indignity of inspection, like caged carnivora in a zoo."

But it would be a mistake to represent her either as an automatic praiser—she is robustly dismissive of Toulouse and the vulgarity of Lourdes, of false decoration and meretricious bedizening—or as a mere building-broker. Her landscapes are vivid, and peopled with a peasantry she attends to carefully, if lyrically. When she writes of Pyrenean hill-country men "so disciplined by industry, yet so romantically free," or of the French provincial face provoking "the same kind of interest as a work of art," she is not just another rich urban foreigner charmed by local colour. What she finds in these glimpsed physiognomies is what she also seeks and celebrates in old buildings: something that carries the imagination back in a direct flight. She is aware that the motorist who arrives in the uttermost parts of France with an expectation of modern plumbing and Maple furniture is also finally a menace to the "independence and simplicity of living," the "thriftily compact traditional life" which has over centuries formed and defined the landscape's inhabitants. What she celebrates about France on the human side is its civic order and elegance, the amenity of manners, the vivacity, good temper, and intelligent enjoyment of life. These terms are always comparative. Today the motorist will find the approaches to French towns no more "romantic or stately" by road than they are by rail; and just as there is a commercial clutter of Mr. Bricolage and his confrères disfiguring the outskirts, so there is more of an overlay to the perceptible character of the people. We can no longer see back as clearly as she could.

Wharton and James agreed about much, but not everything, of what they visited together. Each had an aesthetic in which Italy was the touchstone; they liked their old buildings old, and were suspicious of restoration. She is more wholehearted in admiring the Graeco-Roman remains of Provence. He had judged the Pont du Gard finally "a little stupid" (an adjective also applied to the Tour Magne at Nîmes, and to the round towers of Chambord), and was lordly in his diminishment of Roman architecture: "The Roman rigidity was apt to overshoot the mark, and I suppose a race which could do nothing small is as defective as a race that can do nothing great." She thought Avignon engagingly Italianate; he had loathed it, finding the Palais des Papes "as intricate as it is vast, and as desolate as it is dirty." For once he would happily applaud the arrival of the restorers, "for they cannot well make it less interesting than it is at present." But their most instructive disagreement came at Bourg-en-Bresse, whose principal attraction was and is the church at Brou.

James's account begins with a sentimental evocation of Matthew Arnold's then-celebrated poem about Brou. He twits and pardons Arnold for his geographical inexactitude, sketches the flamboyant piety that lay behind the construction of the church, dabbles with his guidebook, describes the famous tombs, gives them little butter-dabs of approval—admirable, admirable, charming, exquisite, splendid, ingenious, elaborate, precious—before concluding that, though fine, the monuments are not quite so fine as their rivals in Verona. He makes a slightly arch mother-in-law joke, marvels that the whole edifice wasn't destroyed in the Revolution, and segues effortlessly into a rhapsodic description—more fun for us, and, one senses, for him too—of the simple yet epicurean lunch of boiled eggs, bread, and local butter that he subsequently consumed in Bourg.

Wharton's account makes no reference to James's text of 1882, any more than it does to his living presence beside her in the Panhard twenty-five years later. It must have been intimidating to address an unchanged subject already discussed by an accompanying Master. No doubt she had read *A Little Tour;* though when last, we do not know. How could there not be, at some level, an element of competitiveness in her description? She too begins with a jocund treatment of Arnold's poem, wondering if he could ever have seen the church at Brou, so inaccurately does he locate it. As for the edifice itself: for a start, it disobeys Wharton's precept that old buildings should look old—this one is "scrubbed, scraped and soaped as if its renovation were a feat daily performed by the 'seven maids with seven mops' on whose purifying powers the walrus so ingeniously speculated." Externally, it is "a celluloid toy." Internally, it reminds her of the Albert Memorial, all pious expense and little taste. It is "pastrycook's art." Alongside this informal mockery resides her precise architectural sense. Where James murmurs suavely that Margaret of Austria's shrine is "the last extravagance of a Gothic which had gone so far that nothing was left it but to return upon itself," Wharton makes the same point in a more vernacular style ("the last boiling-over of the heterogeneous Gothic pot"), emphasizes her extra knowledge ("One sees the same result in almost all the monuments of the period, especially where the Spanish-Netherlands influence has added a last touch of profusion"), and seals it with a memorable metaphor: "Expiring Gothic changed its outline as often as the dying dolphin is supposed to change his colours—every ornament suggests a convulsion in stone." And whereas James moves lightly on to lunch, Wharton moves seriously on to a comparison with the mourning sculptures on the tomb of Jean-sans-Peur in Dijon, which she values highly (and which James had found of "limited interest"). A leery mind might hazard that despite her true reverence for James, she is out to pull architectural rank; while also ensuring that her freshness of tone impresses him—and us—with her modernity.

James occasionally made fond mock of Edith Wharton's travel-fever, portraying her as a bossy bird of prey swooping down on the more sedentary and bearing them off "on india-rubber wings." But they were clearly excellent and devoted *compagnons de voyage.* James reported that on the motor-flight he had "almost the time of my life," and looking back he gave out gratified exhalations. "Ah, the lovely rivers and the inveterately glorious grub." "Ah, the good food and good manners and good looks everywhere!" For her part, Edith Wharton declared that "Never was there a more admirable travelling companion, more ready to enjoy and unready to find fault—never bored, never disappointed, and never (*need* I say?) missing any of the little fine touches of sensation that enrich the moments of the really good traveller." No sooner had they got back to Paris than she whisked him away for another brief flight. And in April 1908 James responded enthusiastically to the idea of meeting in Amiens with the suggestion of "a little *tournée,* under motor-goggles, in Normandy." He had a specific and powerful destination in mind: "& oh, will you take me to Croisset, by Rouen, as a pendant to Nohant?" It would indeed have been a fitting pendant—first Sand's house, then the vestiges of Flaubert's—but the plan fell victim to the complications of Wharton's emotional life.

One final motor trip should, however, be mentioned. Shortly after the publication of *A Motor-Flight Through France* the two novelists were driving from Rye to Windsor when James suggested making a detour to Box Hill to visit the aged George Meredith. Wharton was at first unwilling, as she judged herself unlikely to shine in such impromptu circumstances; then she agreed to the route-change but insisted upon staying in the car at Box Hill. Determinedly, James overcame her objections and took her with him into the house. Meredith, terminally ill, deeply deaf, and "statuesquely enthroned in a Bath chair," had great difficulty cracking the identity of this unknown woman who had turned up unexpectedly with Henry James. It was, she later recalled, "a laborious business, and agonizing to me, as the room rang again and again with my unintelligible name." Eventually, Meredith twigged; whereupon he picked up the book lying open at his elbow, and held it out with a smile. "I read the title, and the blood rushed over me like fire. It was my own *Motor-Flight Through France,* then lately published; and he had not known I was to be brought to see him, and he had actually been reading my book when I came in!"

(6)

Tour de France 2000

"To the memory of Tom Simpson, Olympic medallist,
World champion, British sporting ambassador,
died 13th July (Tour de France 1967)"

In early July, as the first Tour de France of the new millennium meandered joustingly down the flat western side of the country, I visited a small cycling museum in the mid-Wales spa town of Llandrindod Wells. Halfway round this testament to curatorial obsession, among the velocipedes and the 1896 Crypto Front Wheel Drivers, the passionate arrangements of cable clips and repair-outfit tins, there is a small display window containing the vestimentary leavings of the British cyclist Tom Simpson. A grubby white jersey with zippered neck, maker's emblem (Le Coq Sportif), big Union Jacks on each shoulder, and discoloured glue bands across the thorax indicating the removal of perhaps a sponsor's name, perhaps the coloured stripes awarded for some previous triumph. Black trunks with PEUGEOT embroidered in surprisingly delicate white stitchwork across the left thigh. Chamois-palmed string-backed cycling gloves with big white press-buttons at the back of the wrist, and the fingers mittenishly cut off at the first joint. This is what Simpson had been wearing on 13 July 1967, during the thirteenth stage of the Tour, when he collapsed on Mont Ventoux, the highest of the Provençal Alps. Thirty-three years to the day of his death, the 2000 Tour was due to climb the mountain again.

Back in 1962, Simpson had been the first British rider ever to wear the race leader's yellow jersey (only three other Britons have acquired it since); he'd been World Champion in 1965, and in 1967 had already won Paris-Nice, the early-season classic flatteringly known as "The Race to the Sun." He was a strong, gutsy cyclist, popular with fellow riders, the press, and the public. He also played up cheerfully to the Englishman's image, posing emblematically with bowler hat and furled umbrella. The memorial to him near the summit of Mont Ventoux lists his achievements as "Olympic Medallist, World Champion, British Sporting Ambassador," and the last of these three is no sentimental piety. If sport increasingly becomes a focus for slack-brained chauvinism, it also, at its best, acts as a solvent, transcending national identity and raising the sport, and the sports person, above such concerns. Simpson was one of those transplanted stars (like John Charles in Italy, or Eric Cantona in Britain) who managed to win over a foreign public, and thus did more to harmonize Europe—or at least, reconcile diversity—than a thousand Brussels suits. His martyrish suffering on a French mountain added to the myth. His name is still widely remembered in France—more so, probably, than in Britain.

Mont Ventoux, which rises to just over nineteen hundred metres, doesn't appear especially sharp-sided or rebarbative from a distance. For those on foot, it is comparatively welcoming: Petrarch climbed it with his brother and two servants in 1336, and a local hiking firm offers night-time ascents for the reasonably fit with a promise of spectacular sunrises. For the Tour rider, it is another matter. Other mountains in the race may be higher or steeper, but seem more friendly, or more functional; or at least more routine, being climbed most years. Ventoux is a one-off. Its appearance is perpetually wintry: the top few hundred metres are covered with a whitish scree, giving the illusion of a snowbound summit even in high summer. A few amateur botanists may scour its slopes for polar flora (the Spitzbergen saxifrage, the Greenland poppy), but there is little other recreational activity on offer here. Ventoux is just a bleak and hulking mountain with an observatory at the top. There is no reason for going up it except that the Tour planners order you to go up it. Cyclists fear and hate the place, while the fact that the Tour only makes the ascent once every five years or so increases its mystique, builds its broodingness. In his autobiography, *It's Not About the Bike*, Lance Armstrong called the

Tour de France "a contest in purposeless suffering"; the climb of Mont Ventoux illustrates this implacably.

When the tree line runs out, there is nothing up there but you and the weather, which is violent and capricious. Legend has it that on the day Simpson died a thermometer in a café half-way up the mountain burst while registering fifty-four degrees centigrade (officially, the temperature was in the nineties Fahrenheit). But there is one thing cyclists fear as much as heat: wind. One task of the support riders in a team is to protect their leader from the elements; they cluster round him on windy stretches like worker bees protecting the queen. (This abnegation is also self-interested, for in the Tour the monarch is also a cash crop, his prize money being divided among the team at the race's end.) But on the mountains, where the weaker fall away, the top riders are often left to themselves, unprotected. And Ventoux, where the mistral mixes with the tramontane, is officially the windiest place on earth: in February 1967, the world gusting record was set there, at 320 kilometres per hour. Popular etymology derives Ventoux from *vent,* wind, making it Windy Mountain; appropriate but erroneous. The proper etymology—*Vinturi,* from the Ligurian root *ven-* meaning mountain—is duller but perhaps truer. Mount Mountain: a place to make bikers feel they're climbing not one peak but two; a place to give bikers double vision.*

As I drove towards the mountain the day before the Tour climbed it, there was cloud hanging over its summit, but otherwise the day felt clear, if breezy. This changed quickly on the upper slopes. Cloud covered the top fifteen hundred feet or so; visibility dropped to a few yards; the wind rose. By the side of the road, hardy fans who had arrived early to claim their places were double-chocking the wheels of their camper vans and piling stones halfway up the rims for extra security. The Simpson memorial—

---

*Edith Wharton thought there were two candidates for the title "the sublimest object in Provence": the Pont du Gard and Mont Ventoux. For her, the Pont du Gard finished (a close) second.

the profile of a crouched rider set on a granite slab—is placed where he fell from his bike, a kilometre and a half from the summit on the eastern side. Its handsome simplicity is subverted by the clutter of heartfelt junk laid on the steps in front of it. Some mourners have simply added a large white stone from the nearby slope; but more have strewn the site with a jumble of cycling castoffs: water bottles, logoed caps, T-shirts, energy bars, a saddle, a couple of tyres, a symbolic broken wheel. It is part Jewish grave, part the tumultuous altar of some popular if dubious Catholic saint. All this was difficult to take in because the cold and the wind were pulling so much water into my eyes. It felt locally strange to be attempting some vague act of homage while being barely able to stand; more largely strange in that the winds—gusting at more than 150 kilometres per hour that day—seemed to have absolutely no effect in dispersing the cloud. After a few minutes, I got back into the car and drove down the mountain to Bédoin, where I found that the bones of my fingers and toes still ached from the cold. I craved a whisky. An hour or so later, snow fell on the summit.

When Petrarch set out on his ascent, he encountered, like any modern journalist, a quotable peasant who just happened to have climbed the mountain himself fifty years previously. However, the fellow "had got for his pains nothing except fatigue and regret, and clothes and body torn by the rocks and briars. No one, so far as he or his companions knew, had ever tried the ascent before or after him." Petrarch's brother headed for the summit by the most direct, and therefore hardest, route; while the poet, being wilier or lazier, kept trying other paths in the hope of finding an easier way. Each time the trail proved false, and such shameful halfhearted-ness brought Ovid to the climber's mind. "To wish is little: we must long with the utmost eagerness to gain our end." For Petrarch, the excursion up the Ventoux turned out to be a metaphor of the spiritual journey: it is uphill all the way, and there are no shortcuts.

But bikers, like hikers, are always looking for shortcuts. Next to the Simpson display window in Llandrindod Wells, I saw a publicity photograph of Mrs. Billie Dovey, a prewar cycling belle promoted as "the Rudge Whitworth 'Keep Fit Girl.'" This smiling, bespectacled icon pedals towards us in sepia innocence, an advertisement for comradely physical improvement, *mens sana in corpore sano*. But, as in most sports, the higher and the more professional you go, the less Corinthian it becomes. Various factors led to Simpson's death on 13 July 1967: the heat, the mountain, the lack of support (he was riding with a weak national team), the pressure on a rider approaching thirty to win the Tour before his time passed. But the prime cause of Simpson's heart attack on Mont Ventoux was the use of amphetamines, which helped his body ignore sense, and made his last words a dying plea to be put back on his bike. Traces of amphetamines were found in Simpson's body and among his kit. Speed kills, the moralists asserted. But Simpson's case was hardly egregious. Amphetamines—famously used to keep bomber crews alert on long missions—were widely consumed by cyclists in the postwar years. Their explosive effect caused them to be nicknamed *la bomba* in Italian, *la bombe* in French, and the somewhat more sinister *atoom* in Dutch. In the late Fifties, the legendary Italian rider Fausto Coppi was asked on French radio if all riders took *la bomba*. "Yes," he replied, "and those who claim the opposite aren't worth talking to about cycling." "So did you take *la bomba*?" the interviewer continued. "Yes, whenever it was necessary." "And when was it necessary?" "Practically all the time." The five-time Tour winner Jacques Anquetil told the French sports daily *L'Equipe* in the year Simpson died, "You'd have to be an imbecile or a hypocrite to imagine that a professional cyclist who rides 235 days a year can hold himself together without stimulants."

Benjo Maso, the Dutch sociologist and historian of cycling, enlightened and depressed me about the prehistory of drug use. In the early days, this meant mainly strychnine, cocaine, and morphine,* though there were also folksier pick-me-ups, like bull's

---

*The most popular stimulant was the innocently named "American coffee": caffeine in combination with strychnine, cocaine, ether, and nitroglycerine.

blood and the crushed testicles of wild animals. An Englishman named Linton died from his exertions in the Bordeaux-Paris race of 1896; his death was generally attributed to the use of morphine. In the 1920s, riders fuelled themselves with "incredible amounts of booze." Maso cited another Bordeaux-Paris race (the event called for herculean stamina, being run in a single stretch, right through the night) in which one team's allowance per man was a bottle of eau-de-vie, some port, some white wine, and some champagne. These alcoholic habits continued; there are photos of Tour de France riders refuelling in bars and cafés. At Bédoin, where the Ventoux climb begins, Simpson supposedly complicated his body by stopping off with other riders for a drink; rumour has served him with a whisky and a pastis. This may sound foolishly self-defeating now, but at the time Tour regulations permitted the riders' support staff to give them liquid only at certain intervals; moreover, there was a general belief in the *peloton* (the main bunch of riders) that alcohol taken during the course of an event did you no harm, since it was quickly sweated out. Athletes and alcohol: when Captain Webb swam the English Channel in 1875, he washed his breakfast down that day with claret, and sustained himself on the way to Calais with brandy and "strong old ale." So has it always been going on, I asked Maso. "Well, they had breath tests for alcohol in the ancient Olympic games," he replied.

This all seems less shocking when you look at the terrain and remember that the riders have to cover 3,630 kilometres in three weeks, with only two rest days. The Tour de France is easily the most punishing endurance event in the athletic world. A triathlon, by comparison, is a fun-run. (Armstrong was a triathlete before becoming a professional cyclist.) The British rider David Millar, a Tour débutant this year, summed up a day that for him had consisted of eight and a half hours in the saddle, followed by a two-hour traffic jam to get to a hotel where the restaurant had closed and he was unable even to get a massage: "Sado-masochism." If driving down the Ventoux to Bédoin leaves you croaking for a whisky, you'd certainly need one if asked to cycle up it; even the

Rudge Whitworth Keep Fit Girl might take a snifter. The nearest equivalent to her on the Tour de France was perhaps Gino Bartali, Coppi's great rival, who won the race twice, in 1938 and 1948. "I didn't need drugs," he once said. "Faith in the Madonna kept me from feeling fatigue and pain." But such Petrarchianism was rare; for many riders miracles existed only in capsule form. With amphetamines, there was even a certain rough justice: they helped get you up the mountain one day, but exacted their price the next. Both Coppi and Simpson were known for their *défaillances*, their days of weakness; though doubtless climbing Ventoux without chemical help would leave you pretty tired the next day anyway.*

Such speedy, boozy days now seem almost innocent; and they were innocent in that Coppi's use of *la bomba* didn't contravene the cycling regulations of the day—amphetamines were declared illegal only in the mid-Sixties. The quantum leap came when drugs designed to stimulate were replaced—or, in real terms, joined—by drugs designed to fortify, notably growth hormones and EPO (erythropoietin). Instead of helping suppress pain and giving you the illusion that you were stronger than you actually were, the new drugs really did make you stronger. In addition, Maso explained, "There are no bad days, as with amphetamines." From the early Nineties, EPO became the drug of choice among many professional cyclists. Its function is to raise the red-blood-cell count, which sends more oxygen to the tissues, thus increasing your endurance and powers of recovery. If there are two riders of equal ability, the one taking EPO will always beat the one who remains

---

*There was an Italian rider of the postwar years called Brambilla, who was famous for his masochism. When riding badly, he used to hit himself round the head with his cycle pump, and deny himself water. In 1947 he lost the Tour on the very last day. In response, he punished his bike, by burying it at the bottom of his garden: a deed he was not allowed to forget. "Is it true?" André Brulé asked him, as the riders were rolling out one day in a subsequent Tour. "Why did you do that?" "The bike had wooden rims," Brambilla replied sarcastically, "and I wanted to grow some poplars in my garden." "Lucky you didn't plant your water bottle as well," said Brulé, "or you'd have grown a pharmacy."

clean; it really is as simple as that. And until this year, the presence of EPO was not detectable; only its suspicious consequences were.

There is a down-side, of course. Bike riders, like other top athletes, are so fit that their heart rate is preternaturally low; EPO thickens the blood, making it harder to pump around the body, and also more liable to clot. In the early days of EPO there were a number of mysterious deaths—usually from a heart attack, usually in the middle of the night—of otherwise healthy cyclists. The assumption was that their heart rate had dropped during sleep and had become simply insufficient to pump the blood. To counter this, some EPO-takers got up in the middle of the night and did exercises. Some even used a kind of thoracic alarm clock, which woke them when their heart rate fell too low.

If you want to put a date on the final loss of innocence (ours, not that of the inner cycling world), you could do worse than suggest 8 July 1998—a century on from Linton's morphine-fuelled win in Bordeaux-Paris. Willy Voet, *soigneur* to the Festina team, was stopped by customs officers at the Franco-Belgian border. *Soigneur* means healer, and the job traditionally consists of giving massages and overseeing the day-to-day fitness of the riders. Voet was on his way to join the start of that year's Tour and was found to be transporting, in two refrigerated bags, "234 doses of EPO, 80 phials of growth hormones, 160 capsules of testosterone, and 60 capsules of Asaflow, an aspirin-based product which fluidifies the blood." During a subsequent three-year ban, Voet published a memoir in which he set out dispassionately, and with rather unconvincing remorse, the drugs he administered: amphetamines, corticoids, growth hormones (clenbuterol, creatine, nandrolone), and of course EPO. Voet explains that each drug has a specific function for the different parts of a stage race: thus, sprinters would take Trinitrine five or six kilometres before the finish to help them launch their final attack. *La bomba* has given way to *le pot Belge* (Belgian mixture), whose typical contents might be amphetamines, antalgics, caffeine, cocaine, heroin, and sometimes corticoids. This is a world in which the phrase "caffeine injection" refers not to a double espresso but to something with a needle on the end which helps you get through a time trial in the mountains. The *soigneur* is constantly tinkering and adjusting, in full collusion with his charge. (Here the notion that riders are sometimes slipped wicked substances without their knowledge is thoroughly mocked.) Voet describes Richard Virenque, the highly popular French leader of the Festina team, fretting about his preparation for a time-trial stage during the 1997 Tour de France. But Voet knew that everything was under control: "Given his regular treatments of EPO and especially growth hormones, he was as ready as he would ever be. All he needed was a well-timed injection of caffeine, plus Solucamphre (to open his bronchial tubes)."

In this world, the dunces and losers are those who pit their cleaner physiques against the smarter cheats. Voet cites the case of Charly Mottet, a top French rider of the Eighties and Nineties. When he joined the RMO team, they discovered to their amazement that "the bloke was clean." Mottet had, in many people's view, the talent to win the Tour, but Voet recognized that he lacked "the wherewithal to make it happen." In other words, he refused the tempting pharmacopoeia. Mottet was known for his weakness over the final third of the Tour, and the *soigneur*'s conclusion is as sad as it is hypocritical: "Yes indeed, Charly never had the career that he deserved."

Voet's disclosures after his arrest led to a police raid on the Festina team, and its ejection from the Tour in mid-race. Six other teams quit in protest—though their departures were open to alternative explanation. One by one, Festina riders admitted illegal drug use, though Virenque adamantly protested his innocence from the start. The only note of unintentional comedy that year came during a judicial hearing in Lille, when the judge put it to him that, "You must have known what was going on because you were the leader." Virenque, in a panicky mishearing, replied, "Me a dealer? No, I am not a dealer." (The same two English words are used in French.) Whereupon Virenque's lawyer interjected, "No, Richard, the judge said *leader*. It's not an offence to be a leader."

Voet explains the mechanics and use of EPO. The *soigneur* takes a blood sample from a rider, puts it in a portable centrifuge, and obtains a reading of the haematocrit, or red-blood cell, level in percentage terms. An average man might have a level of 44 per cent, which would fluctuate with exertion, dehydration, blood loss, altitude, and other conditions. The *soigneur* would therefore monitor his charges in the run-up to a big race and administer EPO if the blood needed boosting; he would also adjust accordingly throughout the event. In 1997, the International Cycling Union fixed the legal limit at 50 per cent. But since *soigneurs* would examine their riders' blood daily, only foolish overenthusiasm or bad calibration would make you fail an official test.

In racing terms, EPO led to what was christened "the two-speed *peloton*"—those using it and those not. It also produced a blurring of the traditional distinction between endurance men and climbers. All of a sudden, riders of quite chunky body profile were motoring up hills previously the preserve of the quail-bodied climber. Recent Tour history cannot be rewritten, but needs to be annotated with Voet's casual asides—for instance, that such-and-such a rider, famous for such-and-such an exploit, was known in the *peloton* as Mr. 60 Per Cent.

The 2000 Tour was largely decided on the Pyrenean climb to Hautacam, on Monday, 10 July. After five hours of cycling, 191 kilometres, and two high mountain passes, Lance Armstrong, the 1999 winner, climbed the final fourteen kilometres at such a pace as to put all his main rivals at least four minutes behind him in the overall classification. Virenque was one of those overtaken in Armstrong's exhilarating attack: "He came upon us like an aeroplane." During that previous year's win, Armstrong had faced some scepticism from the French press. How could a promising, aggressive, but often unthinking rider, after receiving treatment for testicular cancer, which had already metastasized into the lungs and brain, return and not only ride the Tour but actually win it? Renewed determination, a body outline refashioned by chemotherapy, a greater acceptance of suffering, and a wiser tactical approach—these were not sufficient answers for some. Perhaps the cancer drugs had inadvertently beneficial side effects? Ironically, Armstrong's doctors had at one point given him EPO (which, as the synthetic version of a naturally occurring hormone, is often prescribed for dialysis and chemotherapy patients).

Armstrong spent much of 1999 reiterating "I'm clean" at press conferences, and felt that journalists deliberately misconstrued him when he spoke French. His revenge in 2000 was to speak only English and let the French press get on with it. He is a lean, prickly, single-minded character, whose stance before the microphone implies that tact is for girls; he is after victory, not popularity. This approach did little to wash away doubt. Daniel Baal, the president of the French Cycling Federation, said after Hautacam, "I would love to know what is happening today . . . I do not know if we must speak of a new method [of doping] or of a new substance. The controls have had some impact, I saw many riders in difficulty on the climbs and that was good. But then must I have enthusiasm for how the race is being won?" Baal's problem was simply this: to know what he had seen.

Despite what might appear to outsiders a vast moral taint, the Tour remains extremely popular in France. This is the more surprising given that the last French victory, by Bernard Hinault, came fifteen years ago. Since then the race has been won by two Americans, two Spaniards, an Irishman, a Dane, a German, and an Italian. In 1999, not a single stage was won by a Frenchman; in 2000, they managed just two out of twenty-one. Such robust zeal for the victories of others confirms the suspicion that the French sports fan tends to be as much a devotee of the sport itself as of the team or nation, to be more of a purist than his Anglo-Saxon equivalent.

This is probably non-demonstrable, but here is my own evidence. In 1993 the French soccer team was on course for the finals of the next year's World Cup. All it required was one point—a mere draw—out of its final two qualifying matches, against Israel and Bulgaria. Astonishingly, the team lost to Israel. I watched the deciding game against Bulgaria on television in a French provincial hotel in the company of two off-duty waiters. At first, all went well: France took the lead. Then Bulgaria equalized—still, all was well enough, for time was running out. At the death, against the run of play and most versions of justice, Bulgaria scored a winning goal. In Britain, this might have led to domestic violence, or the torching of any nearby Bulgarian car or restaurant, if one could be found. There, one deeply despondent French waiter said to another, "It was a pretty goal."

Purist does not, however, mean moralist. Footage of French police thundering into cyclists' hotel rooms in mid-Tour may delight editorialists but it offends many domestic cycling fans. The name of Richard Virenque was painted on the tarmac of the Ventoux climb as often this year as any other. There is an instinctive French anti-authoritarianism that causes many to side unflinchingly with their heroes against the judiciary, the gendarmerie, and suddenly outraged politicians. But cycling is also different in one key respect. In other sports, fans go to a stadium, where there are entrance fees, tacky souvenirs, overpriced food, a general marshalling and corralling, and a professional exploitation of the fan's emotions. With the Tour de France, the heroes come to you, to your village, your town, or arrange a rendezvous on the slopes of some spectacular mountain. The Tour is free, you choose where you watch it from, bring your own picnic, and the marketing hard sell consists of little more than a van offering official Tour T-shirts at sixty francs a throw just before the race arrives. Then you get to see your heroes' grimacing faces from merely a few feet away; every seat is a ringside seat. These aspects make the Tour unique, and still rightly cherished by the French.

Some play it as a *jour de fête,* part of a communal thrill in small village or country byway; the more hard-core will spend a couple of buffeted nights on the Ventoux in an ad-hoc trailer park, suffering the wind and cold in fellow-feeling with the riders; the fan who wants to know what is actually happening will follow the live TV feed from helicopter and motorbike cameras. The satellite dishes clamped to many of the camper vans indicate that methods two and three are often combined, but most go for one and three. So on 13 July—by which time the wind had dropped, and the temperature at the top of Mont Ventoux had risen to a generous six degrees centigrade—I headed for Saint-Didier, a small village east of Carpentras. The main bunch would reach here after half an hour's riding, at some time between 12:27, if they were averaging thirty-eight kph, and 12:39, if they were dawdling along at thirty-four kph. Their route, down a plane-lined alley towards a handsome 1756 belfry gate, was marked out by chunky red-and-white barriers. The kerbside tables at the Bar du Siècle had been bagged early; outside Coiffure Salon Martine the eponymous hairdresser and her friends sat in white plastic chairs sipping white wine; there was minimalist bunting in the trees and a *peloton* of tots with *tricolores* painted on their cheeks being inducted into the mystery of the Tour. A couple of policemen were genially ignored as they tried to stop the crowd edging into the road.

First comes the publicity caravan and the team cars, bikes mounted on their roofs, spare wheels rotating idly; then a ten-minute warning of the race's arrival, and the approaching clatter of the TV helicopter. Then, at 12:35—indicating a slowish tempo—it goes like this: two riders suddenly appear round the bend and are past, *whoosh*, before you can turn your head—thirty seconds—three main groups—*whoosh whoosh whoosh*—three small groups—a few dropped riders—the very last one a member of the Cofidis team, because by now your eyes have adjusted—you also note he has ginger hair—then *whoosh* he is gone—and a swift two minutes are concluded with the blaring horns of the final race cars. I had expected it to go quickly, but in trying to take in everything I had seen virtually nothing. I hadn't recognized a single rider, because I hadn't specifically looked out for Armstrong or Virenque or Marco Pantani, the 1998 winner. They were in amongst the lean and gaudy figures going faster than I was prepared for. Only when they clustered in groups did I recognize team colours: the pink of Telekom, the blue-and-white of Banesto, and the Spanish-omelette colours of Mapei. Still, I had at least seen almost nothing from just a few feet away, and in a spirit of benign fellow-feeling. That was the point of the *jour de fête*. Then I drove off to find a television while Coiffure Salon Martine reopened and the Bar du Siècle clattered on with more drinks.*

Two and a half hours later, after making a long loop without ever losing sight of the Ventoux, the race reached Bédoin, where Simpson had his last drink. The remnants of an early escape were chased down; Armstrong sent his U.S. Postal Teammates Tyler Hamilton and Kevin Livingston to the front, a discouraging pace was set, and what the French call *la grande lessive* (the big wash—or, perhaps, the great rinse) began, as rider after rider was slowly dropped. With ten kilometres left, the cleansing had reduced the leading group to six (Armstrong, the second-placed Jan Ullrich, and Virenque among them), with Pantani—the tiny, bald, earringed Italian climber—hanging off the back. They passed Danish flags painted on the road, though the Danes had little to cheer this year; then another national enclave marked BELGIUM DYNAMITE and blazoned with the name of the Belgian sprinter Tom Steels, who had dropped out earlier in the day and didn't get to read his own name; there were signs for Polti and Rabobank, Pantani and Virenque. The crowds gradually thickened as the mountain exerted its mute thrall.

The previous time Armstrong had ridden up Mont Ventoux, in the Dauphiné Libéré earlier in the year, he had cracked and lost over a minute to Tyler Hamilton. The experience had left him apprehensive. This time, however, he watched as others cracked. At Hautacam he had produced a great attacking ride; here, for most of the ascent, he showed how enthralling a great defen-

---

*In the antepenultimate chapter of *Tender Is the Night* Dick Diver watches the Tour pass in the South of France. In the late Twenties the race evidently went more slowly, as he is able to distinguish expressions on the faces of the riders. After they have passed, Fitzgerald pertinently has Diver notice "a light truck [which] carried the dupes of accident and defeat." This is the "broom waggon," which sweeps up those who, like Diver, are forced to abandon a gruelling competition.

sive ride can be. He stayed with his main rivals for the yellow jersey, keeping a steady pace, showing no weakness, and implicitly telling them: You want to win this thing? Then you'll have to attack me. And none of them was strong enough to do so—except an intermittently revitalized Pantani, who had started the day more than ten minutes behind Armstrong. The race leader allowed him to climb ahead, carried on monitoring Ullrich and Virenque, and then, with 3,000 metres to go, left his defensive posture and raced across to Pantani, taking a full half minute out of Ullrich and Virenque in the process. He passed the Simpson memorial without so much as a nod. Alongside Pantani, he kept telling him, *"Plus vite! Plus vite!"* and the two rode to the summit together, where in the last few feet Armstrong eased to give Pantani the day's victory. It was a *geste de seigneur,* French commentators agreed. To the rest of the field, Armstrong's ride up the Ventoux simply said: I'm the boss. They believed it; and apart from a bad afternoon on the Tour's final mountain five days later, he rode as boss to Paris and final victory.

Pantani won another stage before retiring from the race, perhaps to concentrate on his forthcoming criminal trial at Forlì, in central Italy, for the use of banned substances back in 1995. The final mountain stage was won by Virenque, soon to be up before the beak at Lille, charged with "complicity to supply, incite the use of, and administer drugs"; also with "complicity in their import, possession, supply, transport, and acquisition."* How many of those I had watched who went up the Ventoux were taking something fortifying yet legal, or illegal yet undetectable, or illegal yet detectable yet worth taking the risk for? The evidence is always contradictory. Riders who are notoriously clean, like Chris Boardman, a world-class time-trialist regularly defeated by the mountains,

*On the second day of his trial Virenque finally admitted his drug-taking, while still deploying the evasions of metaphor: "It was like a train going away from me and, if I didn't get on it, I would be left behind. It was not cheating. I wanted to remain in the family."

never seem to notice anything going on. Whereas the whistle blowers, the drug-takers, and the drug-givers offer a picture in which everyone is doing it and only the naïve or the ridiculously principled abstain. Benjo Maso remembered a French rider from the Seventies called Dominique Lecroq being asked on French television what percentage of riders took drugs in his day. "One hundred and twenty per cent," he replied, meaning that the masseurs, *soigneurs,* mechanics, and support staff would be doing so as well. Voet confirmed this social overflowing of the drug habit, but his own estimate was that sixty per cent of the *peloton* were users.

The world portrayed by Voet is enclosed, secretive, furiously competitive, and not too bothered about moral questions. Chris Boardman says, "My own reasons for not taking drugs are ultimately more practical than moral. Why should I risk it?" To which the seductive answer comes: Because with this new drug it isn't a risk; you'll be ahead of the game in both senses. Voet describes Virenque approaching a hospital biologist and trying to get some synthetic haemoglobin (which oxygenates the blood without raising the haematocrit level); according to one source, it is already being deployed widely in Italian sport. Voet also derides the notion that a foolproof test for EPO will clean up the Tour: "EPO is already being supplanted by other forms of doping, both cellular and molecular." During Voet's last weeks at Festina, the team doctor was busy studying the sporting application of the cancer drug interleukin. It would be ironic indeed if Armstrong, medical victim and sporting hero to many, had inadvertently redirected attention from laboratories to hospitals.

Does it matter, finally, if a leader swaps consonants and becomes a dealer? Cyclists use bike technology to beat one another; they use performance labs and wind tunnels to discover the best aerodynamic positions; they are "computer slaves," as Armstrong puts it. The U.S. Postal Team riders have two-way radio contact and wear heart monitors so that their team director can tell them to adjust their pedalling accordingly. Would it matter if they also used drug technology to acquire that additional edge?

It matters, I think, for three reasons. Sentimentally, we want there still to be some connection, however thinned, between the world of the Rudge Whitworth Keep Fit Girl* and that of the professional cyclist. Morally, we are still Petrarchians, and recognize that certain shortcuts are wrong. Sport's history is bleakened when we remember those defeated by steroidal shot-putters, testosteronic East German women swimmers, or American sprinters whose body profiles thickened alarmingly in close-season training. In cycling's case, we need only quote Voet's epitaph for Charly Mottet: "Yes indeed, Charly never had the career that he deserved." Finally, and practically, it matters because the complex relationship between spectator and athlete, fandom's *pot Belge* of explosive emotions, depends at bottom on truth and trust. The Tour de France may be an example of "purposeless suffering"; it is also, as Armstrong says, "the most gallant athletic endeavour in the world." Whether we are the puzzled president of the French Cycling Federation on Hautacam, or Martine of Coiffure Salon Martine sitting by the roadside in Saint-Didier waiting for two minutes of lurid lycra to pass, what we need and what we want is simply this: to know what we have seen.

*Shortly after this piece appeared, I received a letter from the Honorary Life Vice-President of The Fellowship of Cyling Old-Timers pointing out that Mrs. Billie Dovey was both still alive and an active member of the club. As yet, no Fellowship of Old EPO-takers exists. Meanwhile, the court at Forlì gave Marco Pantani a three-month suspended sentence for a thwocking 60.1% haematocrit level; the conviction was overturned when a higher court in Bologna decided that doping "is not seen by the law as fraud." Chris Boardman retired from competition. From the start of his career the Englishman had suffered from a naturally low level of testosterone, which caused a condition similar to osteoporosis. The cycling authorities would not allow him to boost the level and continue in the sport. The *Guardian* announced the news with the wry headline: "Boardman quitting to take drugs."

In 2001, Lance Armstrong won his third successive Tour de France (and spoke French to journalists again); and Tom Simpson's memorabilia were moved to a museum in his home village of Harworth, Nottinghamshire.

(7)

The Pouncer

Georges Simenon with all his needs
(the maid is off camera), 1930s

In his book on the Lucan affair, *Trail of Havoc*, Patrick Marnham made one of the most vivid calculations in modern British biography. Lucan, he explained, was a very unadventurous eater. In his days as a house player at the Clermont Club, his taste ran to nothing but smoked salmon and lamb cutlets. The latter were grilled during the cold months, and served *en gelée* in warmer times. The biographer therefore estimated: "If Lord Lucan ate four lamb cutlets a day, for four days a week, for forty weeks a year, for eleven years, and if there are seven cutlets in a sheep, then he would have despatched 1,006 sheep."

Marnham has been schooled to write well about Georges Simenon: he has forensic, journalistic, and francophonic expertise. But an additional qualification must be a small numerological kink. Figures stud Simenon's life as pungently as cloves in an orange. The 400-plus books he wrote; the 55 cinema and 279 television films made from them; the 500 million copies sold in 55 languages; the 1,000,000 francs he took one Sunday morning in cash, in a suitcase, to buy back from Fayard the subsidiary rights to his first 19 Maigrets. He moved house 33 times; when separated from his eldest son he wrote him 133 letters in three weeks; when interviewing for a bilingual secretary he got through 180 candidates in a single afternoon. Then there is his famous estimate of having bedded 10,000 women. Even in laundry he was not modest: at his Swiss retreat there were six washing machines in continuous operation. This blizzard of numbers also invites us to make our own lamb-cutlet calculation: if Marnham was commissioned to write his biography shortly after Simenon's death, and if it took two years to complete, and if biography is half research and half writing, and if research is half reading and half interviewing, then in order to have read all the Belgian's books Marnham must have despatched them at a rate of more than two a day.

Writers are dangerous. They are also, frequently, not very nice. When they become famous, they can be not very nice in the manner of other famous people—vain, tyrannical, inflexible, and so on. But they can also be not very nice in a way specific to writers: by exploiting the one skill which sets them apart from others, by making clear that it is they who fix the official version of events. Those who live close to writers sooner or later inevitably strike against this discouraging truth:

> Whatever happens,
> They have got
> The typewriter
> And we have not.

Among Simenon's published works are a psychopathic number of autobiographical texts: twenty-seven in all. There is no obvious justification for leaving more words of autobiography than Chateaubriand: Simenon was little concerned with public events, foreign travel, or the society around him. These *Dictées* are made up instead of relentless self-explanation, guilty confession, and cocky boasting—the testimony of a man incapable of being bored so long as he remains the topic of conversation. Though cast as restless seekings after truth, they amount to an obsessive seizing of the historical record from those around him. To rub it in, Simenon also endowed a vast archive of professional papers in his native city of Liège.

The human race, Simenon told his mother in 1934, is divided into the *fesseurs* and the *fessées:* the spankers and the spankees. He added that it was his intention to be *un fesseur.* What the novelist had not yet discovered when he proposed his theory is that this division can exist within the same person, either running concurrently or, as in Simenon's case, consecutively. His life falls into two clear parts: the rise and rise of the super-spanker, followed by the slow decline of the spankee. You could make a moral tale out of it if you wished, and it is to Marnham's credit that he declines to do so. In this he is following Simenon's own example. One of the distinctions of the fiction, especially of the *romans durs*, is to show sympathetic understanding for driven, obsessed, morally affectless characters who inflict and sustain often terrible damage. The refusal to moralize makes them less distant, less safely other. Simenon in one of his more engaging moments said of himself: "Maybe I am not completely crazy, but I am a psychopath." Calling in the ethical police doesn't particularly help understand psychopaths.

The rise of the super-spanker began in Liège in 1903. He had an indulgent, invalid father and a dominant, unsatisfiable mother: Henriette, a woman who "found unhappiness where no one else had suspected its existence." As a child he knew the morally unsignposted world of a country first occupied, then liberated. He escaped quickly, through journalism and through marriage, to Paris, where he learned the local rules: "I now understand everything one has to do to win success in Paris. And I will do it. But I am appalled at what I will have to do." Pulp fiction brought him money, the Maigret series world fame, and the *romans durs* serious critical acclaim and the sometimes embarrassing admiration of Gide, Cocteau, Thornton Wilder, and so on. Cars, houses, boats, parties, booze, snobbery, posh friends, and bucketsful of women: prostitutes, dancers (up to Josephine Baker), occasionally mistresses—though he did not like the involvement—and always the housemaid. One new employee enquired of another girl, as if checking the job description, *"On passe toutes à la casserole?,"* whose pungency is rather lost in the English "Do we all get laid?"

Late in life, and bubbling with senile sexual pride, he told John Mortimer in a *Sunday Times* interview about the 8,000 prostitutes he had known: "I treated them with consideration and like a gentleman. I always let them have their pleasure first. And of course I

was enough of a connoisseur to know if their pleasure was faked."
The connoisseur, the gentleman: elsewhere he presents himself as
the big-game hunter, and the tourist among women. Naturally,
though, Simenon didn't exceed the number of Casanova's con-
quests merely out of sport, or even a pure love of sex. As he told
Fellini in an interview: "It wasn't at all a vice. I have not the slightest sexual vice, but I have the need to communicate." Later, he
elaborated: he did it "because I wanted to learn the truth . . . I do
not know these women any longer, I have forgotten them . . . but
with these 10,000 women I am beginning to know 'the' woman."

Here is a typical sexual encounter from the Twenties, at the
time of the writer's engagement to his first wife:

> With Simenon, early one morning, lying awake in the Hotel
> Berthe, the need was so great that when he heard a chambermaid
> outside in the hallway cleaning the guests' shoes, he got up,
> opened the door, lifted the girl's skirt and possessed her on the
> spot—while she was brushing away. She did not even stop what
> she was doing but merely said: "Oh Monsieur!"

Now skip two marriages, forty years, and nine thousand-odd
other women, and catch the truth-seeker's first sexual encounter
with Teresa, his final housekeeper-companion:

> A month after she started work at Echandens, I unexpectedly
> walked into a room and found her bending over a table that she
> was polishing. The sight was too much for me. I advanced upon
> her, feverishly pulled down her knickers and penetrated her . . .
> Teresa did not play the coquette. She had an orgasm as violent as
> mine, still bent over the table, with a duster or chamois leather in
> her hand . . . We did not even look at each other. I just walked out
> of the room and locked myself in my office.

Simenon doesn't elaborate on which particular truth he was confirming on this latter occasion—perhaps that the conscientiousness

of domestic staff had not declined over a period of forty years. But the encounters are typical of Simenon's vaunted manner: the sudden pounce, the rapid penetration, the unfailing female orgasm, and the retreat into the study. There his technique was not all that different: literature's pouncer, he wrote each novel in a swift, uninterruptible burst. For once, psychobiography provides the perfect fit.

A whirl, a riot, a debauch, but also a controlled one, marked by regular, driven work. Marnham quotes Bernard Pivot as saying that for most writers sex is a distraction from work, and adds that with Simenon it was the other way round, work being a distraction from sex. This is neat, but does not seem to fit the facts: Simenon had enviably more than enough time for both activities. By the late 1930s his life was a display-case of literary, financial, and sexual success. The spanker had triumphed, and spanked everyone: professionally, by bossing his publishers, even up to a 50-50 split on gross profits; domestically, by running his home and his sex life on his own uniquely favourable terms. His marriage survived his being busted in mid-siesta with the maid: Simenon's way of discouraging his wife Tigy from sacking the woman was to tell her he had already been unfaithful hundreds of other times, "frequently with people she knew, including her friends." Tigy, a robust and impressive figure, agreed to continue in marriage and motherhood. Simenon, blaming the victim, later wrote: "A man never forgives a woman who forces him to tell lies."

In the traditional story, settled, conveyor-belt love may be disturbed by the ferocious intrusion of sex; with Simenon, settled, conveyor-belt sex was disturbed by the ferocious intrusion of love. Yet at first, when he exchanged Tigy for Denise, a 25-year-old French-Canadian he met in New York in 1945, it must have seemed to him that he was trading up. For whereas Tigy reluctantly permitted a *ménage à trois*, Denise gleefully encouraged a *ménage à quatre;* where previously his brothel visits had to be hidden from Tigy, Denise now came along as companion and cheer-leader, even packing the novelist back upstairs for a second bash if she hadn't finished her conversation downstairs. Two of her powerful attractions for him were that she smoked with an American pout and had a "vaginal voice." But by loving Denise, by finding the only woman in his life with whom "love and sex were merged," Simenon gave her power; he became a potential spankee. She was more than his match at drinking, hitting, quarrelling, and lying. He got what he wanted; also, if you are feeling briefly moralistic, what he deserved.

In this second part of his life, with Denise and their three children, the disappointments and the embitterments slowly arrived. The professional ones were trivial—like the failure of "the cretins" in Stockholm to give him the Nobel Prize, or his inability to reciprocate the lavish praise offered him by Gide, Wilder, Henry Miller and others (better, after all, to have it this way round). But the personal ones wrought real damage. Denise, after years of mocking inertia during sex (*"Fais vite!"* she would instruct, and not as a turn-on), finally announced that "I no longer enjoyed making love to him. And that I think was the end of him." Their marriage collapsed, much aided by drink and jealousy; Denise had a nervous breakdown, they separated, but the battle continued. She attacked him in her pointedly-titled memoir *Un oiseau pour le chat;* he replied with the 250,000-word *Mémoires Intimes*—like using a neutron bomb in a cold war. He would never permit a divorce, and for a quarter of a century, as she put it, "he hated me as *possessively* as he loved me." Their daughter, Marie-Jo, caught in the crossfire, also had a breakdown (which the novelist typically used as material for a novel) and then shot herself through the heart with a rifle. Finally, implacably, like some terrifying Shakespearean mother returning to curse her boy who has usurped the neighbouring throne, Henriette made her reappearance. On a visit to his Swiss fortress, she cried poor, daring him to be ashamed of her; she handed back all the money he had ever sent her throughout the previous forty years and embarrassingly quizzed the servants about whether the house was really paid for. When his brother died in Indochina, Henriette grieved thus: "What a pity, Georges, that it's Christian who had to die." In 1970 she herself lay dying back in Belgium; her first words to him were, "Why did you come, son?" She declined to be impressed right up to the end—to his face, at least—and those attracted to the theory that artists are driven by the hope of securing approval from their unloving or at least outwardly unimpressable parents will find support in the story of Georges and Henriette. Perhaps her implacability sparked both his frenetic fiction-writing (each book saying to her: "Like me! Like me!") and his frenetic philandering (each conquest saying to him: "She likes me! She likes me!"). Within a year of her death he had abandoned fiction altogether and thereafter wrote nothing but look-at-me memoirs.*

The spanker spanked? Proper punishment for a career of self-gratification? Even if we resist this line, there is something very poignant and pathetic (not tragic—the tragedy belongs to Marie-Jo) about the elderly Simenon pottering through the Swiss streets on the arm of his final maid, his wealth irrelevant, his paintings all in the bank, his home a bare apartment with no carpets or book-cases and overlooked by a supermarket car park. The erotic communicator had failed the key female member of three separate generations: he had failed to please his mother, failed to satisfy his wife, failed to protect his sole daughter from her demons. The only communication he had achieved was that deeply intimate yet deeply indirect one, with the readers of his books, telling them about obsession, jealousy, dark thoughts, alcoholism, marital pain, violence, and crime in a direct, easy, spare, swift, rich manner.

Two numerical afterthoughts. 1) Women: the second Mme Simenon thought the figure of 10,000 grossly engorged, and

---

*Truffaut greatly admired Simenon's twice-yearly confessional effluvia, and wrote to tell him so, adding that Jean Renoir "adored" them too. Truffaut also judged *L'Etranger* inferior to every single one of Simenon's novels. But then he also preferred Charles Trenet and Boby Lapointe to Georges Brassens.

detumesced it to 1,200. 2) Cutlets: I have consulted more than one butcher on the Lucan calculation. There are indeed seven, or occasionally eight, cutlets to be had off a decent sheep, but this is seven or eight from *each side* of the beast. So Lucan would have despatched only half the estimated number of sheep.

(8)

French Letters

Not an Ultimate Peasant but a
sophisticated poet: Stéphane Mallarmé

(a) Baudelaire

Which famous nineteenth-century French writer am I describing?

Born 1821, into a professional family. Expelled from school. In young manhood went on a voyage to exotic places which shaped his sensibility. A keen frequenter of prostitutes, he contracted syphilis and for much of his life was in a precarious state of health; one doctor he consulted pronounced him a hysteric, a judgement he considered sound. His widowed mother held a key psychological place in his life—a mother he always sought to placate, and who always remained insufficiently impressed by his writing. She was also unimpressed by his handling of money: he appalled her with his tailors' bills, and ended his life financially ruined. In his writing he sought only Beauty, and believed that Art should not have a moral goal. In matters of politics, he was suspicious of democracy, loathed the mob, and often expressed a hatred for contemporary life. His first and most famous work was prosecuted for obscenity by State Attorney Ernest Pinard in 1857, a trial which brought useful publicity. For many years he was torn between living quietly in Normandy with his mother and living more vibrantly in Paris. He described himself as an Old Romantic, considered he was old at forty, and greatly disliked steel-nibbed pens.

Are zebras cream animals with black stripes, or black animals with cream stripes? This rough grid of a life, which sounds so much as if it belongs to Flaubert, also turns out to fit Baudelaire. At times the parallels are eerie; at times, you almost feel sorry for Ernest Pinard, now remembered only for shooting himself in the foot twice in the same year.

But the lives of Flaubert and Baudelaire diverge sharply as soon as it comes to practical literary matters: the process of composition, the relationship between character and work, the matter of career politics. In composition, Flaubert (despite ritual protests) worked hard and fluently—he was like the camel, he observed, and once started was very hard to stop; Baudelaire was more like an old jalopy on a winter's morning, always whirring and coughing into feigned life, and likely to be started in the end only by a sharp kick, either from its owner or from an irritated passer-by. In matters of character, Flaubert sought to subdue the neurotic side; Baudelaire, looking back on his life in his private notebooks, commented: "I cultivated my hysteria with pleasure and terror."

In literary politics, Flaubert observed the writer's proper pride. His attitude is mainly: here is my work, take it or leave it; his letters catch him out in ostentatious careerism only when he tries to become a dramatist. Baudelaire, even by the low standards of nineteenth-century French literary life—and despite having as high a concept of Art as Flaubert—is a fawner and a wheedler, a calculator and an operator. There are pages in his letters which, even if you allow for the gap in time and culture, and for French epistolary style, make you embarrassed on Baudelaire's behalf, make you blush for literature. When Sainte-Beuve patronizes his art, calling it "a bizarre kiosk which the poet has built for himself at the tip of the Kamchatka of Romanticism," Baudelaire grovels in reply (to the subsequent double distaste of Proust). When Vigny receives the poet during his hopeless attempt to get elected to the Académie Française, Baudelaire writes in thanks: "You are yet another proof that a vast talent always involves great kindness and exquisite indulgence." The fact that Baudelaire turns out to be a bad and often counterproductive literary operator, that his attempt to become an Academician is disastrous, that he is beaten down by publishers, that he chooses the wrong man as his agent, that his assiduous cultivation of Sainte-Beuve never produces the major article Baudelaire anticipates, makes it all the more pathetic.

Are novelists "nicer" than poets? Flaubert, who sought objectivity in art, who proclaimed the necessary invisibility of the author, who declared in 1879 that "giving the public details about oneself is a bourgeois temptation that I have always resisted," has despite all this been thoroughly investigated since his death and found to be a generally noble and genial fellow. Baudelaire, whose art is soaked in egotism, whose poetry gave the public details about himself ceaselessly, and who longed for the caress of fame, has been no less thoroughly investigated and turns out to be a deluded heap of spleen, lassitude, and self-pity, obsessed with the blot inflicted on his honour at the age of twenty-three when his financial affairs were (very wisely) taken out of his own hands, never to be returned.

Their differing attitudes to literary glory are instructive. At the time of *Les Fleurs du mal*, Baudelaire drew a caricature of himself gazing at a bag of gold flying towards him on a large pair of wings. He longed, he wrote to his mother in 1861, to know "some degree of security, of glory, of contentment with myself" (it is an odd triple wish: two modest, normal ambitions, and one extreme one; but then glory, like freedom, is indivisible). In a rather oddly phrased comment, perhaps suffering the contortion of envy, the poet refers to "Gustave Flaubert . . . who has so strangely achieved glory at his first attempt." Compare the following encounter between Louise Colet and Flaubert. One day, under the trees at Mantes, she told him that she wouldn't exchange the happiness she was feeling even for the glory of Corneille. It was intended, no doubt, as a harmless, flattering lover's phrase, but it riled Flaubert: "If you knew," he later wrote to her, "how those words shocked me, how they chilled me to the very marrow of my bones. Glory! Glory! What is glory? It is nothing. A mere noise, the external accompaniment of the joy Art gives; 'The glory of Corneille' indeed! But—to *be* Corneille! To feel *one's self* Corneille!"

Are novelists nicer than poets? Could it be a rough truth that poets are egotists who write mainly about themselves, whereas novelists diffuse their personalities and are therefore more familiar with the action of sympathy? "I'm as self-centred as children and invalids," Baudelaire writes; and later, to the Second Empire beauty Apollonie Sabatier, "I am an egotist and I use you." Philip Larkin used to say that he gave up fiction for poetry because he stopped being interested in other people. On the other hand, perhaps a novelist's egotism is just as great, but expressed less raucously; while "being interested in people" can turn into a frigid and parasitical activity. Novelists can also diffuse themselves so much that they cease to be there: V. S. Pritchett remarked on what boring company novelists are because they're always half-listening to the next conversation and half-thinking about their own work. At least with a poet you know where you are. Perhaps in love it's best to avoid both, and marriage bureaux should stamp on the application forms of writers Flaubert's remark to Louise Colet: "If I were a woman, I wouldn't want myself for a lover. A fling, yes; but an intimate relationship, no." Isherwood, writing of Jeanne Duval, observed, "Few of us would really enjoy a love-affair with a genius."

In his life, and for long stretches of his letters Baudelaire is his own worst enemy: at a low, comic level when he despatches yet another complaint to his publisher and declines to frank the envelope on grounds of poverty (never make your publisher pay the postage is the first rule of literary life); at a higher, more psychopathic level when he admits, "It's part of my nature to abuse my friends' indulgence." Abuse it he does, mostly about money. "I am writing to you as my last two logs burn" is the refrain of Baudelaire's letters. He is always, as it were, on his last logs. The poverty was no doubt real, but also largely self-inflicted by a profligate early manhood, and prolonged by an inability to get down to work. (How the poet envied Balzac, and astutely observed that you do not necessarily start off with talent and intelligence and then set to work; as appetite comes with eating, so talent and intelligence can come, as with Balzac, through toil.)

In recent times we have invented the (possibly spurious) concept of celebrities who "invade their own privacy." Something parallel may occur in a published correspondence, with the letter-writer unintentionally assassinating his own character. Letters, even the most solemn, are written for the moment; their function is individual, not sequential or cumulative; they normally involve a variety of recipients. But when the letters become a book read with an objective heart by a single dweller in a later civilization, then what a cold judgement may ensue—the colder because the confession is written in the accused's own hand. The sequential printing of letters spotlights every moment of sly hypocrisy and blatant contradiction. So on one page Baudelaire is fulsomely congratulating Ernest Feydeau on *Fanny* ("Contrary to those who complain that your novel violates modesty, I admire the decency of expression which increases the depths of the horror and that excellent art of allowing so much to be guessed"); six months later he is telling his mother, "*Fanny,* an *immense success,* is a disgusting book, an absolutely disgusting book, an absolutely disgusting book." He calls George Sand "a genius" when writing to ask her to fix a job for an actress friend of his; she does her best, fortunately ignorant of the opinion Baudelaire confided to his *Intimate Notebooks:* "She has, in her moral concepts, the same profundity of judgement and delicacy of feeling as a concierge or a kept woman . . . It is indeed proof of the degradation of the men of this century that several have been capable of falling in love with this latrine." Baudelaire wrote a flattering review of *Les Misérables,* then roundly despised Hugo for taking it at face value: "The book is disgusting and clumsy," he reported triumphantly to his mother, Mme Aupick.

"On this score I've shown that I possess the art of lying. To thank me he wrote an utterly ridiculous letter. That proves that a great man can be a fool."

But of course, in proving that a great man can be a fool, Baudelaire is equally demonstrating that a major poet can be a hypocrite and a toady. Neither Hugo's gullibility nor Baudelaire's smirk makes what they wrote less good, and part of the reader's job is not to let his or her reactions to the poet's life and character short-circuit estimation of the poems. This may prove difficult, since Baudelaire's life is deeply infused in the work, and since the ideal of beauty he pursued in *Les Fleurs du mal* was both "sinister and cold," as he proudly put it in a letter to his mother. The temptation is to translate our moral queasiness about the life into aesthetic queasiness about the work. But then we are doing no more than Baudelaire's sailors do to the albatross: grounding the bird and mocking it, incredulous that something so majestic in flight could struggle so awkwardly on the ground.

Baudelaire was not a great letter-writer; his correspondence contains no equivalent of the Flaubert-Colet love letters (his addresses to Apollonie Sabatier read like the lifeless exercises of one taking an amatory correspondence course), or of the Flaubert-Sand exchanges on aesthetics; when he writes about his work he is more likely to be complaining about misprints—even the thickness of a character in one word of a dedication—than about the nature or meaning of a poem. And yet, and yet . . . as this correspondence proceeds, for all the cadging letters and tedious procrastinations about why the poet can't go and live with his mother, something almost heroic begins to emerge. As things get worse, as time begins to run out, as illness increases, as Baudelaire becomes ever more starkly the victim of his own personality, as it becomes clear that each new and frantic plan to sort out his finances is doomed to fail and that glory with its winged bag of money is never going to fly through the window like the angel of the Annunciation, something tragic and clarifying comes over the correspondence. I once knew a neighbourhood greengrocer who had suffered all his life from a disfiguring skin disease; his children knew his face only as a piece of gaudy patchwork. In his late fifties, he got cancer. The drugs he was given had the unexpected side effect of clearing up his skin complaint: so as he lay dying, his children were able to see their father's true face for the first time.

Something like this happens with Baudelaire. The egotism remains sturdy, but is increasingly purified of affectation. "After he left me," the poet writes about a visit from Charles Méryon in 1860, "I wondered how it was that I, who have always had the mind and the nerves to go mad, have never actually gone mad." "Oh my dear mother," he writes the next year, "is there still *enough time* for us *both* to be happy?" Clearly not; and the attainability of that long-sought glory (let alone "security" or "contentment with myself") is receding too. "Something terrible says to me: *never,* and yet something else says: *try.*" It is evidently to be never—or never in his lifetime, at least. In an extraordinarily powerful letter of 6 May 1861, in which he characteristically rails at his mother for not appreciating his work, and uncharacteristically celebrates his happy childhood with her, the brutal intransigence of this mother-son bond is put in the plainest terms:

> We're obviously destined to love one another, to end our lives as honestly and gently as possible. And yet, in the awful circumstances in which I find myself, I'm convinced that one of us will kill the other, and that the end will come through each of us killing the other. After my death, you won't go on living: that's clear. I'm the only thing you live for. After your death, especially if you were to die through a shock I'd caused, I'd kill myself— that's beyond doubt.

In these last years the reflex of professional grovelling continues, as does the relentless solipsism: when Manet writes to say that he has contracted cholera, Baudelaire gives the matter two dutiful sentences of sympathy before plunging into his own publishing problems and his own bouts of neuralgia. But the self-obsession is tempered by self-knowledge. It is now that he writes, "It's part of my nature to abuse my friends' indulgence"; now that he confesses to being, at the age of forty-three, still at the stage of the "ashamed child" with his mother; now that he compares himself to Shelley in terms of memorable unlovability. During these final years, spent in Belgium, an unexpected humour emerges, too, as if, having loathed the world and its imbecilities so long and so hard, exhaustion has thinned hatred to a splenetic chuckle. "Rubens is the only kind of gentleman Belgium could produce, by which I mean a churl clad in silk." Mme Meurice "has fallen . . . into democracy, like a butterfly into gelatin." "All I've got out of my trip to Belgium is the chance to get to know the stupidest race on earth . . . and the habit of continuous and complete chastity . . . *a chastity, moreover, that has no merit whatsoever,* given that the sight of a Belgian female repels all thoughts of pleasure." (Things had obviously changed by Simenon's day.) There is even the odd comic incident: "Would you believe that *I* could *beat up* a Belgian? It's incredible, isn't it? That I could beat up anyone is absurd. And what was even more monstrous was that I was completely in the wrong. So, my sense of justice taking the upper hand, I ran after the man to give him my apologies. But I couldn't find him."

These lighter moments are brief, and deceptive: merely another patch of skin clearing up while elsewhere the cancer rages. In March 1866 a stroke paralysed Baudelaire and left him speechless. When Nadar came to visit him and argued against the immortality of the soul, the poet could only point his fists at the sun in impotent protest. He died in 1867. The following year his mother had a copy of his *Oeuvres complètes* sent to Flaubert. The novelist with the parallel life replied: "I am very touched by your sending me the works of your son, whom I greatly loved and whose talent I appreciated more than anyone." Mme Aupick, twice widowed and now having endured the death of her son (why isn't there a verb for that catastrophic event?) herself died in 1871. Another year and she would have completed the chronological symmetry: Mme Flaubert died in 1872.

(b)   Courbet

In 1991 the Musée Courbet in Ornans held an exhibition of the
"erotic" work of André Masson. It was mostly grim stuff: juvenile,
facile, and often plain nasty, a reminder that dredging the male sub-
conscious sometimes brings up little but dead dogs and rusty
torture equipment. But for those who trudged through the gallery there was an unexpected reward at the far end. Alone and
unsignalled was Courbet's rarely seen *The Origin of the World:* a
splayed female nude, from breast to mid-thigh, painted for the
Turkish diplomat Khalil Bey, and which latterly hung in Jacques
Lacan's country house.* Despite decades of subsequent erotica
and pornography it is still extraordinarily potent. Edmond de
Goncourt, who for decades loathed Courbet's work, finding *"ce
Jordaens moderne"* altogether too vulgar, his nudes "untrue," and
who after attending a joint private viewing in 1867 of Courbet's
tribadic *Le Sommeil* and Ingres's *Bain antique* (both also painted for
Khalil Bey) dismissed the two painters as *idiots populaires*, was won
round by *The Origin of the World.* He saw it for the first time in
1889, ten years after Courbet's death, and offered "honourable
amends" to one who could render flesh as well as Correggio. It is
painted with a lush delicacy, and the effect is intimidatingly realistic. No, it's not like that, it's like this, the painting seems to declare.
And the fact that it continues to make this declaration when surrounded by twentieth-century erotica, that it is capable of rebuking the future as well as its own past and present, is a sign of how
alive Courbet's work remains.

He was always a great rebuker, a setter-right in both art and

---

*It is now in public hands: "Courbet's oil, *L'Origine du monde*, was owned / by
Madame Jacques Lacan and through some tax / shenanigans became the Musée
d'Orsay's. / Go see it there. Beneath the pubic bush— / a matted Rorschach
blot—beneath blanched thighs / of a fat and bridal docility, / a curved and rosy
closure says, 'Ici!' " From John Updike's characteristically titled "Two Cunts in
Paris" (*American and Other Poems*, 2001).

life. No, it's not like that, it's like this: the head-on sky-billowed seascape, the cocky self-portrait, the dense female flesh, the dying animal in the snow, all are imbued with a corrective as well as a descriptive zeal. He is an in-your-face realist, aesthetically assertive. "Shout loud and walk straight" was apparently a Courbet family maxim, and throughout his letters, which cover the whole of his adult life, he shouts loud and listens contentedly to the echo. He calls himself "the proudest and most arrogant man in France" (1853). By 1861, "I have the entire artistic youth looking at me and at the moment I am their commander-in-chief." By 1867, "I have astounded the whole world . . . I triumph not only over the moderns but over the old masters as well." "The attention I get is tremendous" (1872). "On my side I have all of democracy, all women of all nations, all foreign painters" (1873). He cannot go stag-hunting in the hills outside Frankfurt without reporting that his exploits "aroused the envy of all Germany."

Though much of this arrogance seems natural, it was also tailored to the market. Courbet, who was born in Ornans in the Franche-Comté in 1819, came to Paris at the age of twenty, and had his first picture accepted by the Salon five years later, created, or adapted to his use, the persona of the boisterous, belligerent, subversive, shit-kicking provincial; then like a TV pundit of steroidal "personality," he got stuck with this public image, which became indistinguishable from his true nature. Courbet was a great painter, but also a serious publicity act. He was a pioneer in self-marketing; he sold photographs of his pictures to help spread their fame; he issued press releases when a painting of his sold for a large amount of money; he planned the first permanent exhibition centre devoted to the work of a single artist—himself. In the Franco-Prussian war he even managed to get a cannon named after him; whereupon he wrote to a newspaper caricaturist giving details of the "schedule and route" of "Le Courbet," asking him to "cover it for one of the newspapers at your disposal."

For all his Proudhonism and anti-establishment beliefs, his genuine desire to cleanse the mucky stables of French art, there was more than a touch of Yevtushenkoism about him, of the approved rebel calculating how far he could go, and knowing how to turn outrage to his own advantage. When *Return From the Conference* was refused for the Salon of 1863 (by no means his first rejection), Courbet commented with perhaps more complacency than was appropriate, "I painted the picture so it would be refused. I have succeeded. That way it will bring me some money." He was skilled at, or at least noisily involved in, the politicking which surrounded both the acceptance and the hanging of pictures at the Salon; he wanted to be accepted and to be refused at the same time.

He also wanted to accept and refuse, most notoriously with the *Légion d'honneur.* He needed to be offered the decoration so that he could be publicly and proudly offended. He nearly got his wish in 1861, until Napoleon III irritatingly struck his name from the list, and had to wait until 1870 for the desired insult to arrive. He turned it down—in a letter to the newspapers, naturally—with high Gallic pomp: "Honour is neither in a title nor in a ribbon, it is in actions and the motivations for those actions. Respect for one-self and for one's ideas constitutes the greater part of it. I do myself honour by staying true to my lifelong principles [etc., etc.]." It's worth comparing the case of Daumier, who had been offered the *Légion d'honneur* earlier that year and refused it dis-creetly. When Courbet upbraided him, Daumier, the quiet repub-lican, replied, "I have done what I thought I ought to do. I am glad I did, but that is no business of the public's." Courbet shrugged his shoulders and commented, "We'll never make anything of Daumier. He's a dreamer."*

The ego and self-belief revealed in the letters are, of course, no more than a confirmation of what the work proclaims. Courbet's self-portraits are painted with an attentive sensuality verging on erotic love, while the pose he arranges himself in is often deliber-

---

*Flaubert's maxim: "Honours dishonour, titles degrade, office-holding ossi-fies." By the time he wrote this, however, he had already accepted the *Légion d'honneur.*

ately Christlike. (Proudhon was not shy of the comparison either; witness his remark, "If I find twelve weavers, I am sure of conquering the world.") In *The Meeting* Courbet's friend and patron Alfred Bruyas is depicted as only slightly less deferential towards the painter than his own servant. Bruyas has just removed his hat to greet Courbet, whereas Courbet's hat is already in his hand because that is how he as a free artist chooses to walk; Bruyas lowers his eyes in greeting, whereas Courbet cocks his head and points his beard like an implement of interrogation. To make a further point, the artist carries a stick twice as big as that of his patron. There is no doubt at all about what is happening: the artist is auditioning his patron for suitability rather than the other way round. How far we have come from the days when the patron or donor of a painting was depicted kneeling shoulder to shoulder with the saints, while the painter might at best disguise himself among the peasantry on the sidelines.

Or take *L'Atelier* (1854–1855), the "Real Allegory Determining a Phase of Seven Years of My Artistic Life": friends and patrons to the right, wider and lower world to the left, artist with attendant nude model in the middle. Courbet called it "the moral and physical history of my atelier," as well as, naturally enough, "the most surprising picture imaginable." He delighted in its riddling quality: critics would "have their work cut out," the picture would "keep people guessing." And it still does. Who are these figures, placed in inert uncommunicating groups, and clearly other than a plausible cross-section of visitors to Courbet's studio? Where does the light come from? Why is there a model present if he is painting a landscape—and why is he painting it in his studio? And so on. But however we try to solve, or over-solve the mystery—is it a political cartoon? does it have Masonic embellishments? (if in doubt, always wheel on the Masons)—there is no disputing the intense focus of the picture: the figure of Courbet himself at work. It seems a relatively small physical area to support the focus of such an enormous picture; but the depiction of the master aiming his brush is clearly thought powerful enough to do the job.

It's helpful to see *L'Atelier* hung in the Musée d'Orsay directly opposite Courbet's earlier great painting *Burial at Ornans*. The latter is in design a grand frieze, tightly framed, with the ripple and dip of the mourners echoed in the distant cliffs above; then the painting is abruptly cut off at the top, with only a low strip of sky allowed, enough just to accommodate and set off the raised crucifix. This severity and close focus point up the comparative sprawliness of *L'Atelier*, and especially the fact that two-fifths of the painting lies above the line-up of human figures, occupying a vast area of scumble and mud. Structurally, *L'Atelier* might remind us of a medieval triptych: Heaven and Hell on either side, with the vast empyrean above. And in the middle, what have we got? Christ with Mary? God with Eve? Well, Courbet with a model, at any rate, sitting there, reinventing the world. And perhaps this helps answer the question of why Courbet is painting a landscape in his studio rather than *en plein air*: because he is doing more than reproducing the known, established world, he is creating it himself. From now on, the painting says, it is the artist who creates the world rather than God. ("I paint like *le bon Dieu*," Courbet once said to Francis Wey.) Read like this, *L'Atelier* is either a colossal blasphemy or a supreme claim for the importance of art, depending on your viewpoint. Or both.

We are dealing not just with an ego and a career, but with a mission. Baudelaire wrote that Courbet's 1855 debut, at the show he organized himself after both *L'Atelier* and the *Burial* had been turned down for the Universal Exhibition, took place "with all the violence of an armed revolt." And from then on, the painter's life and the future of French art are deemed to be indistinguishable. "I am winning my liberty. I am saving the independence of art," he writes, as if the second statement were merely an elaboration of the first. After the "dragging-down" from its pedestal of painting based on "ideas and stereotypes," after the "great burial" of academic and Romantic art (the stock symbols of Romanticism— guitar, dagger, hat with feather—lie discarded in the foreground of *L'Atelier*), Courbet outlined the new art in his open letter of 1861 to the young artists of Paris. His main demands were contemporaneity of theme (artists were not to paint the past or the future), individuality of manner, concreteness, realism (he once praised one of his own stag paintings for being "mathematically precise," with not "an ounce of idealism" in it), and beauty. This beauty was to be found in nature, and carried "within itself" its own artistic expression, which the painter had no right to alter or amplify: "Beauty provided by nature is superior to all artists' compositions."

This *profession de foi* is generally believed to have been written by Courbet's friend Jules Castagnary. Courbet seems to have fancied himself as a theoretician, but he had a practical rather than abstract cast of mind. In any case, we should always trust the painting rather than the trumpeting manifesto. The call for concrete realism doesn't rule out allegory or suggestiveness, as in *L'Atelier*. Equally, the bellicose public aesthetic doesn't prepare us for either the delicacy or the sheer romping variety of Courbet's work: from the Bellini-esque early portrait of his sister Juliette to those confrontational seascapes which at their best have a power beyond realism, to the complex and torpidly erotic *Demoiselles au bord de la Seine*. Courbet was accused of beating "the tom-tom of publicity" with the latter picture (no doubt he was), but now that its history as provocation has passed, it remains a tensely compelling image. The scene is set in shade, yet gives off oppressive heat; the seemingly languid atmosphere is denied by bright, almost gaudy coloration; while the prone woman's sleepy, half-open eye contrasts with the frank gaze we as spectators are allowed to bring to her and her companion. This gaze of ours is also intrusively close, since the picture is framed with forceful tightness; the lush trees sit preternaturally low over the recumbent figures, and the spray of leaves in the bottom right-hand corner binds in this image of sultry enclosure. There is a further loose structural rope thrown round the picture too. The boatman who has rowed these women down the Seine to this quiet spot has slipped away, leaving his hat abandoned in the boat moored at the back of the painting. Where has he gone? Presumably he has padded out of the frame in a soft semicircle and is now standing where we are, slyly observing his two pouting passengers. If the boatman does not actually merge with the spectator, he certainly stands close by, complicit and greedy-eyed, pressing back into the picture.

Just as there are weighted absences in several of Courbet's greatest pictures—the owner of the hat in *Les Demoiselles*, the out-of-shot corpse beneath the spectator's feet in *Burial at Ornans*, Mme Proudhon in the pellucid homage to her philosopher husband—so there are powerful silences in Courbet's letters. Of course, the survival of correspondence is a haphazard and unrepresentative process, but even so it's hard to think of a major painter who shows less interest in, or appreciation of, the work of others. No thrilled accounts of seeing a great painting for the first time, no encouragement of contemporaries (except to be like Courbet). The world divides into "the ancients," i.e., those unfortunate enough to have been born before him, and "the moderns," i.e., himself. He socialized with Boudin, was financially generous to Monet, has a good but brief word to say for Corot. He does cite Titian—but just as a point of comparison for his own work. The only person, or rather persona, before whom Courbet quails is Victor Hugo, the one Frenchman even he would have to admit was more famous, and to whom he writes uneasily ingratiating letters.

Courbet was a socialist (pre-Marxian, admittedly) who dabbled in the stock market and was keenly acquisitive of land. Similarly, for all his millenarian convictions, his attitude to women was pungently that of his time and class: brothels, mistresses, and unreflecting laddishness. "Women should concern themselves only with cabbage soup and housekeeping," he writes; though he does try to raise their status with a gallant if complacent aphorism: "It is the ladies' task to correct, with their feelings, the speculative rationality of men among themselves." He intermittently declares that his art leaves him no time for marriage, and just as intermittently tries to get married. In 1872 he settled on a young girl from his native

Franche-Comté, grandly declared that he and his family were not bothered by "the social differences" between them, and blithely continued, in his letter to a go-between:

> It is impossible that Mlle Léontine, despite the stupid advice she may receive from the peasants, may not accept the brilliant position I am offering her. She will be indisputably the most envied woman in France and she could be reborn another three times without ever coming across a position like this one. Because I could choose a wife from all of French society without ever being refused.

Mysteriously Mlle Léontine declined to become the most envied woman in France, and left Courbet huffing and puffing about the rustic rival he had lost out to, and about "village sweetie pies" in general, who have "an intellectual worth about equal to that of their cows, without being worth the money."

More ironically revealing is Courbet's exasperated reaction a decade earlier to the news that his mistress—coincidentally another Mlle Léontine—has been deceiving him. As an artist and thinker he believes that "marriage must be free," a notion he finds compatible with the idea that "woman . . . must be subject and faithful to man." And when she isn't, the bohemian comes over all bourgeois, the utopian turns Outraged of Ornans. He rages over rumpled sheets and rebukingly charts his growing suspicions to Mlle Léontine: "Another evening my head was cold. You gave me the nightcap, but it didn't fit anymore, the person who had slept there the night before had a smaller head than mine and had tightened it by five or six holes. With you I was only ever jealous of my personal dignity . . ." He certainly seems to have lost it here; and perhaps the painter found it especially and historically galling that Mlle Léontine was betraying him in bed with a new kind of realist image-maker—a photographer.

Under the Second Empire Courbet fought a noisy, obstreperous, and admirable campaign for the democratization of art in its funding, administration, and teaching. The irony was that when he obtained what he wanted, when he finally held artistic power during the Siege and under the Commune, it led to his undoing. The destruction of the Vendôme Column which proved to be the turning-point in Courbet's public life, is at times strangely fore-shadowed in these letters. In 1848, writing to his family, he reassures them that he is "not getting very involved in politics," but that he will "always be ready to lend a hand to destroy what is ill established." The next year he tells Francis Wey, "I have always felt that if the law took it into its head to accuse me of murder, I would definitely be guillotined, even if I were not guilty." And the next year: "If I had to make a choice among countries, I admit that I would not choose my own." Two decades later Courbet was the instigator of the campaign to demolish the "ill-established" Vendôme Column, a symbol of Napoleonic imperialism; the law accused him, and though perhaps not technically guilty (certainly less guilty than some, since he wasn't a delegate to the Commune at the relevant time), he was sentenced to six months in prison, later topped up with a ruinous indemnity of 286,549 francs and 78 centimes; whereupon the prospect of further imprisonment for debt forced him to make his choice among countries. He opted for Switzerland.

Courbet accepted moral responsibility for the destruction of the Column; but neither this, nor his reminder that during the Siege and the Commune he had saved many national art treasures from possible loss, worked as mitigation. He seems not to have understood the extent to which by 1871 he had become a perfect target for the incoming government. A charismatic public figure, a professional provoker of the established order, a socialist, an anti-clerical, a Communard delegate, a man who raised artistic independence to a political creed, who could write of Napoleon III, "He is a punishment that I do not deserve," whose closing line in his call to the artists of Paris in April 1871 had been "Farewell old world and its diplomacy"—what more apt and exemplary victim for the "old world" when it returned to power? And when a state decides to persecute an individual for reasons of public policy, it has more than the normal advantages of money and organization; it also has the formidable advantage of time. The individual may get tired and depressed, feel his talent being affected, his years running out; whereas the state rarely gets tired and imagines itself immortal. The French state in particular can be unforgiving after wars, especially civil ones.

By 1876 Courbet is still uncomprehending about what has happened, or rather why. "Was it," he asks senators and deputies in an open letter, "to punish me for having refused the decoration under the empire that I must carry a cross of a different kind?" This is perhaps no more than a turn of phrase, though an interesting one from the painter who called one of his self-portraits *Christ with Pipe*. If the French state didn't crucify Courbet, it certainly did its best to break him: his property was requisitioned, his pictures stolen, his assets sold, his family spied upon. He continued to paint, and to fight his corner, from Switzerland. Occasionally he would summon up all the old boastfulness: "At this moment I have more than a hundred commissions. I owe it to the Commune . . . The Commune would have me be a millionaire." But his last years—cut off from family and friends, increasingly obsessed with those who had betrayed and denounced him—were sad and stressful. Eventually, worn down, he agreed to a negotiated deal with the French government according to which he promised to pay off the cost of rebuilding the Vendôme Column over thirty-two years. "I must go to Geneva to get a passport at the consulate," he wrote optimistically in May 1877; but renewed turmoil in France kept him an exile until his death that December.

If you sit at one of the café tables on the Place Humblot in Ornans today and look across the clear, shallow, fast-flowing Loue, you will notice on the side of Courbet's *maison natale* the faded letters of the word BRASSERIE. This is apposite. Alfred Stevens told Edmond de Goncourt that the painter's consumption of beer was "terrifying": thirty *bocks* in an evening. He also preferred to lengthen his absinthe not with water but with white wine. On various occasions Courbet's friend Etienne Baudry sent 62-litre barrels of brandy to the exile (Courbet's sister sent only "splendid socks," to which he replied with gifts of a sewing machine for her and a pepper-grinder for his father). Alcoholic abuse resulted in dropsy, causing the painter's body to swell to enormous proportions. The fearsome new technique of "tapping" produced twenty litres of water, marginally more effective than the older system (steam-bath plus purging), which had rendered "eighteen litres from the anus." There is an extravagance and challenging realism about Courbet's end, as there was about his life and his art.

(c) Mallarmé

In 1896, on the death of Verlaine, Mallarmé was elected Prince of Poets by the review *La Plume*. He accepted the honour but declined the dinner. It was, at this moment of public triumph, an entirely typical gesture. In part it reflected his finely calibrated sense of propriety—the death of a great poet should not be even the indirect cause for celebration—but it also had a wider, longer echo. Mallarmé had devoted much of his existence to Refusing the Banquet.

Compared to other nineteenth-century French writers, Mallarmé had scarcely any "life" at all. No legend attached to him; there is no syphilis or bankruptcy, no exotic travel or homosexuality; set beside the rackety, dissolute, self-deceiving life of his co-partner in Symbolism, Villiers de l'Isle-Adam, no existence could seem more measured, more careful, more buttoned-up. His rebellion against his upbringing consisted of giving up the traditional family career in the Records Office and becoming a schoolmaster. (His three-volume English grammar, *Thèmes anglais*, belongs next to Arthur Koestler's *Encyclopedia of Sexual Knowl-*

edge in the library of unexpected hack work.) He married at twenty-one. His rebellion against this marriage, twenty years on, came in the form of a liaison with the former actress Méry Laurent. But Méry had an American protector in Thomas Evans, one-time dentist to Napoleon III; Mallarmé exquisitely withdrew. His life was one of flights untaken and feelings suppressed, the inner life and the late-burning lamp. If he weren't so French he could easily be English.

Gauguin etched him as a bureaucrat, or perhaps a fastidious convict; Manet painted him in a boneless, deliquescent slouch; Munch made him look like Conrad (Mallarmé's daughter thought the portrait resembled a head of Christ printed on a handkerchief); Degas had him leaning against a wall, hands in pockets, looking down at Renoir in a stiffness of pose explicable by the fifteen-minute photographic exposure. All show him as late-middle-aged, which is normal, given the operation of fame, but also apt. From his earliest letters he sounds like a fifty-year-old waiting to grow into that age.

Aesthetically and emotionally, his life was fixed early on: a mixture of daunting maturity and premature renunciation. At twenty he met his wife, Marie, a German governess dangerously close to him in temperament. "She's unhappy . . . and bored," he explained to his friend Henri Cazalis, "I'm unhappy and bored. From our two melancholies we could perhaps make a single happiness." They ran off together to England—"the country of the false Rubens paintings"; she declared herself ruined; he suffered acute guilt; they married. Icily clear-minded, Mallarmé wrote to Cazalis:

> If I married Marie to make myself happy, I'd be a madman. Besides, can happiness be found on earth? And should one seek it, *seriously,* anywhere but in dreams? . . . No, I'm marrying Marie solely because she couldn't live without me and *I* would have poisoned her limpid existence . . . I'm not acting for myself, but for her alone.

It doesn't take much hindsight to observe that such emotional altruism at age twenty is storing up trouble for later; but it's all part of Mallarmé's deck-clearing and hatch-battening. He became a schoolmaster even though he didn't much like teaching: he commanded little respect in his post at Tournon and was frequently "worsted by paper darts and cat-calls." He became a husband even though he believed that "serious marriage is too primitive" and that the best way to look on the institution was as a means of acquiring "a home, that's to say a little peace, and a 'tea-maker,' to quote De Quincey." Happiness lay in the dream, and the dream was poetry.

Side by side with the rather self-inflicted personal and professional adulthood comes the genuine and astonishing maturity of his aesthetics. The "new poetics" he was to proclaim and pursue all his life are there from the beginning. It is a twenty-two-year-old provincial schoolmaster who announces the famous dictum: "Paint, not the object, but the effect it produces." Over the next months he declares reflection more valuable than impression as the source of art; lauds concision and arrangement as key elements in the poet's method; admonishes Romanticism by asserting that a writer may have a literary temperament quite distinct from his human temperament. Even his formal innovations are in train: when he writes in 1865 that "the most beautiful page of my work will be that which contains only the divine word *Hérodiade*," he is already predicting the tweezer-careful layout of *Un Coup de dés.*

Some of this "maturity," however, felt more like old age. He is "splenetic and miserable" in Tournon, temperamentally "sterile and crepuscular"; he declares himself "an old man, finished, at twenty-three." Lethargy and self-disgust quicken into nervous exhaustion and a full-blown spiritual crisis, a struggle with "that old and evil plumage" as Mallarmé—characteristically painting not the object but the effect—refers to God. The young poet thought he had his life successfully compartmentalized, but the lids are lifting on all the pots at the same time. Socially, he is longing for the metropolis ("I need men, Parisian women friends, paintings, music"); emotionally, he is discovering the fallacy of trying to construct a single happiness from two melancholies; physically, he is exhausted; spiritually, he is in revolt; aesthetically, he is elaborating a difficult and rarefied poetic, dreaming a Work which will (he announces with no sense of vanity, but rather of impersonal inevitability) be the third leg of Beauty whose first two parts are the *Venus de Milo* and the *Mona Lisa*. The pots boil over at the same time, all across the stove; the art is made from a fearsome scalding. "And now, since I've reached the terrible vision of a pure work of art, I've almost lost my reason and the sense of the most familiar words." He is twenty-six.

Mallarmé's poetry, like his life, began by selecting what it had to reject. For a start, Hugo (or Hugolianism), personality verse, poetry as a vent for the emotions. He gives a whack of the cane to his friend Eugène Lefébure for writing love poetry: "The truth is that Love is only one of thousands of feelings that lay siege to our souls, and mustn't take the place of fear, remorse, tedium, hatred and sadness." This is a rather ambiguous rebuke, given Mallarmé's domestic circumstances; but then, literary principles often spring from psychological compromises. His other main rejection was of those aspects of poetry deemed novelistic: poetry as documentary, as narrative. In the first half of the nineteenth century the novel—despite Balzac—was still a junior literary mode. Poetry was dominant, imperialistic. If this created a problem for novelists—until Flaubert led the liberation struggle—it did the same for those poets who saw their art as less sweeping and less proprietorial. Writing to Zola in 1877 to congratulate him on *L'Assommoir*, Mallarmé offers a double-edged compliment: "It really is a great work and worthy of an epoch in which truth has become the people's version of beauty!" Mallarmé's art is not concerned with "the people's beauty," any more than it is with "thinking" or "meaning" as conventionally understood:

> I think that to be truly a man, to be nature capable of thought, one
> must think with one's entire body, which creates a full, harmo-

nious thought, like those violin strings vibrating directly with their hollow wooden box. As thoughts are produced by the brain alone . . . they now appear to me like airs played on the high part of the E-string without being strengthened by the box—which pass through and disappear without *creating* themselves, without leaving a trace of themselves.

As for "meaning," Mallarmé explains his poem *"La nuit appro-batrice"* to Cazalis thus:

> It is inverted, by which I mean that its meaning, if there is one (but I'd draw consolation for its lack of meaning from the dose of poetry it contains, at least in my view) is evoked by an internal mirage created by the words themselves. If you murmur it to yourself a couple of times, you get a fairly cabbalistic sensation.

The key phrase in this—and a fairly crude one by Mallarmé's normal standards of diction—is "dose of poetry." It makes the poetic act sound like the plying of a magic syringe. Some poor, untrained clump of words is hanging out at the track, wondering if it will ever make the grade; then along comes Mallarmé with the *pot Belge* and the EPO.

Elimination, concision, impersonality ("My personal work which I believe will be anonymous, since the Text would speak by itself and without the author's voice"), the broadening of "thought," the narrowing of "meaning," the "dose of poetry." Naming an object, he was to say in a newspaper interview of 1891, destroys three-quarters of the pleasure of poetry: thus the swan trapped in the ice in *"Le Vierge, le vivace et le bel aujourd'hui"* is first evoked as *"le transparent glacier des vols qui n'ont pas fui"* ("the crystal ice of flights never taken"). The point of such indirection isn't to create a crossword puzzle (though that aspect is inescapably present), but to create space, dream-time, between the reader and the subject. In *"Toute l'âme résumée,"* Mallarmé's light, self-mocking *art poétique* of 1895, the injunction to débutant poets runs:

> *Exclus-en si tu commences*
> *Le réel parce que vil*
> *Le sens trop précis rature*
> *Ta vague littérature.**

Poetry should be like cigar smoke: that's to say, our attention is directed not at the puffing, personalized, Hugolian smoker, or the glamorous, red-burning cigar-end, or the gathering ash, but metonymically at the curls and wisps of grey-blue sweet-smelling smoke. What is the true poetry? It is *"plusieurs ronds de fumée / Abolis en autres ronds"* ("a few smoke-rings which disappear into other smoke-rings").

And as there is a drawing-back from naming, so there is a drawing-back from the domination, the unambiguity of syntax. *"Le Vierge,"* for instance, demonstrates the twin techniques of compacting, whereby *"magnifique"* implies *"qui a été magnifique,"* or *"se délivre"* implies *"qui essaie en vain de se délivrer,"* and grammatical loosening. In the final line of the sonnet, *"Que vêt parmi l'exil inutile le Cygne"* ("Donned in useless exile by the Swan"), *"inutile"* manages to modify both *"l'exil"* and (adverbially) *"le Cygne."* Thus propinquity counts as much as syntax; the words respond to one another chemically rather than grammatically.

In 1866 Mallarmé described himself as "a sacred spider" spinning his thread into "wonderful lace"; the following year, as "a diamond which reflects everything but which has no existence in itself." Peter Quennell's image of the poet, in *Baudelaire and the Symbolists* (1929), connects technique with effect in a fanciful but memorable way:

> He was industrious and workmanlike; day by day, on little, carefully torn squares of paper, he noted down his linguistic discoveries, storing them with others in a big wooden tea-chest against

---

*"For a start leave out / The real, because it's cheap / Too much precision will wreck / The dreaminess of what you write."

the moment when they should be embodied in a poem. For when he wrote, it was methodically; he constructed a skeleton, significant words deliberately scattered over his maiden sheet, pre-arranged schemes of rhyme . . . and within these limits the poem had only to build itself! He was like the magician whom the anthropologist sees, stringing up a row of frail hempen slip-knots, in which he means to snare a favouring wind or entrap the wandering spirits of the dead.

Of course, the anthropologist has to trust the magician. That's a favouring wind you've snared there, is it? Mallarmé is one of the least translatable of the French poets: reading him in English is often like listening to a chamber work for boys' choir in a transcription for brass band.

In Huysmans's *A Rebours,* that Baedeker of decadence, Mallarmé is the favourite modern poet of Des Esseintes. (What would be the contemporary equivalent to this cultural puff? Perhaps a whole evening of televised homage.) Huysmans delights in Mallarmé's withdrawal from a world of "universal suffrage," "commercial greed," and "raging folly," in the way he just sits there

> taking pleasure . . . in the caprices of his mind and the visions of his brain; refining upon thoughts that were already subtle enough, grafting Byzantine niceties on them, perpetuating them in deductions that were barely hinted at and loosely linked by an imperceptible thread.

Mallarmé liked to deny the charge of obscurity: replying to a generous assessment of his work by Edmund Gosse in 1893, he wrote, "The only quibble I have to make is on obscurity; no, my dear poet, except through awkwardness or clumsiness, I'm not obscure . . . Of course I become obscure if the reader makes the mistake of thinking he's opening a newspaper!"

We might jib at this claim (just as we jib at Graham Greene's repeated claim to be a failure), and at the reclassification of most

French poetry as journalism; but Mallarmé always defended his position. Poe made the distinction between obscurity of expression—the sin of novice poets—and the expression of the obscure. "There must always be enigma in poetry," Mallarmé (Poe's translator) wrote in 1891. "That is the aim of literature." Difficulty, yes; obscurity, no. Elsewhere, Mallarmé speaks of the need for a "system of defences at the entrance to the shrine of art," which would "keep out those who do not love it enough." Here difficulty is a more active notion: it helps keep the muddy-footed amateur reader out of the nice clean library.

In 1865 Mallarmé wrote to Cazalis sympathizing with his friend for having had to endure ignorant critical comment from an aunt. Hearing about this *lèse-majesté* distressed Mallarmé, "so deeply do I feel that art is for artists alone. If only you knew how it hurts me to water down my thought and weaken it to make it instantly intelligible to a room of indifferent spectators!" Art, then, not just for art's sake, but for artists' sake, a further (and more limiting) refinement. Huysmans imagined the perfect Mallarméan prose poem becoming "an intellectual communion between a hieratic writer and an ideal reader, a spiritual collaboration between a dozen persons of superior intelligence scattered across the world, an aesthetic treat available to none but the most discerning." Such exclusivism was endorsed by the fine-binding aspect of this literary movement: Mallarmé wanted his edition of Poe produced with "pious sumptuousness"; Des Esseintes's account of *"L'Après-midi d'un faune"* is two-thirds textual analysis, one-third crypto-sexual gloat over the exquisite Japanese felt book covers and twin-hued bookmarks. This section of *A Rebours* concludes:

> The truth of the matter was that the decadence of French literature, a literature attacked by organic diseases, weakened by intellectual senility, exhausted by syntactical excesses, sensitive only to the curious whims that excite the sick, and yet eager to express itself completely in its last hours, determined to make up for all the pleasures it had missed, afflicted on its death-bed with a desire

to leave behind the subtlest memories of suffering, had been embodied by Mallarmé in the most consummate and exquisite fashion.

In his understandably appreciative response, Mallarmé told Huysmans that there was "not an atom of fantasy" in his book, and called the novelist "more strictly documentary than anyone else." Mallarmé's letters divide as firmly as his life did into two periods: provincial obscurity and Parisian success. The correspondence of the neurotic, ambitious schoolmaster is in fact more enthralling than that of the urbane and revered man of letters. After he reaches Paris there is less annotation of his work and less elaboration of his feelings (though many of his letters to Méry Laurent remain embargoed); instead, Mallarmé is courtly, wise, and unfailingly—even irritatingly—appreciative of other writers' work. Paris, and Parisian success, brought out his skittishness, his teasing and schmoozing. The Selected Letters should be accompanied by the Selected Envelopes, composed at a time when the leisurely postman would respond good-naturedly to an address in conundrum-form:

> *Va-t'en, messager, il n'importe*
> *Par le tram, le coche ou le bac*
> *Rue, et 2, Gounod à la porte*
> *De notre Georges Rodenbach.**

The poet of *"L'Après-midi d'un faune"* was also editor of the fashion magazine *La Dernière Mode* and wrote sixty-one little verse offerings to accompany gifts of glacé fruit at the New Year. This playful aspect is given visual corroboration by two of the strangest literary photographs ever taken. They show Mallarmé, in three-piece suit, floppy butterfly tie, and broad black hat, posing as

---

*"Hence, messenger / by tram, coach or ferry—it doesn't matter— / And take this to No. 2, rue Gounod / Home of our friend Georges Rodenbach."

a French peasant against a painted rustic backdrop. In one shot he is wearing clogs, carries a hay rake over his shoulder with lunch pail attached, and is trying to look like a jaunty farm labourer. The poet of ultimate refinement playing at "real life":

Exclus-en si tu commences
Le réel parce que vil . . .

"I need men, Parisian women friends, paintings, music . . ." While still marooned in the provinces, Mallarmé criticized Taine for his view that "an artist is merely man raised to his greatest possible power, whereas I believe that it is perfectly possible to have a human temperament utterly distinct from one's literary temperament." This notion—so baffling to the reductive biographer—is confirmed by Mallarmé's own case. Where the work is erudite and abstruse, the man was courtly and accessible. Such a mix is often a powerful social aphrodisiac: Mallarmé became one of the most admired and loved writers of his day, the familiar of Manet and Degas, Whistler and Swinburne; the young Gide testified to his enormous charm.

After he was elected Prince of Poets in 1896,* the newspapers had a label to stick on him, "a kite's tail with which I try to escape in the streets, having no other means of hiding myself than by joining the Mardi Gras parade." Celebrity meant that the press was free "to make the hermit a buffoon," and the poet of "intellectual communion between a hieratic writer and an ideal reader" was approached for his views on the bicycle, and for his contribution to a symposium on whether or not the top hat was ugly. He obliged good-humouredly, indeed seriously: "A bicycle," he told readers of *Le Gaulois*, "is not vulgar when wheeled out of the garage, and

---

*They ordered these things more efficiently in France. In Britain, thirteen years later, Yeats had to make his own pronouncement on the death of Swinburne: "I'm the King of the Cats now." Compare Berryman's uncertainty on the death of Robert Frost: "Who's Number One?"

soon becomes sparkling in its rapidity. Yet whoever mounts it, man or woman, reveals something disgraceful, that of human being reduced to mechanical object, with a caricatural movement of the legs. Too bad!"

"Among these exquisites, these dandies of word and syntax, there is a madman madder than the rest, and that is the nebulous Mallarmé, who maintains that one should never begin a sentence with a monosyllable." Edmond de Goncourt can always be relied on for the contrary view, and his splenetic exasperation in the *Journal* is comical, but not absurd. Mallarmé wasn't mad—few writers can have been so high-minded and purposeful—but his extreme refinement, his ethereal costiveness, strained vitality from his work. The more poetry moves towards music, the farther it moves away from life; though of course Mallarmé's aesthetic is well defended, and one person's "life" may be another person's "unpoetic vulgarity." In the middle of an aesthetically anguished and grammatically contorted letter to Cazalis, for instance, after announcing his "Work" as the third great beauty to follow the *Venus de Milo* and the *Mona Lisa*, Mallarmé drops in this paragraph:

> Since we've reached these heights, let's go on and explore them, then we'll do our best to descend from them. This is what I heard my neighbour say this morning, as she pointed to the window on the opposite side of the street from her: "Gracious me! Madame Ramaniet ate asparagus yesterday." "How can you tell?" "From the pot she's put outside her window." Isn't that the provinces in a nutshell? Its curiosity, its preoccupations, and that ability to see clues in the most meaningless things—and such things, great gods! Fancy having to confess that mankind, by living one on top of the other, has reached such a pass!!

The poet's nose-holding fastidiousness extends equally to sex. When Cazalis is fretting over whether or not to marry an English girl called Ettie Yapp, Mallarmé, the connoisseur of renunciation, recommends the acquisition of a "tea-maker" but rebukes his friend for overemphasizing the physical: "You see it [marriage] too much in terms of lingam fiction." Not just the statement, but the phrasing, is significant; sex is one of those things best left to people in hot climates.

Huysmans, via Des Esseintes, praised Mallarmé's "lofty scorn." A refined aesthetic which declares itself above the battle is intrinsically conservative. In 1863 the poet went to a meeting in support of Poland (where the rebellion against Russia had recently been crushed) and was primarily struck by the way in which the workers applauded frenetically when addressed as *"gentlemen."* "I don't like workers: they are vain." What of the bourgeoisie? "They are hideous, and it's quite plain that they have no soul." Which leaves the aristocracy, by which he means "the nobility and the poets." "As long as the former have money and the latter have beautiful statues, everything will be fine."

The poet, for Mallarmé, is a statue owner rather than an indulger in lingam fiction, and his answer to the old poser about what you would save from your burning house is predictable: "Henri, don't you think that the man who made the *Venus de Milo* is greater than the one who saves a race, and wouldn't it be preferable that Poland should fall rather than see that eternal marble hymn to Beauty lying in pieces?" Happily, such choices don't often arise (and if they did twenty-one-year-old aesthetes would probably not be consulted). Polish freedom against the *Venus de Milo*? Shouldn't the Poles have a vote in it?

The "lofty scorn," combined with a topographical preference for "the purest glaciers of Aesthetics," produced moments of farcical solemnity, especially when Mallarmé was in league with Villiers de l'Isle-Adam, whose grip on reality wasn't always tenacious. In 1867 they planned an attack on that reliable enemy, the bourgeois, to show him

> that he has no existence independently of the Universe—from which he thought he could separate himself—but that he is one of its functions, and one of the vilest at that—and I'll show him

what he represents in that Development. If he understands it, his joy will be forever poisoned.

The plan seems to have been to write a book which the bourgeois would gobble up but then choke on (the scheme has zoomed off into metaphor already): "I'm eagerly awaiting your sugary mixture, which will make him feel so nauseated he'll vomit himself: you're right, we'll avoid the courts, all the art will lie in making him judge himself unworthy of living." The idea that Mallarmé and Villiers (of all duos) might come up with something to make the bourgeois auto-destruct with self-loathing must be filed in the most arcane section of the Department of Empty Threats.

Poets, in order to write great poetry, don't need to see as much as novelists must in order to write great novels. If literature is a spectrum (and Hugo hogs the rainbow), then Mallarmé is working in ultra-violet. Nowadays we probably honour him more in the breach than in the observance. Anthropologists, we hunch over the wise-looking magician, and take what he does much at his own estimation; but capturing a sacred wind with an array of hempen knots is only one of poetry's skills. If the *Mona Lisa* ate asparagus, it would show in her urine; and this would make her richer, both as a woman and as a subject for art.

(9)

Flaubert's Death-Masks

Flaubert's death-mask

(a)   Biographer

Alcoholism softens the flesh—or at least, it did in nineteenth-century France. When Verlaine died, Mallarmé watched a cast being taken of the face of this staunchly self-destructive drinker. He reported to the poet Georges Rodenbach that he would never forget "the wet, soggy sound made by the removal of the death-mask from his face, an operation in which part of his beard and mouth had come away too."

After the morticians, along come the biographers: they, too, carefully mould the wax to preserve every last tuck and wrinkle, aiming to convey the final, decisive expression on the lips; but sometimes the flesh is soft, and the reverent process proves destructive. Bits of Flaubert's moustache, for instance, have been coming away for a century. When he died in 1880, the *Times* obituarist confused him with his brother Achille and said he had once trained as a surgeon (the Paper of Record also retitled his last novel *Bouvard et Peluchet*). The first proper study of Flaubert, by Emile Faguet (1899; Englished in 1914), firmly and misleadingly declared that the writer's affair with Louise Colet "may be considered as the only sentimental episode of any importance in Flaubert's life." In 1967 Enid Starkie prefaced her two-volume account with a portrait of "Gustave Flaubert by an unknown painter"—thereby managing to rip off his entire face in one go, since the picture was in fact of Louis Bouilhet. Sartre was less of an impression-taker, more an imposer. In *L'Idiot de la famille* he seared the novelist with a terrifying theoretical grid—like an imperious chef branding false scorch-marks on to a steak after it's been cooked.

In 1859, Ernest Feydeau wrote to Flaubert asking for biographical details to pass on to a journalist. It was an inept request. "I have no biography," Flaubert replied, and went on to complain:

> As soon as you become an artist, it seems that grocers, legal registrars, customs clerks, bootboys and others feel themselves obliged to take a personal interest in your life. And there are others to inform them whether you are dark or fair, witty or melancholic, how many summers you have lived, and whether you are a devotee of the bottle or keen on playing the mouth-organ. I, on the other hand, believe that a writer should leave behind him nothing but his works.

It was a vain hope; and it would be little comfort to Flaubert that the disobedient pursuit of every detail of his life has on the whole been carried out by scholars and critics. They were, for him, the moral equivalent of bootboys and customs clerks; all his life he trawled their work for idiocies high and low to include in the "Copie" of *Bouvard et Pécuchet*.

Yet to a certain extent Flaubert might still be able to say today, "I have no biography." There was no early fact-dredging, no tracking-down of the faithful servant, the reticent mistress, the garrulous supplier of cabbages. So the interpreters, the dreamers, and the wonky theorists got in there without the sifters and sorters having first done their business. The best biographers in English either stopped half-way (like Francis Steegmuller) or were too brief (like Philip Spencer).

Now comes Herbert Lottman, the diligent biographer of Camus. Pre-eminently a dredger and sifter, an archive-pounder and source-badgerer, Mr. Lottman arrives approximately a hundred years too late, yet still needed. He arranges the known facts about Flaubert's life, and the known opinions of his contemporaries, with an efficiency that has not been seen before. As against this, he writes badly, translates awkwardly, has no apparent opinion on Flaubert's works, and has little feel for the nineteenth century; he alternates stretches of drab invisibility with outbursts of perkily certain judgement, and is often crassly up-to-date. When Flaubert gets the pox, Lottman comments pompously: "The modern reader will be struck by the absence of respect for personal prophylactics . . ." Given the messy history of Flaubertian biography, this book has a certain value. But its formidable irritations confirm that the chuckling curse Flaubert put on his biographers hasn't lost its power.

He was modern literature's archetypal rewriter; he told us that prose is like hair—it shines with combing. Mr. Lottman's text is a tangle of nits and knots, a flour-bomb of dandruff, a delta of split ends. Flaubert, to begin with (line one), isn't a great writer but "a seminal figure." His family roots in Champagne are swiftly outlined—perhaps too swiftly, Lottman worries: "Indeed, we have hardly made this Champagne region seem attractive. It is a countryside of chalky soil whose perfect grape, when dealt with in a certain way, becomes that fizzy wine." Gustave grew up in Rouen: "One would love to be able to see the world as this child saw it." At the age of six or seven, he passed a recently-employed guillotine and saw bloodied cobbles: "Surely every child can call up at least one unbearable memory, even if guillotines and heads in baskets are harder to find now." Later, his education began: "Gustave went to school during the tail end of romanticism, which explains how romanticism was able to enter the classroom." And so on.

Having reassured the timid reader that champagne comes from Champagne, Lottman similarly tickets and dockets the French nineteenth-century literary scene. *Les Fleurs du mal* is an example of "the liveliest modern writing"; Musset was once "a young star of French letters" (who also lacked the proper respect for prophylactics); Juliette Adam is "this premodern feminist"; the European phenomenon of Byronism is reduced to "Byron's works in French translation were among the best-selling books in the country in the decade preceding Flaubert's schooling"; while Louise Colet is jauntily characterized as "the poetry hustler." This last phrase indicates the comparative shallowness of Lottman's depth of field: what strikes him as "hustling" was normal behaviour then (and still hasn't exactly died out). If Louise Colet was a hustler, so were Baudelaire and Mallarmé.

Then we come to the books. "The novel can be read for the story," Lottman tells us of *Madame Bovary,* and this is, alas, his most incisive remark. His one-paragraph plot-summary also includes the sentence: "Meanwhile, Charles moves from one professional humiliation to another, despite the paternal counselling of the village pharmacist, Homais." Perhaps "because of " would have been apter than "despite"; though this would, of course, mean something entirely different. Similar plonkingness affects Lottman's brief account of *Bouvard et Pécuchet. Trois contes* is "a book of three remarkable short stories"; and the third chapter of *Saint Julien l'Hospitalier* is summarized as follows: "When he discovers that he has indeed slain his parents, he abandons everything to beg, then befriends a leper and goes to Heaven." Rarely can the process of attaining sanctity have been made to sound so jog-a-jogly routine; presumably Mr. Lottman thinks that the process of "befriending" a leper normally involves lying naked on top of him, chest to pustulated chest, mouth to mouth, warming him up with your body. Wisely in the circumstances, Lottman doesn't try too ambitious a plot-summary of *La Tentation de Saint-Antoine.* He also gets by without any mention of *style indirect libre.*

Nor for that matter does he quote the Flaubertian motto *ne pas conclure*—no doubt advisedly. On the contentious topics of Flaubert's private life—such as epilepsy, homosexuality, and anti-Semitism—Lottman is briskly conclusive when brisk conclusion is not just unwise but impossible. Zola was disappointed on first meeting the author of *Madame Bovary* because *(inter alia)* he found his hero had a taste for paradox; and Lottman has a similar aversion to the unresolved, the ambiguous, the self-contradictory—the human, in other words. For instance, Flaubert is famously reported by Amélie Bosquet as having said: *Madame Bovary, c'est moi.*

Lottman, in his pertly titled chapter "Louise Takes a Ride," refers us to Flaubert's letter to Louise Colet of 6 July 1852, in which he mocks Musset and the idea of making art by setting one's personal feelings to music. This, Flaubert conceded, had been his failing in *La Tentation:* "In the place of Saint Antony, you find me." Lottman at this point comments: "He would not make that mistake again. (So much for one remark attributed to Flaubert, that *Madame Bovary, c'est moi.*)" *So much for . . .* The comment must therefore have been invented, QED. Alternative factors Mr. Lottman might have considered: 1) Writers are frequently inconsistent in their statements about their art, and a gap is common between theory and practice; 2) The remark was intended to describe the almost psychopathic closeness which sometimes develops between novelist and character (Flaubert felt nauseous when Emma took poison); 3) It was a joke, the wearily ironic response of a writer fed up with being pestered for the "real" identity of his most famous creation; 4) It was a reference to Cervantes's supposed remark on his deathbed, declaring himself to be the original of Don Quixote; 5) All of these at the same time.

The toughest part of Lottman's book to read is the first half, since what is known of Flaubert's life up to about 1860 has been much-repeated, and there is little for him to add: but after this point, he grinds a grudging recognition from his victim. He is particularly informative on the non-artistic aspects of Flaubert's life: on his exact financial position at various times, his relationship with his publishers, his "hustling" to promote his niece's career as a painter, and his own fiasco in the theatre. If you want to know where Flaubert was at a particular time, what he was doing, what he wrote to friends, and what those friends were saying behind his back, then this is the first book you should turn to. And if Mr. Lottman doesn't always make the desired point, he at least provides the facts from which the point can be made. For instance, Edmond de Goncourt, leaving an ill-attended Sunday afternoon *chez* Flaubert, discussed with Zola the "lack of radiance" around their host, for all his bonhomie and fame. Was this just a typical bit of Goncourt depreciation? How might this "lack of radiance" be quantified? Later, when Flaubert dies, Zola estimates the number of mourners at about three hundred. This may remind us of another funeral in the same city 120 pages earlier, that of Bouilhet (fellow Rouennais but a far less successful writer): it was attended by two thousand mourners. Lottman allows us to make such comparisons simply by including everything he knows.

One particularly successful strand to the book concerns Flaubert's relationship with Juliet Herbert, the English governess who first came to Croisset in 1855, and with whom Flaubert seems to have pursued a liaison for a quarter of a century, right up until his death. It is a story full of absences and negatives: their regular meetings in Paris have to be deduced from his regular lies, the dates of her summer holidays, his anonymous sexual boasting, plus stray hints in letters to his niece. The evidence was remarkably and convincingly assembled in 1980 by Hermia Oliver *(Flaubert and an English Governess)*, on whom Lottman naturally relies. But the simple insertion of Juliet Herbert into the novelist's larger life (instead of her standing as a story by herself) allows us to judge more fairly how much weight to give her in his overall emotional life: more than we ever imagined, is the answer. It also offers us a comparison of evasions: between the excuses the young Flaubert used to put off meeting Louise Colet and the excuses the old Flaubert used to find space in his year for his *rendezvous* with Juliet Herbert.

Flaubert said of *L'Education sentimentale* that he wanted "to hold the ocean in a carafe." Lottman's Flaubert is more like a ship in a bottle: all the working parts are there, but what it is doing in the bottle, what waters it inhabits, and where it might be sailing are mysteries. Two small but interesting matters remain unground by Lottman's gizzard: Flaubert's height, and the colour of his eyes. On page 44 the novelist is "just under six feet," and on page 78 his passport shows him at ¾ m 83 (which tallies); but by page 142 Flaubert is quoted as telling Mlle Leroyer de Chantepie that he is "five feet eight inches" tall. Has he shrunk by four inches? Is he perhaps playfully fictionalizing to a correspondent whom he was never actually to meet? Neither: Flaubert didn't say he was "five feet eight inches," he said he was *cinq pieds et huit pouces.* Over the years the *pied* and the *pouce* have varied slightly in size as units of measurement, and at this time didn't translate exactly into their English equivalents.

As for the eyes: on page 51 Flaubert has "sea-green" eyes, which change, without comment from Lottman, to "blue eyes" on page 78. The first colour was supplied by Maxime Du Camp in his memoirs (the English translator of these added yet another tint, wildly translating *ses yeux enormes, couleur vert de mer* into "large eyes grey as the sea"). The second colour comes from Flaubert's passport. Which do you prefer?

(b)　Novelist

What does Madame Bovary look like? We know that she has dark hair and eyes of a complicated colour, but what of her nose, her chin? Does she tuck neatly into your shoulder? Are her ankles trim? How do you visualize the set of her shoulders?

Of all the great fictional heroines, Emma is probably the one about whose appearance readers are most likely to disagree. We cannot, as with Dickens, refer to some foxed engraving in an early edition, since Flaubert hated and forbade illustration of his works. Nostalgic moviegoers might picture Emma as Jennifer Jones, but since this would entail Flaubert himself resembling James Mason, it doesn't take us very far. Mario Vargas Llosa fell deeply in love with Emma from the moment he first read *Madame Bovary*—in Paris in 1959—and at the start of *The Perpetual Orgy,* his unconventional, shiningly intelligent, and fiercely sensible homage to Flaubert, he confesses that ever since he has been in thrall to Emma's social rebelliousness, her erotic power, her vulgarity, and her promise of violence. But at no point does he describe her physically. Is it possible to be in love with a woman and not know what she looks like? Or perhaps he is jealously guarding his image of her from the rest of us.

It is important to take Vargas Llosa's opening declaration of love seriously, not as a mere critical conceit, a smart way into the book for him. "A handful of fictional characters," he observes, "have marked my life more profoundly than a great number of the flesh-and-blood beings I have known." One advantage of fictional characters over real ones is their summonability: they can always be brought to life and friendship again, anywhere, any time, merely by snapping open the book. Their power can be as decisive as the power of real people, too. Purveyors of generous-hearted commercial fiction occasionally report that fans have thanked them for saving their lives, for stopping the suicidal hand. This is an extreme extension of one useful function of the novel, that of saying you're not alone out there after all. But this salvationist capacity doesn't necessarily stop when you enter the Classics section of your bookshop. Vargas Llosa explains without any affectation how, when he was in despair and even tempted by suicide, the story of Emma—and in particular the death of Emma—brought him "consolation and a sense of proportion, a revulsion against chaos, a taste for life . . . The fictional suffering neutralized the suffering I was experiencing in real life."

Others might, when in despair, be more tempted to listen to the direct voice of Flaubert in his letters ("Sadness is a vice," he tells us, for instance) and even be surprised by the notion of a consolatory Emma. But then others are not quite so in love with her as Vargas Llosa is. Others will also note that his portrayal of her in his first section seems slightly Hispanicized, even Carmenized: he stresses her melodrama and flashiness. There is a wry comparison to be made between Flaubert's expressions of weariness with Emma in his letters ("a woman of false poetry and false sentiments") and Vargas Llosa's paean to the woman who flamencos around in his mind and memory. If Emma Bovary came off the page and into his life, she would run through his money in a few months, bore him stiff with her chatter, and decamp with his best friend. But you sense that he knows this already, and would almost savour the humiliation.

The love for Emma expands into a love for Flaubert: not the simple business it might seem. Loving a writer often results in a ferocity of defence not evidenced in "more serious" areas of life, like politics or marriage. Vargas Llosa recounts how in 1960 a friend told him that there were two subjects on which he refused to give an inch: Cuba and Flaubert. Fourteen years later (*The Perpetual Orgy* first appeared in 1974) he finds he can tolerate criticism of Cuba, but remains adamant on the author of *Madame Bovary*. For the lover of Flaubert, other writers and critics are judged by their response to the great novelist. Vargas Llosa, for instance, rightly loathes Barbey d'Aurevilly (the nineteenth-century critic and novelist who wrote that Flaubert would pollute a stream by washing in it). For myself, I find it hard to forgive Thackeray for finding *Madame Bovary* "heartless" and "coldblooded."

Most of *The Perpetual Orgy* is a discussion of the genesis, execution, structure, and technique of *Madame Bovary*. It is the best single account of the novel I know. Flaubertistes will instantly set it alongside Francis Steegmuller's 1939 classic *Flaubert and Madame Bovary;* students of literature who want to know how a novel works could not be better advised than to watch and listen as Vargas Llosa hunches over this masterpiece like some vintage car freak over the engine of a Lagonda. Yet it's more than a question of valves and pumps and tubes—of sophisticated engineering. Vargas Llosa rightly and keenly stresses the irrational factor in writing, the organic element, the part that may hide itself even from such a scrupulous and self-conscious creator as Flaubert.

His discussion of sources, for instance, is impeccably instructive. The writer—any writer—absorbs information from many different levels (the novelist as sponge); this information is processed into a transformed substance (the novelist as Magimix). Sources, once used, become unimportant and uninteresting to the writer, who may end up knowing less about them than a ferreting biographer. With a novel such as *Madame Bovary* there are many possible sources for incidents and characters, often conflicting with one another; but where a thoughtful critic might dutifully weigh up one against the other and conclude that the one true source of so-and-so was such-and-such, Vargas Llosa, having seen the business of fiction from the other side, takes what he calls a "liberal, maximalist" position. "Everything convinces me, except exclusivism." This may irritate those who see novels as things to be solved, like crossword puzzles; but it more accurately reflects the reality of making fiction.

Vargas Llosa enlightens us on so many aspects of the novel: on Emma's mannishness, on Emma as prototype of the twentieth-century consumer, on the *style indirect libre* (that subtle rendering of indirect thought which Flaubert never refers to in his correspondence, yet which we now consider his greatest technical achievement), on the puzzle of the "we" narrator who opens the novel and vanishes after seven appearances. Central to *The Perpetual Orgy* is a large, well-argued section on the "descriptive frenzy" of Flaubert's realism, in which things are described as carefully as people, and emotions like happiness and nostalgia become things. This "reification of the human" and its counterpart, the humanizing of the object, also help explain how we may come to differ over what Emma Bovary looks like: for the novel evokes her as much in terms of her clothes as in terms of her person. We get a rhapsodic account of her hair style where another novelist might offer a long description of her face; her parasol is as important as her fingertips, and equally seductive.

Rival lovers of Flaubert are bound to quarrel over a few things. Some will pause over Vargas Llosa's ascription to Louise Colet of a "willing obedience" to Gustave's amatory rules, or over his odd dismissal of *Salammbô* as "dated." But the only area where I would seriously part company with *The Perpetual Orgy* is in the matter of Flaubert's epilepsy. Following Sartre, Vargas Llosa maintains at several points that the novelist "chose" his illness, that at some deep level he "willed" it. Sartre on Flaubert followed Freud on Dostoevsky, suggesting that his subject's epileptic symptoms, while real, were the product of neurosis rather than a brain lesion: they offered "the option of hysteria" (which in Flaubert's case made it easier for him to evade life and become a writer). Current opinion among epileptologists, however, is that the concept of affective as against organic epilepsy is a sensational fabrication. Flaubert "merely" had epilepsy: it was as simple as that.

Flaubert left no direct literary descendants, though any number of paternity suits have been brought against him over the last hundred years. Vargas Llosa discerns two streams of claimants: on the one hand, realists and naturalists (who all too often lack Flaubert's sense of form), and on the other, formalists like the proponents of the *nouveau roman* (whose interest in theme is often dismayingly minimal). Might there be an argument that Flaubert, like Milton, was a great writer who had a bad influence? Perhaps. But among his other descendants are writers who hear very precisely what he says yet do not necessarily obey. The true influence of a great writer is to say, simply and repeatedly, across the years: Go thou and do otherwise.

(c)   Theorist

Jean-Paul Sartre's *The Family Idiot,* an intense, unfinished, three-volume growl at Flaubert, is mad, of course. Admirable but mad—to abduct Sartre's own phrase about Villiers de l'Isle-Adam. A work of elucidation couched in a lazily dense style; a biography seemingly concerned with externals but in fact spun from inside the biographer like a spider's thread; a critical study which exceeds in wordage all the major works of its subject put together . . . *"On n'arrête pas Voltaire,"* de Gaulle said of Sartre in 1968; and perhaps those down at Gallimard imagined they heard a pun. One does not arrest Voltaire . . . and you can't stop him either.

Who started him? Roger Garaudy, it seems, with an inviting bet in 1954: "Let's try and explain the same character, I according to Marxist methods, you according to existentialist methods." So began a project whose aim Sartre expresses on the first page of *The Family Idiot* as: "What, at this point in time, can we know about a man?" To which he gives the answer: a lot more than you might imagine. The traditional, academic approach to biography—the search for documentation, the sifting of evidence, the balancing of contradictory opinions, the cautious hypothesis, the modestly tentative conclusion—has run itself into the ground; the method has calcified. Sartre decides to reinvent the genre, using three principal techniques: Marxist analysis of the social background, Freudianish analysis of the personality, and freewheeling imaginative hypothesis to fill in any gaps. Not surprising, then, that it took a decade of his life, or that it brought upon the comrade of 1968 certain inevitable reproaches.

But why Flaubert? After all, Sartre recorded in *Les Mots* how, as a child, he was "poisoned" by the "old bile" and the "abstract hatred of mankind" of Flaubert, Gautier, and the Goncourts: they were responsible for confusing "literature" with "prayer." A harsh excommunication was also pronounced in *Qu'est-ce que la littérature?* It was Flaubert's dazzling correspondence which converted Sartre from antipathy to empathy; moreover, the letters struck him as ideal psychobiographical material—an almost perfect example of free-associating from a pre-Freudian couch.

There is, also, a personal element in the choice of Flaubert. *The Family Idiot*, for all its "scientific" method, is a tellingly personal, almost autobiographical work as well: psychoanalysis, whatever else it does, in part defines the psychoanalyser. Sartre liked to fob off comparisons between his childhood and Flaubert's, but the evidence was against him: in particular, his own evidence, *Les Mots*. Both writers came from provincial bourgeois families—austere, hard-working, traditional, practising virtue without too much believing in it. Sartre's maternal grandmother, in her seventies, was still complaining about the leek salad she and her husband had shared at a station buffet on their honeymoon half a century earlier: "He took all the white and left me the green." A way of life rich in matured rancour. Sartre also records how his paternal grandfather, a country doctor, discovered on the day after his wedding that his wife's family—supposedly rich Périgord landowners—were in fact penniless. From that moment on, the deceived doctor never spoke to his wife again, expressing himself at table by means of gesture; undaunted, the couple still contrived to produce three children, and lived together for forty years; in their old age the grandmother used to refer to her unforgivingly silent husband as "my paying-guest." This sort of family texture, acrid and enduring, was shared by the two provincial novelists, while some members of their immediate families also echoed one another. Sartre's god-like grandfather, who amused himself by crushing the life out of his sons, recalls Flaubert's father Achille-Cléophas—or, more precisely and more interestingly, recalls Sartre's portrait of Achille-Cléophas; while the pinched virtue of his grandmother, who "thought straight and thought wrongly," reminds us inevitably of Mme Flaubert.

Sartre liked to argue that there was one great and significant difference between himself and Flaubert: he was loved and pampered as a child, whereas Flaubert was *mal aimé*. Even if we accept this thesis (which is, of course, Sartre's own, in both cases), its effect, paradoxically, is to bind the two men together as biographer and biographee even more closely: for Sartre in a way envied Flaubert his unlovedness. Sartre's infancy was shamelessly happy, as he recalls in *Les Mots:* but after reading *L'Idiot de la famille* it's hard not to feel that this early happiness was in part begrudged. How selfish and irredeemably unfair of this bourgeois family to have inflicted untarnished contentment on the future Marxist, Existentialist, and creator of Roquentin. The Flaubert family, on the other hand, was more properly bourgeois and supplied the correct degrees of trauma and unhappiness which Sartre was deprived of. His father died, it is true, before Jean-Paul was aware of him, but even this (he makes clear in *Les Mots*) was a deeply fortunate occurrence: while every other male child was an Aeneas slogging around with an Anchises on his back, he alone was free—free and filled with loathing at the sight of all those invisible progeni-

tors astride their sons for the whole of their lives. For there is a hor-
rid shadow to his fatherless felicity: "The speedy departure of my
father deprived me of a proper Oedipus complex." The tone is
amused, ironic, of course: but not that ironic. What is a properly
instructive bourgeois upbringing without an Oedipus complex?
Every home should have one.

So a subsequent incident from Jean-Paul's childhood curiously
prepares the ground for *L'Idiot de la famille*. The boy, encouraged
to believe that "a book can never do harm if it is well written," asks
his mother for permission to read *Madame Bovary*. "My mother put
on her most musical voice: 'But if my little darling reads these sorts
of books at his age, what will he do when he grows up?' " The
young Jean-Paul retorts precociously, *"Je les vivrai"* ("I shall live
them out")—a reply which proved a lasting success. Even more
durable, in fact, than his family imagined. First, Sartre lived out the
threateningly anti-bourgeois life described in the dangerous classics. Now, for long tracts of *L'Idiot de la famille*, he is able to go
even further: he lives, relives, the author himself.

Flaubert's line of life, in Sartre's version, runs like this: idiocy,
passivity, interiorization, neurosis, breakdown (the famous incident at Pont-l'Evêque in 1844—fainting, epilepsy, or Sartrean "false
death," according to your terminology and interpretation), then
genius. How to explain what Sartre calls "this scandalous occurrence: an idiot who becomes a genius"? And how, *a fortiori*, to
explain it when the documentary evidence is thin, misleading, fictional, or piously shuffled together after Flaubert's death?

"We recognize at the outset that we cannot know the vicissi-
tudes of his intrauterine life." Not even Sartre will invade Mme
Flaubert's womb. And there are some other frustrations for the
investigative psychobiographer: "the nursing, the digestive and
excretory functions of the infant, the earliest efforts at toilet training . . . about these fundamental givens, nothing." If only Gustave's parents had had the foresight to preserve one of Gustave's
earliest stools; if only the fossilized excrement had been passed
down to the Musée de Rouen . . . Ironically, just before *The Family*

Idiot came out here, De Beauvoir was publishing *La Cérémonie des adieux*, in which she usefully records the bladder malfunctionings which set in during Sartre's final illness.

But there are few other areas where Sartre fails to tread. As he prowls round the infant Gustave—necessarily mute from such a distance—he sometimes reminds us of another French experimenter and theorist: Jean-Marc Itard, who spent years trying to make the Wild Boy of Aveyron talk. In the same way, Sartre prods and pokes at Gustave, treats him alternately with kindness and frostiness, and is everywhere indefatigable.

The psychoanalytic insights offered by Sartre are always Olympian and frequently crass. The father of Flaubert's mother died when she was ten: this makes it inevitable that "she would only marry her father." Her mother had died in giving birth to her: consequently, when she suckles her first daughter, "*she gave herself the breast* in order to obliterate from the present the indestructible frustrations of the past; she made love to herself so that she could at least *give* the tenderness that she had not received." Achille, Gustave's elder brother, is naturally kitted out with an off-the-peg Oedipus complex. Unfortunately for him its working-out goes wrong. When the father, Achille-Cléophas (head of the hospital at Rouen), falls ill, he instructs his elder son to operate on him. In the course of the operation he dies. Sartre comments: "The most unexpected result of this relationship is that the old man, by giving himself up to the knife, deprived his elder son of even the possibility of deliverance through the classic murder of the father; certainly Achille killed him, but he made himself the docile instrument of a sacred suicide." The proof that Achille has been cheated out of the necessary liberating murder comes in the next paragraph: when he stepped into his father's shoes as head of the Hôtel-Dieu, Achille also stepped into his father's old goatskin coat. This garment, the argument runs, was already eccentric and unfashionable when his father had worn it on his rounds: it would have been "aberrant" by the time the son took it on. Yet he could not now avoid this flapping symbolic mantle. "Polished, refined by his new friendships, he was urbane in the salons, a clod on his rounds; in both instances, actually, he *perpetuated* the paterfamilias." Or maybe he just liked the coat . . .

There is a matching inflexibility in Sartre's Marxist analysis of Flaubert's social origins. His parents were mere functioning units going through their bourgeois programme; the ambitions, social behaviour, attitudes to property and family of this "semi-patriarchal community" can all be easily predicted. The Flauberts automatically pursue their dream of upward mobility (as if anyone ever pursued a dream of downward mobility), and the relations between Gustave and Achille-Cléophas "incarnate the drama of French society." Moreover, the sly wrong-footing of Marxist criticism is also in evidence: characters can first be reduced to easily comprehensible social automata, with scarcely an atom of free will, reliant (like Flaubert's father) on the chance mutation of intelligence in order to advance themselves; and then these ruthlessly conditioned social automata can be despised for not being more humane, more enlightened, more twentieth-century. Thus Sartre, of Achille-Cléophas's (undocumented) firmness with Gustave when teaching him to read: "125 years later, better-informed about the nature of childhood, we accuse the medical director of having aimed too high, too quickly, and of having bewildered his unhappy pupil by allowing him to see his exasperation."

"We accuse . . ." Yet perhaps this arrogance is not quite what it seems. There are times—many times—when Sartre seems impatient and scornful of Flaubert's immediate family, when he seems to want that family to be in as great a state of postulated discord as possible, when he seems to cry openly, with Gide: Families, I hate you. But perhaps this is to overemphasize Sartre's political and biographical presence in *L'Idiot*, and to underestimate his literary presence. In part, the biographer adopts the bullying, chivvying tone he does because the characters under examination are his own creation. He has revived them and fleshed them out, so he naturally awards himself extra rights in their behaviour. Thus he is at the same time the scientific, unsurprised Marxist and the intuitive but

irritated novelist. It is easy to forget this ambivalence, to underestimate the fictional alloy present in *L'Idiot,* though the literary
company Sartre keeps sometimes looks a bit seedy. Take the
account of Mme Flaubert's pregnancy, which led to Gustave's
birth:

> Nine highly agitated months. She must have imagined every-
> thing, poor Caroline, she must have hoped and despaired, some-
> times welcoming a future daughter as celestial manna, at others
> spitting into the ashes to deny the imminent son. No doubt these
> agitations of the soul remained hidden. But she could not dis-
> semble her ardent wish to have a girl, to re-create herself . . .

Given that paragraph blind, where would you place it? Somewhere in the Imagine-the-Heartbreak school of popular biography, I should imagine, where the word "must" is always a
giveaway.

Of course, to say that swathes of *L'Idiot* are fiction is not to
deny them the possibility of truth. Nor, on the other hand, is it to
assert that they are well written. *L'Idiot* is, indeed, an outstandingly
badly-written book (the dust-wrapper of Carol Cosman's translation disarmingly warns us that it conveys all the nuances of
Sartre's style "from the jaunty to the ponderous"). The contrast
with *Les Mots,* swift, supple, and economical, is saddeningly
instructive. But then Sartre was always fighting against the allure
of lucidity, against the guilt induced by pleasing the reader. There
is a warning exchange in *La Cérémonie* where de Beauvoir quizzes
him on the value of good writing. "Sometimes even," she begins,
"you were disgusted with literature; you used to say, Literature is
shit. What exactly did you mean? And from time to time, more
recently, you have said to me: after all, it's stupid to work at
expressing oneself; you seemed to be saying that one only had to
write, as it were, any old how. Moreover you told me that this is
how you wrote your Flaubert, which isn't entirely true." Sartre
growls back: "It isn't true." De Beauvoir retreats with, "There are

many felicities in your Flaubert," and Sartre replies: "I write faster now. But that comes from having worked at it."

No one, of course, would admit that he wrote *worse* than he used to, especially not by design. I just write differently, that's all, more quickly; but then, as Sartre goes on, "I believe that the best writing is always done without too much working over." However generously we feel inclined to interpret the ageing Sartre's remarks, his is an ironic conclusion to reach while engaged on a study of the finest, the most literary, and the least *engagé* of French nineteenth-century novelists. *"La littérature, c'est de la merde."* "Oh yes, who are you working on at the moment?" "Flaubert, of course." This makes shocking, almost insulting, the rare occasions in *L'Idiot* when Sartre chooses to quote Flaubert: suddenly we are reminded that it is perfectly possible—indeed, it seems actively desirable—for high intelligence, piercing insight, and scrupulous concentration to be combined with extreme lucidity of expression. One of the rogue myths of criticism is that difficult ideas can only be expressed or elucidated in dense and difficult language. When one falls routinely on sentences like "Praxis becomes the *efficacy of the passive* because the child's conditioning strips him of any means of affirming himself, even the positive act of negativity," it pays to remember the first act of practical criticism inflicted on the young Flaubert. When Louis Bouilhet and Maxime du Camp rubbished his ornate first version of *La Tentation de Saint-Antoine,* they reminded him of La Bruyère's advice: "If you want to say that it is raining, say: 'It is raining.' "

As you machete your way through the prose, however, the jungle partly begins to clear. The heart of the first volume is a rich and plausible imaginative hypothesis about the inner life of the young Flaubert, with its profitable passivity and fecund neurosis. The evidence is of two sorts: occasional documentation (Flaubert's letters, his niece's memoir of him), and internal evidence drawn from the adolescent stories (largely inaccessible to English readers). In his exposition of these stories Sartre is at his most resourceful: a swift and ruthless pursuer of the subtext and the Freudian implication (here Flaubert is shown wanting to kill his entire family; there just his brother; over here Satan represents Gustave, God represents Achille-Cléophas). No one will now be able to read these texts without bearing in mind Sartre's psychological parallels, and the "proud confessions" of hatred, envy, and sublimated murder which he discerns.

Whether Sartre's critical reading is *right* is another matter, of course. It is frequently plausible, but it is vigorously one-sided in method. These early stories—rancid items of romantic sex and violence, for the most part—are highly derivative, sometimes direct parodies or exercises. The scented influence of writers like Petrus Borel is paramount. Yet Sartre declines to discuss literary genesis, to examine how far the motifs he interprets as being Gustave's private neuroses writ public are in fact provided ready-made by the writers he imitates. Sartre's reason for not doing so is curt: of course Gustave is being imitative—but the real question is, what made him choose to imitate *this* rather than something else? His unconscious clearly directed him to rewrite, parody, expand items of direct psychological concern to him. Perhaps; yet how wide was the choice of imitable texts—the real, likely choice, given Gustave's age, reading, and surroundings? Is it all that surprising for an adolescent to produce stories littered with sex, madness, and death when he lives above the morgue, and when from the age of six he had been taken for educative walks by an uncle who liked to drop in at the lunatic asylum and then linger in the prostitutes' quarter? And what, furthermore, is the likelihood of Sartre *not* being able to read envy and revenge into whatever adolescent stories Flaubert might have written?

As for the documentary evidence, even Sartre admits that it is thin and unreliable. His starting-point for this whole enterprise— for the presumption of the young Gustave's "idiocy"—comes from a piece of "decorous gossip" written by Flaubert's niece, Caroline Commanville, after his death. She reports the family tradition that he was slow in learning to read (adding, however, that he was "avid for knowledge and his brain was always working");

then records that he would often as a child sit "for hours, one finger in his mouth, absorbed, looking almost stupid," and that once, when he was six, "a servant called Pierre, amusing himself with Gustave's innocence, told the boy when he pestered him: 'Run to the kitchen . . . and see if I'm there' "—which the child duly did.

Not much, is it? Yet Sartre immediately applies the magnifying glass and expands the child to "pathologically credulous"; while his parents, we are assured, "searched his features and feared he was an idiot." Is Gustave's instant departure towards the kitchen *that* credulous? How many parents would back their own six-year-olds not to fall for a similar straight-faced wheeze? As for the idiocy: Gustave was, it is true, slower at learning to read than his sister, but the memoir continues with an incident which might well be held to confirm precocious intelligence. Before he was taught his letters, Gustave was often read to by an old family friend called Papa Mignot. Caroline Commanville reports that when there were scenes over Gustave's slowness in learning to read, the child's final argument, "to his mind irrefutable," was "What's the use of learning when Papa Mignot reads to me?" Not quite as good, perhaps, as Jean-Paul's *"Je les vivrai,"* but hardly the sort of response to have parents scanning the infant face for signs of idiocy. Sartre ignores this part of the memoir, and supports his thesis more by bullying repetition than anything else. The twentieth-century Freudian orthodoxy is that of the artist as neurotic; Sartre expands this into a wider orthodoxy of the genius as idiot. In fact, it's rather a Hollywood notion, a literary version of Log Cabin to White House, sentimental, and a bit vulgar. "I see it all . . . the small boy, his thumb in his mouth . . . the great writer having difficulty with his letters . . . and a little wood-burning stove in the background . . ."

Sartre is much stronger on the less contentious subject of Flaubert as neurotic, on the big, strapping youth mysteriously laid low by spiritual scurvy. The passivity, the pessimism, the malice, the "option of hysteria," and the "precocious senility" are fictionalized together into a convincing flow. I'm not sure the lengthy result is more vivid than Flaubert's own deliberations on the subject: he once described his adolescent self as "a mushroom swollen with boredom." But then Sartre seems unwilling—too jealous, even—to give Flaubert his head in quotation.

"*Critic.* Always eminent. Held to know everything, to have seen and read everything. If you disagree with one, call him Aristarchus, or eunuch." Flaubert's definition from the *Dictionnaire des idées reçus* doesn't exactly come home to roost. Eunuch? Hardly. Aristarchus? Well, Sartre didn't really cut or change bits of Flaubert— rather the opposite, in fact. But his zeal to transform an instance of life into an instance of dogma, a proof of theory, brings to mind the words of the American artist Stuart Davis: "It has been scientifically established that the acoustics of Idealism give off the Human Sound of Snoring, whereas Reality always says 'Ouch!'" Sartre could also be accused of not having learnt one lesson taught by the object of his study. Flaubert died in 1880; Sartre in 1980. Flaubert left unfinished *Bouvard et Pécuchet,* in which he sought to enclose the whole of knowledge, the whole of the world, the whole of idiocy; Sartre left unfinished *L'Idiot de la famille,* in which he sought to enclose and subdue Flaubert, master writer, master bourgeois, the sage, and the enemy. Sartre condemns *Bouvard et Pécuchet,* first as "colossal and grotesque," later as "vast and monotonous." All four adjectives can safely be transferred to his own work. It is a vast folly, erected with "admirable but mad" single-mindedness. There it stands, and surely, you think, the view from the top must be splendid. But no: Climb up and you only see a little more than you do from the road.

(10)

Not Drowning But Waving:

The Case of Louise Colet

Louise Colet in riding costume,
by Courbet

Who burned Louise Colet's letters to Flaubert? For a century it was taken for granted that the destroyer was Flaubert's niece Caroline, the inheritor of his literary estate. Caroline, the stiff, correct, high-bourgeois protector, *"la dame si bien,"* who in publishing her uncle's correspondence cut out any passages she deemed intimate or indecent, suppressed uncomplimentary opinions, changed his punctuation, and tidied up his phrasing; who wouldn't allow the expression *"tenir le bec hors de l'eau"* ("keep your snout above water") in a letter to Turgenev, gentrifying it into *"tenir la tête hors de l'eau"* (head). Such editorial interventionism was of the period: when negotiating with Louise Colet's equally proper daughter, Mme Bissieu, Caroline received permission to publish 138 of Flaubert's letters to Louise (and none of the more unbuttoned ones) on the condition that she changed *tu* to *vous* throughout. What could be likelier, in this suppressive, censoring, cleaning-up ambience, than that Caroline, while adjusting her uncle's image into something more Pantheonic and less fun, should dispose of the no doubt licentious outpourings of the notoriously pesky Louise?

Hermia Oliver's *Flaubert and an English Governess* quietly but pertinaciously queried this assumption. Caroline may have offered the public a pasteurized version of her uncle, but her tampering had an innate probity to it. She deleted and rewrote, but never touched the manuscripts themselves: everything was done in the transcription. Further, Caroline's own niece testified that her aunt's attitude towards the literary estate—manuscripts, notebooks, dossiers, even her uncle's library—was that "it was absolutely necessary to preserve all of them." And finally, while there is no specific evidence to finger Caroline as vandal, there is already one documented destroyer of the novelist's correspondence: Flaubert himself.

In 1877, warned about what might happen after a writer's death by the publication of Mérimée's *Lettres à un inconnu*, Flaubert and Maxime Du Camp burned most of their youthful letters to each other. The correspondences with Ernest Chevalier, Louis Bouilhet, and Georges Pouchet were drastically thinned for similar reasons. Another burning session took place in May 1879. Flaubert wrote to his friend Edmond Laporte: "Yesterday I spent *eight hours* sorting and burning letters, a long delayed job, and my hands are shaking from tying up packets." Hermia Oliver adduces as corroboration a hitherto ignored account by Maupassant in *L'Echo de Paris* of 24 November 1890, in which he recalls a bonfire night at Croisset "a year before" Flaubert's death—i.e., in 1879. Maupassant describes "a little silk dancing shoe," containing a faded rose and a yellowing lace-edged handkerchief, being cast into the flames. This was almost certainly Louise Colet's slipper, as hymned by Flaubert in a love letter to her of August 1846. "It can surely hardly be doubted," Hermia Oliver concludes, that among the letters destroyed that night were those of Laporte, Caroline's English governess Juliet Herbert—and Louise Colet. This conclusion is the point of departure for Francine du Plessix Gray's biography and rescue-act:

> I believe that those last missives . . . were the many hundreds of letters written to Flaubert by Louise Colet. That is why I have written this book. To reinstate a colleague into the annals of her time. To do her justice. To resurrect yet another woman whose memory has been erased by the caprices of men.

Louise Colet was born in Aix-en-Provence in 1810 and came to Paris with her music-professor husband Hippolyte in 1835. She swiftly established herself as a poet, a beauty, and a salon-goer. She won the Académie Française's prize for a poem on a set theme four times, and was awarded a government pension. She found a long-term protector in Victor Cousin, supporters in Béranger and Victor Hugo, lovers in Musset, Vigny, Flaubert, and Champfleury. She posed as Sappho for the sculptor Pradier, and frequented the salon of the ageing Mme de Récamier. She had, as Gray generously puts it, "a reverence for glory." This word, which features much in Louise's life and musings, was the cause of her key disagreement with Flaubert over "the glory of Corneille." He also rebuked her sternly for having "the love of art" but not "the religion of art."

Still, a reverence for glory and a love of art are certainly enough to get a literary career started. Colet was also a sharp exploiter of opportunity. When she approached Chateaubriand for a puff for her first collection of poetry (which just happened to include two poems in praise of the "Homer of Melancholy" himself), he replied rather cannily that his endorsement would not count for much, since "only poets can announce a poet." Undeterred, she simply reprinted his letter as a preface (Chateaubriand, to his credit, does not seem to have taken offence). Sainte-Beuve largely resisted her literary charm, though applauding her novel *Lui* (in which he is given a cameo role as the wise "Sainte-Rive"). A more conspicuous failure was with George Sand, who always kept the younger writer at a distance; if we are to believe an anecdote in *Lui*, Sand once heard Colet recite her work at a salon and afterwards offered the following literary compliment—"Madame, you have the arms and shoulders of a Greek statue." Still, Louise certainly had supporters enough at the start of her career, and knew how to play the Paris game. Victor Cousin, lover, protector, and high government official, used his influence to have Louise's pension tripled and Hippolyte's salary doubled.

Louise was bold and melodramatic, impulsive and self-advertising, admirable yet faintly ridiculous. All these characteristics emerged in her celebrated attack on the satirical journalist Alphonse Karr. In 1840, when Louise was almost nine months pregnant, Karr wrote an article clearly insinuating that Cousin—a regular target of his—had used his official position to get Colet's pension raised (true), and was also the father of her child (which, if not necessarily true, certainly seems to have been believed by both parties at the time). The piece was indubitably caddish, and Louise straightforwardly decided that the journalist must die for it. What's more, it seemed to her self-evident that Hippolyte Colet should be charged with rectifying this insult to her honour.

Hippolyte was a slight and prematurely stooped professor of composition at the Conservatoire; Karr a bulky expert swordsman and one of the best shots in Paris. When Hippolyte "backed off," as Gray puts it (and who can blame him?), Louise went round to Karr's lodgings with a kitchen knife: "To arm myself with a more elegant weapon," she later wrote, "would have been theatrical. I only wished to act with simplicity, as is suitable to any great sorrow." Heavily pregnant as she was, she stabbed Karr in the back, drawing a little blood. The journalist turned round, disarmed her, and (in his version) offered her his arm before calling her a cab.

Through the intervention of Sainte-Beuve, Karr promised not to sue Louise, and in the next issue of his magazine even applauded her "energy" and "courage bordering on nobility." But the occasion was too lushly tempting for any journalist to resist. "I certainly would have been gravely harmed," Karr went on, "if my attacker had struck me with a direct horizontal blow instead of lifting her arm high over her head in a tragedienne's gesture, surely in anticipation of some forthcoming lithograph of the incident." Both come out of the drama well and badly; though Louise probably had more to lose, and did so. Karr kept the knife, and exhibited it in a glass case with the label: "Given to me by Mme Colet . . . in the back."*

---

*Karr (1808–90) later retired to Nice to grow flowers professionally. Now totally forgotten as a writer, he remains an obscure link between the two greatest nineteenth-century novels of adultery. Stabbed by the future mistress of the author of *Madame Bovary*, he was also cited approvingly (on the subject of not invading Prussia) by Prince Shcherbatsky ten pages from the end of *Anna Karenina*. His name is commemorated in a tropical bamboo (*Bambusca glaucescens Alphonse Karr*), though rarely attached to the dictum he gave the world in 1849: *"Plus ça change, plus c'est la même chose."*

Louise Colet was a prolific writer: of fiction, poetry, biography, history, and travel. What still has life? Francine du Plessix Gray recounts a visit to the Provençal house—now a golf hotel—in which Colet was brought up. The estate's present owner, Paul Révoil, Louise's great-great-grand-nephew, sounds grumpily baffled at being badgered about his scandalous forebear: "You're the third person who's come around this year. Never read a word of hers—was she that good?" To which Gray revealingly replies that she is "awfully interesting." Though her biography is heartfelt and impassioned about the woman, Gray makes no extravagant claims for the work. She seems keener to establish Colet as a pioneer feminist, a "nineteenth-century Erica Jong who splashed her life and loves across her poetry and prose," than as a writer *tout court;* and when it comes to literary assessment, is inclined to quantify the percentage of feminism present and leave it at that.

Colet's novel *Lui* is probably her most enduring work (as well as her only one currently available in English). It was part of that small library of kiss-and-tell fiction set off by Musset's death in 1857. The poet had started it himself with *Confession d'un enfant du siècle* (1836), in which he described his Italian affair with George Sand. Two decades later she replied with *Elle et Lui,* Musset's brother Paul retaliated with *Lui et Elle,* the waggish Gaston Lavalley joined in with *Eux,* and Colet completed the job with *Lui.* This transparent *roman à clef* stars Louise as the glamorous Stéphanie de Rostan, romantically beset by a pair of unsatisfactory suitors: Léonce, the obscure, cold-hearted novelist toiling away at his supposed masterpiece in Normandy; and Albert, the passionate, impulsive, tippling poet-aristocrat whose heart has been crushed by a painful affair with the famous writer Antonia, and who now seeks consolation and amatory rebirth with Stéphanie.

Most of the book consists of Albert/Musset recalling in great detail his affair with Antonia/Sand. This made commercial sense—few, in 1859, would have been interested in a *roman à clef* about Flaubert—but it was also strategically risky. Here was Colet, a former mistress of Musset, giving the dead poet a voice to lament his earlier maltreatment by George Sand (who was, of course, still alive). Despite professions of admiration for Sand's work-rate and reputed kindness, the portrait is not just unsisterly, but disobliging and envious. In her own voice Stéphanie/Louise pulls sartorial rank ("I think wearing men's clothing had hurt her shape"); while through Albert we discover a woman who is bossy and domineering, insincere in bed, and heartless in dismissing lovers, who tainted the purity of her children by behaving licentiously in front of them, and who betrayed Musset with the very Italian doctor brought in to save him from his deathbed. Not surprisingly, Sand told Flaubert that she thought the novel a "chamberpot of a book into which she [Colet] excreted her causeless fury."

Lui still entertains, though largely for non-artistic reasons. It is talky, lush, and hot-breathed, with both the allure and the weaknesses of the *roman à clef*. On the one hand, the thrill of being given the inside dope; on the other, a sense of aesthetic concerns being placed in neutral gear. In a *roman à clef* the reason something happens is generally that it actually did happen, or happened a little bit differently, or might have happened had the author's wishes been grantable by life as opposed to literature. Early on, for example, Albert takes Stéphanie to the zoo. Why the zoo, we might naïvely wonder, and why are we spending so many pages there? Is some parallel being set up with caged passions, with wild nature restrained behind bars? But no: sometimes a zoo is only a zoo. It features because that's where Musset used to take Louise; besides, he once wrote a poem to her about the zoo, and she wants to quote it later on in the novel.

And are we getting the inside dope in *Lui*? Musset is ardent yet essentially ridiculous;* Sand a worthy bluestocking; Flaubert a

---

*Edith Wharton on the naming of her cars after French writers: "One summer, when we were all engaged on the first volumes of Mme Karénine's absorbing life of George Sand, we had a large showy car which always started off brilliantly and then broke down at the first hill, and this we christened 'Alfred de Musset,' while the small but indefatigable motor which subsequently replaced 'Alfred' was naturally named 'George.'"

glacial manipulator. But Stéphanie? What still rings out from the book like a hunting horn is the vanity of Colet's self-depiction. She ups herself socially to a marquise temporarily fallen on hard times; she prefaces the novel with a chapter whose main function is to give a (swiftly vanishing) narrator the chance to praise Stéphanie's serene wisdom and ravishing beauty. With Léonce the marquise suffers nobly; with Albert, she tries to rekindle his genius while politely but firmly fighting off his attentions and staying true in her heart to Léonce. This is a distinctly glamorized version of events. Musset was clearly unsafe in a cab at any speed, and as Flaubert sardonically reminded Louise, "Convention has it that one doesn't go for a moonlight drive with a man for the purpose of admiring the moon." But Louise went for many moonlight drives with the poet. Musset would turn up drunk and imploring on her doorstep, and—such being her reverence for glory—he eventually got into her bed. *Lui* shows us the relationship ending in the heroic mutual renunciation of two cauterized hearts: "We'll see each other again, but as friends, never again as lovers in waiting." However, Colet's private Mementoes dish the real dope on Musset, the *clef* to the *clef*. "His one sensation," she recorded (an entry apparently indicating erection but no orgasm). Other comments include: "Impotent!"; "Oh Gustave, Gustave, what a contrast!"; and "Certain that he is nearly impotent or that he has only very transient painful erections."

Colet's chief mode was of romanticizing confessionalism; and she wrote with celebrated haste. In their different ways Béranger, Hugo, and Flaubert all gave her sensible advice: to slow down, to be more realistic, to be less vindictive. But sensible advice, whether personal or literary, was something of which Louise was always splendidly heedless: she had the turning circle of a supertanker. In Flaubert's case there is something almost comic about the ultimate hopelessness of his counsel: here was the young devotee of form and priest of the impersonal seeking to redirect a poet who was his polar opposite. In a way, they both knew best: he knew she was working in a sluggish, moribund tradition; she knew that you must write as you can and will, not as anyone else thinks you should.

In the mid-1850s Colet planned an ambitious six-poem cycle on the subject of Woman, only half of which she completed. The first, *"La Paysanne,"* is one of her more surprising works: a touching yet brutal tale of parted lovers, emotional impoverishment, and rural destitution. Flaubert praised it wholeheartedly and spent a good twenty pages of the Pléiade *Correspondance* close-correcting the poem.

Even though Colet resisted his characteristic urging to be "Shakespearean, hideously truthful and cold," the poem has a modern toughness to it: the peasant girl Jeanneton shares a distant kinship with Félicité in Flaubert's much later *Un Coeur simple*. The second poem in the cycle, *"La Servante,"* sees Colet self-indulgently regressing (or wisely returning) to her natural mode. If Flaubert, as self-appointed adviser on *"La Paysanne,"* was like a driving instructor trying to grab the handbrake while his pupil insists on pointing at the view, with *"La Servante"* Colet threw away the highway code he was pressing on her. He told her to recast the poem, and in particular urged her not to include a transparent attack on Musset; then expanded his objections into forty pages of notes. Rarely among the writings of Flaubert sent to Louise Colet, this last document has completely vanished (and there are not many suspects in this particular case).

"La Servante" is the intertwined story of two peasant girls who come to Paris: Mariette, virtuous, lectorally aspirant, inflamed by the notion of love, and Théréson, pragmatic and corruptible about the ways of the world. Both tangle with the debauched Lionel, a poet-aristocrat based on Musset: but while Théréson handles him professionally and survives, Mariette lavishes on him the full dose of doomed Romantic love. After Lionel's death, Mariette goes mad, and is incarcerated in the Salpêtrière. The poem is a mixture—rather like Louise herself—of the charming, the irritating, the dogmatic, the instinctual, the observant, the egocentric, the heartfelt; it has both banality and élan. Calling it "vehemently

feminist" as Gray does and passing on is like matronizingly award-
ing it stars for good conduct: the twentieth century applauding the
past for being on the right side. In fact, for much of its length *"La
Servante"* seems to look a century back rather than forward: it is
moralizing, pictorial, and instructive, more Greuze than Greer.
Thus the wicked aristo Lionel is ethically counterbalanced by the
good miller Julien, who asks Mariette to marry him early on, and
later turns up (in one of the poem's several extravagant coinci-
dences) to save her from drowning. Mariette, in rejecting Julien's
dusty hand and following her awakened heart, is seeking her
Gothic-Romantic fate. She is destroyed not by any particular
action of the cold-hearted and largely indifferent Lionel (we are
not in the Marquis de Sade's territory) as by the exigencies and
false expectations of her own heart.

The closing scene, in which Mariette stands, mute, loose-
haired, and strait-jacketed among the mad and abandoned inmates
of the Salpêtrière, certainly gives us a stern and rebuking image of
woman destroyed. But does it make sense to call *"La Servante"*
"vehemently feminist"? It is in places denunciatory, the literary
equivalent to Colet's own cry in her later years of "How base men
are." But one of the poem's complications is that the women in it
who, unlike Mariette, have some control of their lives, some access
to money and power, are the women of pleasure, the "actresses"
who consort with corrupting figures like Lionel rather than oppose
them. And while on the one hand it is Théréson and her kind who
most openly denounce men, they are in turn denounced by Colet.
She presents them as irredeemably vile and vulgar. Modern
debauchery has lost its former voluptuous glory, and become
something cold, neurotic, and drab.

Is this a rich ambiguity, or an authorial confusion? The palm
prints of Louise's own life are all over *"La Servante,"* and it seems
likely that behind such frosty distaste there lies a personal agenda:
a response and a specific rebuke to Flaubert. She was working on
her poem in the second half of 1854; in June of that year she had
finally persuaded the extremely reluctant Flaubert to show her

his travel notebooks from the Orient. It is, of course, always a mistake for any writer to let his or her lover see their diary; and one of their more lurid quarrels duly ensued. For a start, Louise didn't find sufficient entries devoted to herself. "I was thinking about you often," Flaubert plaintively responds, "often, very often." Worse, she discovered rhapsodic descriptions of his encounters with women of pleasure. (And here Flaubert's defence was pretty jesuitical: since the women with whom he dealt had all suffered clitoridectomy, they couldn't feel anything sexually and therefore, he argued, Louise had no grounds for anxiety.) Beyond jealousy, however, there was a fundamental divide of taste, of aesthetic. What Louise found most disgusting—for instance, the bedbugs Flaubert recorded during his famous night with the dancer Kuchuk Hanem—Flaubert found most enchanting. He had been fascinated by prostitution from an early age: he loved it as a complex, bitter, and luxurious point of human intersection; he loved the lack of emotional contact, the muscular frenzy, and the clink of gold. "And it makes you so sad!" he enthused to Louise in a letter of June 1853. "And you dream of love so beautifully!"

This last paradox was no doubt especially provoking to Colet. Simon Leys has deftly summarized Flaubert's erotic bifurcation thus: "While the beloved incarnates the *reality* of love, and is thus fatally destined to disappoint, the prostitute for her part offers a *representation* of love, that's to say an aid to reverie." During her time with Flaubert, Louise Colet suffered a rare and unenviable pincer movement of jealousy: threatened by both the deeply imagined, in Emma Bovary, and the deeply carnal, in Kuchuk Hanem. In 1869, fifteen years after the lovers broke up, Colet was commissioned by *Le Siècle* to cover the inauguration of the Suez canal; on her journey up the Nile she tried to seek out Kuchuk Hanem in Esna. How should we read this: simple curiosity, masochism, an attempted purging, a heroic if belated attempt to confront a rival? Their encounter would have made a fine—indeed, Flaubertian—moment in a novel. But the courtesan's name meant nothing anymore to the locals, and with the lapse of two decades Louise could find no house to match Flaubert's description.

As she grew older, Louise Colet eschewed mellowness. "Poor *Maman*," her daughter, Mme Bissieu, would later recall, "had a character which made everyone suffer." She became more difficult, more irascible, expert at squandering old friendships. Infuriating, but often admirable: when Victor Cousin died, she renounced a legacy rather than bargain away the philosopher's letters. What can seem, in a literary celebrity and salon beauty, mere gilded egotism, grew into a rather splendid doughtiness. She worked, she travelled, she kept her political principles; and she refused to go quietly. As Gray shows, she championed the cause of Italy, helping Mazzini, hymning Garibaldi, covering the independence celebrations. She remained fiercely anti-clerical, and got one interview away from giving the Pope a good dressing-down. During the Franco-Prussian war she took to public speaking with sudden success. She unequivocally supported the Commune (odd that famous painters tended to back it much more than famous writers), and remained true to her liberalism in almost all areas except that of sex, where she became increasingly puritanical and moralistic, denouncing Queen Christina of Sweden as a "debauched strumpet." She judged harshly, and was harshly judged herself: George Sand, who after *Lui* had no reason to love her, compared Louise's old age to that of Mme Flaubert, and found it "even worse, because it has degenerated into malice . . . She's mad."

She was certainly incapable of matching the stoicism of her glamorized alter ego, the Marquise Stéphanie de Rostan. In *Lui* the marquise reflects sagely from a plateau of emotional wisdom upon her "finest hours," with all their tears and torments, and finds the following exotic comparison: "Doesn't the navigator propelled by fate into the glaciers of Greenland remember fondly some balmy, blooming beach in Cuba or the Antilles?" Colet herself found little consolation in beach memories, and was always particularly unforgiving towards Flaubert. In 1859 she denounced *Madame Bovary* in a poem as "a travelling-salesman's novel whose foul stench makes the heart retch." Though she praised *Salammbô* to Mme Edma Roger des Genettes in 1862, she couldn't help adding her opinion that its author was "ugly, common and as far as I am concerned profoundly evil." Mme Roger des Genettes did not convey all of this to Flaubert, and was rebuked by Louise for her tact: "If you passed on my praise to the author, in all truthfulness you should also let him know the absolute disdain I have for his character and the incredible repulsion I feel for his premature decrepitude." In 1872, eighteen years after their liaison had ended, Flaubert brought out a posthumous collection of verse by Bouilhet (with whom Louise had also had an affair); she sent him an anonymous verse letter calling him a "charlatan thumping the big drum over the grave of his flat-footed friend." Flaubert, by contrast, showed "no bitterness, no resentment" towards Colet (according to the Goncourts in 1862); and when she died he displayed a melancholy, regretful spirit to Mme Roger des Genettes—"I have trampled on so many things, in order to stay alive!"

Was he less vindictive because he had the nobler nature, because his heart had been less engaged (or more easily disengaged), or because of vivid and lasting relief at his narrow escape? Something of each, no doubt. Is it a paradox that she, the vindictive one, preserved his letters, while he, the magnanimous one, apparently burned hers? Probably not: their different actions are entirely consistent with their respective attitudes to privacy and fame. There is, however, a further possible reason for Louise's epistolary reverence. A month after Mme Récamier's death in 1849, Colet had published Benjamin Constant's love letters to Récamier; she similarly raised money soon after Musset's death by selling his occasional verse, and soon after Béranger's by publishing his letters to her. Perhaps she also hoped to outlive Flaubert.

When she died in 1876, Victor Hugo noted in his diary, "Mme Louise Colet is dead. Hers was a generous heart." Du Camp composed a disobliging epitaph ("Here lies she who compromised Victor Cousin, ridiculed Alfred de Musset, vilified Gustave Flaubert, and tried to assassinate Alphonse Karr"); he also devoted several unflattering pages to her in his *Souvenirs littéraires,* which, according to Gray, set off a tradition of "Colet-bashing."

There certainly was such a tradition (consider the mere title of Gérard-Gailly's 1934 study, *Les Véhémences de Louise Colet*), though one less monolithic than Gray makes it sound. A simpler explanation of any comparative forgetting of Louise would be that she had used up her fame in her own lifetime, and wrote no one book which either merit or saleability could sustain in print. Her most durable success was *Enfances célèbres,* an instructive work for younger readers about the childhoods of the famous. Indeed, you could argue that the attention of the Colet-bashers, far from obliterating her, kept her alive. Her memory was preserved—if in a distorted and semi-demonized fashion—by her very association with Flaubert. You could further argue that the self-same moustachioed life-raft also kept afloat Louis Bouilhet and Maxime Du Camp. They are still vividly with us, even though Bouilhet's verse is as out of print as Louise's, and Du Camp's six-volume work on Paris as hard to find as Colet's four-decker on Italy. Is not Du Camp also unfairly neglected? He was an energetic and inquisitive writer, for all his careerism and malice—a description which makes him sound uncommonly like Louise Colet.

Gloria Steinem in her book on Marilyn Monroe identified the "rescue fantasy" provoked in many men by the mere thought of the actress. Something of the same feeling often afflicts us when we peer into the past: not *him* again, we complain, as some Great White Male looms, casting his baneful shadow like a manchineel tree. Still, to call Louise Colet "heretofore obscure," as Francine du Plessix Gray does, only makes sense if we define that phrase as meaning "not previously biographed in English." There are times when she seems to have embarked upon a deeply misconceived rescue fantasy: wading heroically into the sea only to discover that Louise is not drowning but waving.

One of the problems of Colet's case is this: the fact that she was patronized by a generation of male Flaubertistes doesn't make her a better writer or a less infuriating person. The most useful, and touching, parts of Gray's book deal with Colet's later years, when, intrepid, troublesome, and isolated, she carries on working and fighting. But throughout, Gray, though resolutely engaged, cannot help noting her "extreme pride," "frequent rages," "monumental talent for self-deception"; or calling her "this most demanding of women," a "one-woman public relations factory" who was "capable of extravagant name-dropping." You begin to wonder how anyone put up with her for longer than strictly necessary. "She always came too early and stayed too late," was Gautier's view. "She wouldn't have left Flaubert alone with his pedicurist."

But Gray is committed to her defence and vindication, and this frequently leads her into special pleading. Rescuing Louise seems to necessitate demeaning others (Hippolyte, Mme Flaubert, and Flaubert's "buddy network," as Gray terms it). It means accepting the word of this "one-woman public relations factory" far too easily. It means making authoritative statements (such as "He was clearly the first man with whom she enjoyed ecstatic sex") without the slightest bibliographical back-up, and recklessly introducing whole episodes from *Lui* into the narrative as if they were objectively established fact. Sometimes an inappropriate twentieth-century template is fitted over nineteenth-century life; sometimes Gray regards as exceptional to Colet, or to women, circumstances shared by others. When Louise takes up fashion journalism (at which she seems to have been rather good), Gray feelingly writes that she was "bound to be humiliated by her need to grind out harebrained fashion chronicles." Perhaps so, but it was a humiliation shared later in the century by a more famous male poet: Mallarmé.

And if Flaubert studies have skewed our understanding of Colet—as they have—this vindication is also skewed in that it observes Flaubert simply from Colet's point of view. His other relations with women are scarcely mentioned: they were varied, complex, and normally enduring. Louise brought out one side of his amatory nature; she got into his heart and under his skin in a way that no one else ever did. They were, however, severely ill-matched in temperament, sociability, aesthetics, ambitions, and even sexual drive. Flaubert also seems to have been more suited to old love than to new love. In his letters to Louise he often gives the impression of hastening not so much towards further discoveries about the beloved as towards a position of established love—he is looking forward to looking back. Could there ever have been a "happy ending"—and if so what might that have been? Wasn't it just a case of waiting for when the rapture gave way to the rupture? Certainly Louise's plan that she and her daughter should transport themselves to Normandy and make some sort of extended rural family seems the ultimate fantasy. As far as we know, they never met again after the mid-1850s.

Du Plessix Gray is right to assert the centrality of Colet's position in the making of *Madame Bovary,* and the centrality (though not the uniqueness) of her place in Flaubert's heart. But was she "the first to recognize and encourage his genius"? (What about Alfred Le Poittevin, Du Camp, and Bouilhet?) Was she "the love of his life"? (Yes, but so in their different ways were Le Poittevin and Mme Schlesinger.) Did she "offer him a unique self-assurance about his vocation"? (Not to judge by the astonishing artistic confidence of his letters.) In her desire to right what she sees as a historical wrong, Gray finds herself making claims which will stagger any Flaubertiste. For instance, Gustave sent Louise his early work—*Novembre,* the first *Tentation,* and the first *Education sentimentale.* According to Gray: "How grateful Flaubert was for Louise's keen insights into the workings of his talent!" Well: in 1847 Maxime Du Camp wrote to Louise warning her that Gustave had been "profoundly wounded by the extravagant praise" she had lavished on *Novembre.* In 1852 Flaubert wrote to her about the first *Education:* "I am astonished, my dear friend, by the excessive enthusiasm you express over certain parts of the *Education.* They seem to me good, but not very much more so than the other pages you refer to. In any case I don't agree with your idea of cutting out the whole section about Jules and making something separate of it . . . Those pages which you were particularly struck by (on Art, etc.) seem pretty easily done to me." If he was marginally less grudging over her response to the *Tentation*, this was in the context of Bouilhet and Du Camp having previously advised him to throw the work on the fire: "Well, you *are* enthusiastic about *Saint Antoine*. At least I'll have one supporter. Although I don't accept everything you say, I think my friends don't appreciate everything that was in it . . . As for the change you suggest, we'll talk about it—it is *huge*."

Which brings us back to the letters. The way Francine du Plessix Gray tells it, there is no doubt at all over what happened in and around Flaubert's fireplace on that night in May 1879.

> Suddenly, in the middle of a particularly thick packet of letters, he comes across a package tied with a narrow ribbon. He opens it very slowly, takes out a small silken shoe; inside it is a faded rose rolled in a woman's handkerchief, its lace yellow with age. Flaubert kisses these three relics sorrowfully. Then he throws them into the fireplace along with the thick sheaf of letters that surrounds them, wiping his eyes. Dawn has come [etc].

This makes a poignant, precise, and, to some, enraging scene; but it's worth checking back to what Maupassant actually wrote. For a start, he quotes Flaubert as outlining the task ahead of them: *"Je veux brûler toutes mes vieilles lettres non classées. Je ne veux pas qu'on les lise après ma mort."* ("I want to burn all my old unclassified letters. I don't want anyone to read them after my death"). Gray renders this as: "I want to burn most of my old letters, things I don't want anyone to read." Here "all" has become "most": Gray is leaning on the translation to make it accord with what subsequently happens. More culpably, she suppresses that little phrase *"non classés."* In other words, Flaubert has done a previous *triage* of his papers, and this is a further sorting-out of the remainder. Since his relationship with Colet had terminated in 1856, and it is now 1879, should we not at least consider the possibility that Flaubert made his decision on Louise's letters during that earlier classification? He might have a) burnt them then; b) saved them (which points the finger back at Caroline); or even c) saved them then, only to change his mind subsequently and destroy them.

Together, Maupassant and Flaubert then pull out a trunk full of papers. *"Je veux en garder une partie, et brûler l'autre,"* says Flaubert ("I want to keep part of them, and burn the rest"). Gray again leans on the translation. "I want to keep a small part and burn the rest." (The "small" is her invention.) The letters are in chronologically reverse order, later ones on the top, earlier ones underneath: Flaubert therefore embarks on a strange reverse journey through the documents of his life. There are letters from the living and the dead, the famous and the insignificant, from friends and acquaintances; sometimes Flaubert drops a tear, sometimes he barks at the inanities he comes across. Early on, he finds a letter from George Sand, later one from his mother. These are the only two correspondents identified by Flaubert—or, to be exact, remembered by Maupassant as having been identified by Flaubert. The silence here is surely significant. Would Flaubert have burnt several hundred letters from Colet without mentioning the fact? And why should Maupassant not report it if he did? Additionally and alternatively, though the emphasis is on what Flaubert destroyed that night, what about the many papers he saved? After all, in his letter to Laporte he said that the next day his hands were still "shaking from tying up packets."

Then comes the discovery of the three relics. There is a slight problem here. Maupassant describes "a little silk dancing-shoe," but as Hermia Oliver comments, "That slipper was not a dancing-shoe; it was Louise Colet's slipper, or pair of slippers (perhaps Maupassant overlooked one of them)." Perhaps he did; but then it was four a.m., and they had taken "several glasses of old claret" with dinner. Flaubert casts the slipper, singular or plural, into the flames, together with the rose and the handkerchief. He had discovered this sentimental bundle, "in the middle of a particularly thick packet of letters," and he now throws the relics on to the fire followed by "the thick sheaf of letters that surround them." This is what Gray tells us. But this is not what Maupassant tells us, not at all. According to him, Flaubert simply found his souvenirs *"au milieu des lettres,"* i.e., among the letters in the trunk. There is no "particularly thick packet of letters," no "thick sheaf," except in Francine du Plessix Gray's novelistic head. She does it, no doubt, with the best of intentions: to dramatize the incident, to finger Flaubert, to point up what she believes to be the first step in a campaign to blot out Louise Colet, a male conspiracy which has finally brought Gray riding to the rescue. But as Flaubert once observed, you don't make art out of good intentions; and you don't make biography that way either.

(11)

Drinking Ink

Alphonse Karr in his garden at Saint-Raphaël

"An hour of full, frank chat," wrote Turgenev to Flaubert in 1863, "is worth a hundred letters." Maybe to them; but not to us. Sartre's description of Flaubert's Letters as pre-Freudian free association hints at their fluency, profligacy, range, and sexual frankness; to which we should add power, control, wit, emotion, and furious intelligence. The *Correspondance*—which Gide kept at his bedside for five years in place of the Bible—has always added up to Flaubert's best biography. This is partly because it has drawn extraordinarily committed and skilful editors (in France, Jean Bruneau and Alphonse Jacobs; in America, Francis Steegmuller); partly because of the inadequacy of Flaubert's biographers. One of their many problems is the very splendour and quotability of the letters: how do you use them without being manifestly outperformed by them? Sartre's tactic of declining to quote in *L'Idiot de la famille* increasingly works against him: watch the investigating magistrate gag his principal witness and answer for him. As Claude Chabrol put it, Sartre only has to start writing about Flaubert to turn into Homais. There are times, too, when the Letters even surpass biography and veer towards the novelistic. As we read beyond the charismatic hero and his vivid companions, beyond the victories and defeats, the running themes and phrases and gags, we start to watch equally for the crucial activities of the minor characters; we attend to the silences amid the noisy street-cries.

The third volume (out of five) of the Pléiade edition runs from January 1859 to December 1868. In this decade Flaubert publishes *Salammbô* and writes most of *L'Education sentimentale,* while continuing to be fêted as the author of *Madame Bovary*. His social success in Paris increases: the Magny dinners begin, Princesse Mathilde invites him, he receives the *Légion d'honneur*. Though George Sand judges him "one of those rare beings who remain open, sincere, in love with art, neither corrupted by ambition nor drunk with success," his head is visibly turned. This is the period when his least will-you-dine-with-me? letter is carefully preserved; when the provincial novelist fancies himself master of the metropolis; when his mother is shocked by his glove bill.

The literary tone of the *Correspondance* in this decade alters too. Behind lie Louise Colet and the spectacular self-anatomization undertaken while writing *Madame Bovary*. Now he is the established writer, knowing better what he does, seeking to produce another masterpiece, and then another. His references to the composition of *Salammbô* and *L'Education sentimentale* are therefore of a different order, fascinating but generally brief: research notes and queries, complaints of difficulty, pre-emptive doubts. He constantly talks down *L'Education* for the "mediocrity" of its conception, and satirically anticipates the objections to *Salammbô*: "They're bound to slaughter me. *Salammbô* will 1) annoy the bourgeoisie, that's to say everyone; 2) turn the stomach of sensitive folk; 3) irritate archaeologists; 4) seem unintelligible to women; 5) make me look like a pederast and a cannibal. Let's hope so!" In place of creative agonizing there are post-publication fisticuffs—notably with the reasonable Sainte-Beuve and the impudent Froehner over *Salammbô* (where the Flaubertian dictum *faire et se taire*—do your work and remain silent—goes rousingly disregarded).

It is in this decade that Flaubert makes opening epistolary contact with Turgenev and George Sand; but the correspondence with Turgenev does not take off until the 1870s; and while there is some preliminary skirmishing here with Sand, their grand though friendly battle about the purposes and practices of art still lies in the future. What is mainly happening in the course of Volume Three is that the aesthetic hammered out with Bouilhet and bawled at Louise Colet, the aesthetic to be tacitly agreed with Turgenev and argued for with Sand, is "merely" being implemented. Writing consists now of doing again what you've done before: "The poisoning of Emma Bovary made me throw up into my chamber-pot. The assault on Carthage makes my arms ache." But this time round your pains are familiar, both to yourself and to your correspondents, and you are often reduced to burlesquing them: "I'm sweating blood, pissing boiling oil, shitting catapults and belching slingsmen's stones. Such is my condition." Writing consists of laboriously taking out extraneous words ("I've used *faire* four times in a row—oh, *shit*!") and not getting screwed by your publisher. Writing consists of complaining that there are more than the agreed number of lines per page on your proofs—"my style is dense enough without making things even harder for the reader"—and of making sure you get the correct Carthaginian circumflex: "The circumflex on Salammbô shouldn't have any sort of curve to it. Nothing could be less Punic. I insist on you making it more open."

Indeed, Flaubert's dealings with his publisher Michel Lévy provide the most purely comic passages in the volume. When negotiations over *Salammbô* begin, the novelist is fully aware of his power and marketability. Even so, his first and main demand remains exceptional in the annals of authorial vanity and paranoia: it is that Lévy must on no account be permitted to read his manuscript. This had happened to the novelist once before, with *Madame Bovary,* when an editor at the Librairie Nouvelle to whom he had shown the book had had the impertinence to comment favourably on it. "A publisher may exploit you," Flaubert explained to the Goncourts, "but he doesn't have the right to judge you." Lévy's superiority as a publisher on that occasion was "never to have said a single word about my book." Now Lévy has the audacity to expect the right to read *Salammbô.* Flaubert feels "a repugnance and extreme exasperation at being judged by M. Lévy." When Jules Duplan tries to change his mind, Flaubert repeats: "The idea of that blockhead Lévy getting his bloody paws on *my pages* revolts me more than the worst review could do. It's as if he was asking me to French-kiss him." Bouilhet suggests that Flaubert merely read fragments of the book out loud to Lévy, Duplan that the publisher be allowed to contemplate the book only in the office of Flaubert's lawyer; but the novelist is adamant. Though he says he wants 20,000 francs for the novel, he insists on first finding out what Lévy will offer sight unseen. Lévy proposes 10,000 francs, which Flaubert accepts rather than suffer the humiliation of being appreciated. The squabble broadens. Lévy wants a two-book contract, the option being on Flaubert's next "roman moderne." Flaubert tries for just having "volume" in the contract, but Lévy wins out, additionally specifying that by "roman moderne" the parties are to understand "not set before 1750." Flaubert's other inflexible demand—for a fixed sum rather than a royalty (for who, he argues, can ever prove the number of copies sold?)—also works against him. By 1866, when *Salammbô* has been a success for four years, Flaubert is agitating for an *ex gratia* payment to make up for lost royalties.

This volume contains many of Flaubert's famous and echoing pronouncements: on fucking your inkwell, on the religion of despair, the royal chamber of the heart, the folly of wanting to come to conclusions, the invisibility of the writer within his creation, the submission of the writer to a particular subject (rather than his active choice of it), the belief that "a novel is . . . a particular way of living." As always, Flaubert is wonderfully free, vigorous, and stern in his opinions. With his motto *Merde, merde et archimerde,* he dumps on the ineradicable imbecility of his time: on the medieval and despotic nature of socialism; on the chic modern rage to *parler sport;* on Béranger and the wider cult of golden mediocrity; on Musset (a sentimental hairdresser); on the inanities of Pre-Raphaelite theory; on the "infantile" *Les Misérables.* Praise is restricted: to Shakespeare *(le maître des maîtres),* Voltaire (but not Voltaireans), Montaigne, Dickens, Zola. He playfully attributes made-up quotes to those he admires: so *L'Esprit des lois* is given as the source for "that bitch was wanking at the sight of other people's pleasure," and Voltaire rewarded with (the so far untraced and therefore presumably invented) "the history of the human mind is the history of human folly." Flaubert is just as free with his predictions, whose wonkiness flatters posterity's hindsight. During this decade he foresees the death of Islam, the division of France into two like Belgium, and the impossibility of war with Prussia: "As for war, who with? With Prussia? Prussia wouldn't be so stupid." This last is from 1868. An odder, longer-term prediction is that a time will come when mankind will abandon its quest for happiness—"which will not amount to progress, but at least mankind will be calmer."

However, if we read this volume as a book rather than as an assemblage to be filleted for aesthetic dicta and handy tips on the fiction, then it becomes richer and stranger, gayer and grimmer. For a start, we notice the wide range of letter-writers who coexist within Flaubert: he has categories of address according to his categories of friendship. With Ernest Feydeau he is the laddish cocksman, dreaming of depilated cunts beneath an eastern sky; with Amélie Bosquet and Aglaé Sabatier the mischievous gallant, going so far but not, in words anyway, farther ("a thousand kisses in places of your choosing"); with Princesse Mathilde the humble courtier and gift-bearer (one wonders what she did with a delivery of turnip seeds); with Jules Duplan, friend and general gofer, he is the impatient, seigneurial employer, occasionally dispensing robust consolation—"You poor old fellow, you look as if life has given you a right buggering"; with Bouilhet the profound friend, literary operator, and also obscenity recidivist, bursting into lubricity as a sign-off; with his niece Caroline mostly the loving Nuncle; with Mlle Leroyer de Chantepie the wise agony uncle, even though she is old enough to be his aunt; with George Sand the affectionate *confrère*, keen to play down any reputation for vice; with the Goncourts ("I grasp you by all four hands") a slightly edgier *confrère*, keen to play up such a reputation. These constant changes of register sometimes lead to comical rephrasings. Summarizing his difficulties with *L'Education sentimentale* to Duplan in April 1863, he writes: "I'm wanking my brain to no purpose." The next year, for Caroline's benefit, he softens the image: "I have never tugged my poor brain so much." By 1866, still on the same book, he sanitizes the phrase completely for George Sand: "You don't know what it's like to spend a whole day with your hands pressed against your head, just to find a single word."

Once the main lines of the decade are established, the correspondents who make the most impact in this volume are not, surprisingly, Flaubert's literary and social companions, but two of the quieter characters: Mlle Leroyer de Chantepie and Caroline. At first sight, Mlle Leroyer de Chantepie, who wrote to him out of the blue in 1856, seems an unlikely long-term correspondent. Though she admires his work, she is not immune from fandom's twittering, and can be whoppingly wrong-headed (thus "The ending [of *Madame Bovary*] should keep women firmly on the path of duty"). She is a fifty-six-year-old spinster at the time of their first contact, living in Angers with up to eighteen hangers-on who exploit her generosity; she is religious but spiritually blocked, neurotic and repetitively complaining; in the emptiness of her life she ardently seeks Flaubert's advice; but when she gets it, she invariably doesn't take it, and then complains anew about her unchanged moral and spiritual condition. At first it seems that Flaubert is merely indulging himself as the wise author being consulted about life. But his concern is genuine, and the pair of them are less dissimilar than they appear to be. She tells him how she finds reality disappointing and can only live in *idéalité* (for her, religion, for him, literature); he observes that each of their lives is sombre and solitary, marked by a hidden wound. If she seems at times a hysterical old woman, then that is precisely how a doctor once described him—an observation he judged "profound." And so, finding priests an insuperable obstacle between her and God, unable to confess in a church, she confesses with brutal wholeness to Flaubert. The kindliness of his replies and his sympathy for her suffering should temper any reflections on his generalized misanthropy. Her tone is frequently valetudinarian; she fears she will die without going to the opera, like the man in the Nadaud song who thought he would die without seeing Carcassonne. (Why is that city so emblematic, incidentally? The narrator of *The Good Soldier,* Ford's "French" novel, suddenly announces, "I just wanted to marry her as some people want to go to Carcassonne.") They never met, despite mutual assurances that they would. Surprisingly, given that she is always about to expire, she outlived him, dying in 1888 at the age of eighty-seven. It is a touching relationship, a side-story having little to do with Flaubert's creativity. Although when, summarizing her life yet again for her illustrious, unglimpsed correspondent, she writes, "My life has been spent in acts of pointless devotion," we might sense a pre-echo of Félicité in *Un Coeur simple.*

Letters to and from Mlle Leroyer de Chantepie survive in equal numbers; the exchange with Caroline is completely one-sided. This is not a new problem; there are voluminous speaking absences elsewhere in the *Correspondance,* absences where the reader must act creatively, as with a novel. Most of Louise Colet's letters were destroyed, while in the case of Juliet Herbert not a single letter survives on either side (and yet, as Hermia Oliver has shown, the relationship can still be plausibly reconstructed). Flaubert's letters to his niece—tender, proud, hortatory, cajoling—exist in some quantity; only one of her replies has come down to us. There is nothing immediately sinister in this: most of the family letters have disappeared. Bruneau comments: "Flaubert's two nieces were responsible, but not blameworthy. That such letters might be published was unthinkable to the bourgeoisie at that time." But there seems a little more to the destruction of Caroline's letters—and to the survival of the one that exists—than general family *pudeur;* and as we track her in and out of Bruneau's scrupulous annotations, her poignant and instructive story becomes the secret drama of this volume.

When Flaubert wrote to George Sand in 1866 that "I am sometimes truly bothered by how bourgeois I am beneath my skin," he was partly trying to defuse Sainte-Beuve's judgement on him as "depraved." But the years 1859–68 show Flaubert more than ready to exploit the advantages and connections of his place in the upper bourgeoisie, to use his influence, push friends, play the system. This is normal—even *de rigueur*—in French literary life; but Flaubert also had no compunction about nobbling Rouen judges, or putting a word in with Princesse Mathilde to help the husband of a friend of Caroline's get promoted *chef de bataillon*. And when it came to Caroline herself, the bourgeois within him lay very close beneath the skin. He adored her; he brought her up to value the artistic life; he urged her to avoid the un-joined-up thinking he found characteristic of her sex, and paid her the highest compliment of writing to her "as if to a sensible young man." But when the lessons of her artistic upbringing looked like they were being applied in real life—when, still only seventeen, she fell in love with her art teacher Johanny Maisiat, a man twenty-two years her senior and manifestly lacking a fortune—Flaubert conspired with his mother to marry her off to Ernest Commanville and into social safety. Decades later, Caroline wrote in her memoir *Heures d'autrefois* (still for some reason unpublished), "They suggested a proper, honourable, indeed bourgeois marriage"; as a result of which "I was thrown out of Parnassus." Mme Flaubert, a tough old bird, was certainly the chief fixer, just as she brusquely paid off Caroline's banished father when he expressed the unacceptable desire to come to his daughter's wedding; but Flaubert's collaboration, his influence over the effectively orphaned Caroline, was central. In October 1863, two months before the drama, he was recording to Amélie Bosquet his proud loathing of "the assembled cream of Rouen, Le Havre and Elbeuf." In December he sends Caroline a letter which for all its initial non-advice-giving, tells her plainly that "I would rather you married a millionaire grocer than a penniless great man"; better, he says, to be rich in Rouen than a pauper in Paris. Six days after this he writes complacently to Duplan of the crisis, "Everything will work out in the best bourgeois manner."

Caroline's sole surviving letter, written while trying to make up her mind on what was proposed, is a touching, naïve document, revealing deep uncertainty and an equally deep desire to please her uncle. She has played music with M. Commanville, she says; he is harmonious in this respect. "But I'm afraid, so afraid of making a mistake. And the idea of leaving you, my poor old uncle, really hurts. But you'll always come and see me, won't you? Even if you found my husband too *bourgeois,* you'd come to see your Liline, wouldn't you? And you'd always have your own room at my house, with big armchairs just as you like them." No doubt the thoughtful railroading of Caroline into marriage was not so unusual for the time; but she did suffer one extra, humiliating betrayal. Before the marriage Caroline went to her grandmother and explained that she did not want children; Commanville should be informed of her decision and its necessary consequences for him. Mme Flaubert led Caroline to believe that she would square the husband-to-be; but when her granddaughter, dressed in her going-away clothes, found herself in the *pavillon* at Croisset, alone for the first time with her new husband, she discovered that the bad news had not been transmitted. "My avowal to M. Commanville was harsh and cruel," she recalled, "and our honeymoon voyage was a sad one." The marriage was not a success, and Caroline's subsequent life followed the same unfortunate pattern: twice more she fell in love, once more she married, but the two conditions never coincided.

How far should we blame Flaubert? Mlle Leroyer de Chantepie once complained that those who loved her had done her more harm than those who hated her, and this seems to have been Caroline's case; perhaps it always is. Flaubert was certainly in awe of his mother ("So, you are guarded like a young girl?" was Louise Colet's taunt), and the marriage was convenient to him: if Caroline remained in Rouen, she could help him out with mother-care. What the writer wanted most of all from his immediate family was calm. When a dispute arose over Caroline's dowry, he retreated swiftly into the irritable vagueness of the artist who must not be bothered with quotidian concerns. Let everything arrange itself in the best bourgeois manner while he gets on with his work. This might be understandable, and *sub specie aeternitatis* almost forgivable, if he had been writing *Madame Bovary* at the time; but the dismal irony of his role in Caroline's marriage is that the art he needed to concentrate on was that duff *féerie* called *Le Château des coeurs*. The Goncourts' verdict on the play was snobbish but fair. When Flaubert read it to them, they judged it "A work of which we would have judged him incapable, given our opinion of him. To have read your way through every single *féerie* and then produce the most vulgar of all of them . . ."

Everything did, in a sense, for a time, go in the best bourgeois manner. Caroline wrote comforting letters from her honeymoon implying that all was well. She returned to Rouen and settled into the life of "a fashionable young lady much in demand." But a breach with her uncle has been opened. Flaubert now begins to rebuke her for being what he had encouraged her to be: an independent bourgeois wife rather than a dependent and adoring niece. He recognizes her new status by using her increasingly as an intermediary in dealing with his mother; but he also finds that she doesn't do what he expects. She comes to Paris when it would be more useful to him if she stayed and looked after his mother. When Commanville is away in Dieppe and he invites her to lunch, she declines. He rebukes her thus: *"Lui, bon oncle pourtant. Lui bon nègre. Lui aimer petite nièce. Mais petite nièce oublier lui. Elle pas gentille! Elle cacatte! Lui presque pleurer! Lui faire bécots, tout de même."* This retreat into baby-talk, or Little Black Sambo–speak, is peculiar and revealing. By using it, he is seeking to corral his niece back into obedient childhood, but in fact it is he who emerges sounding childish, the whiner not getting his own way.

Caroline continues with the life allotted to her, while Flaubert makes uneasy remarks about her sumptuous carriage and the fact that "Tomorrow Madame is having a big party for all the *grand monde*. Will she even have time to read the love and kisses her poor uncle sends her?" What makes such comments distasteful is that while Caroline is disporting herself with the despised *rouennerie*, *havrerie*, and *elbeuferie*, Flaubert is simultaneously relaying rather self-congratulatory accounts of his own progress in the truer *grand monde*. He ticks her off for abandoning her study of Montaigne, and in the next letter writes preeningly to her: "*Two* princesses made fun of me." This is one of the periods from which Flaubert comes out least well. That solitary, plaintive letter from Caroline contrives to haunt a long stretch of the *Correspondance*, and makes the manner of its survival intriguing. Did Flaubert keep only this single letter from his niece? Unlikely. Did he keep all or most of them, and did she then destroy the rest, preserving only this one? And so should we imagine her burning all those cheerful honeymoon lies while saving this true appeal for help, letting it stand thereafter as a rebuke against her famous uncle?

We could not trace Caroline's story so clearly without the extraordinary completeness of the Pléiade edition. Inevitable moments of repetitiousness are balanced by the way we are allowed to follow the life of even a phrase: how "Fuck your inkwell!" (to Feydeau, 1859) becomes "The inkwell is the true vagina for men of letters" (Feydeau 1859) becomes "Drink ink! it makes you drunker than wine" (Feydeau 1861) becomes "Ink is a wine that makes us drunk, let's plunge into dreams since life is so appalling" (Amélie Bosquet 1861) becomes "Let's get drunk on ink, since we haven't got any nectar of the gods" (Bosquet 1861). Or we may watch the creation of an image: when Mme Flaubert is ill in August 1861, Flaubert reports to Caroline that she is given a vesicatory (an irritating ointment or plaster designed to blister the skin—the dying M. Dambreuse is given one in *L'Education sentimentale*). Two days later she is better; two weeks later the writer has appropriated the image to himself, writing to the Goncourts, "My work isn't going too badly. My literary vesicatory brings relief."

Completeness also allows us to follow the volte-faces, ironic juxtapositions, and quiet hypocrisies that bestrew a long correspondence. Flaubert mocks Michelet in a letter to Gautier, but not long afterwards the historian becomes "cher Maître" (Flaubert also goes into turn-around over George Sand). When Froehner denounces *Salammbô* and also calls it "the illegitimate daughter of *Les Misérables*" we can better imagine Flaubert's double wrath by having read his earlier private trashing of Hugo's book to Edma Roger des Genettes. Equally, the wrong praise can produce a squirm: Flaubert explains to Sainte-Beuve that his approach to antiquity in *Salammbô* is diametrically opposed to Chateaubriand's method; a few months later Maurice Schlesinger innocently congratulates Flaubert on the novel—"People are quite right to compare it to Chateaubriand." And after reading Flaubert's slightly patronizing teases of Caroline over *le grand monde,* it seems like an act of editorial justice when Bruneau helps us understand the figure the novelist actually cut as he joked with his princesses. The comtesse Stéphanie de Tascher de la Pagerie, for instance, in her *Mon Séjour aux Tuileries* (1894) recalled: "Gustave Flaubert . . . was showing off amongst us. He has a penetrating glance, but the complexion of a drunkard . . . His books are heavy-going and so is he." In 1867, after a ball at the Tuileries which he clearly regarded as a social peak, Flaubert thanks the Princesse Mathilde: "The Tuileries ball stays in my mind like an enchanting dream." (Comte Primoli, editing this letter, gratuitously inserted the words, "I felt like Madame Bovary, knocked out by her first ball." A new gloss on "Madame Bovary, c'est moi.")

The reader of Volume Three can wander constructively among text and notes and variants, letters to and from Flaubert, third-party documents, Goncourt Journals, socio-historical background, plus extensive summaries of books to which Flaubert makes brief allusion, and will constantly be amazed and impressed by Bruneau's rage for perfection. A different sort of rage is in order when considering the obstructiveness and pig-headedness of some owners of Flaubert material. This complete edition could have been even more complete. At the very start of his quest, for instance, Bruneau found ten letters to Ernest Chevalier from the 1830s and 1840s, but couldn't get permission to publish them; there is a similar problem with letters to the comtesse de Grigneuseville. Sadly, it's more than just a case of individual owners harbouring their possessions, aware that an unpublished letter may be twice as valuable as a published one. Bruneau, with what the outsider assumes to be the normal academic altruism, allowed Steegmuller to draw on material as yet unpublished in the Pléiade edition for his second Harvard volume; Alphonse Jacobs, splendid editor of the Flaubert-Sand correspondence, allowed Bruneau to reproduce the whole of his text in the Pléiade edition. The problem lies with Flaubert's letters to his publisher Michel Lévy. Bruneau was allowed to reprint in full those which had already appeared in the Conard edition of the *Correspondance*. But every single one of the 102 *Lettres inédites de Gustave Flaubert à son éditeur Michel Lévy* can only be represented in the Pléiade edition by their date and their first line. What are the publishers Calmann-Lévy playing at? Protecting the inevitably sluggish sales of a book published way back in 1965 in an edition of 1,500 (of which I bought copy no. 827 in 1985)? Perhaps it is posthumous revenge on Flaubert for the *hauteur* with which he treated his publisher. Whichever way, it is mean-minded and contemptible. It makes you wish Flaubert had been even more eccentric in his negotiating technique and asked how much Lévy would pay for the right not to publish *Salammbô* as well as for the right not to read the manuscript.

(12)

Two Moles

Turgenev at forty: the age of renunciation

Flaubert and Turgenev met on 28 February 1863 at a Magny dinner; the Russian had been brought along by the Franco-Polish critic Charles-Edmond. Recording the event, Goncourt compared Turgenev to some elderly, sweet-tempered spirit of forest or mountain; there was something of the druid about him, or perhaps of Friar Laurence from *Romeo and Juliet*. The Magny regulars awarded him an ovation. In reply, he discoursed on the state of Russian literature, and impressed his hosts with the very high rates paid by Russian magazines. Then the solitary Russian and the several Frenchmen sealed their mutual regard by praising a writer from a third country: Heinrich Heine.

Goncourt makes no mention of Flaubert's presence or reaction to Turgenev that evening, but we may deduce their immediate attraction for one another: the next day Turgenev sent Flaubert two of his books and asked him to dinner. Thus began a friendship which lasted until Flaubert's death in 1880. When they met, Flaubert was forty-one and Turgenev forty-three; each had written the novel—*Madame Bovary, Fathers and Sons*—for which they are still best known. Though there were many books and years ahead, they already presented themselves as elderly men: Turgenev asserted that after the age of forty, the basis of life is renunciation. Each had settled into a rather neutered existence: Flaubert as the solitary prisoner-son of a dominant mother in the backwoods of Normandy, Turgenev as the tame lodger in the Viardot household. Each believed more in the hope of tranquillity than in the possibility of happiness.

In many ways their natures diverged radically: Turgenev was gregarious, cosmopolitan, footloose, mild, and charming; Flaubert was eremitic, provincial, site-specific, rowdy, and coarse. But they had both arrived, through their separate experiences of life, at similar conclusions about the individual, society, and art. Both believed that mankind was a rather hopeless species, that moral progress was a large illusion and scientific progress an even larger one; each was made cheerful by his pessimism. Most importantly, they were in general accord on aesthetic matters. "We are a pair of moles burrowing away in the same direction," the Russian famously writes.

In the same direction, but not at the same speed, or with the same digging power. Turgenev chides himself for being lazy, while also finding that writing comes rather easily to him; Flaubert is famous for his vast labour, his fervent rewriting, his groaning search for perfection. Turgenev is happy to cultivate a broad social life alongside his writing; Flaubert is someone who, as Anita Brookner has put it, "asserts with terrifying intensity that nothing but writing exists for him, and his case is undoubtedly a morbid one." Despite these differences of method and artistic temperament, their aesthetic principles are close. Whereas Flaubert's exchanges with other writers tend to be combative, that with Turgenev is full of shared assumptions. It is the most peaceful, chummy, and uncontentious stretch of his entire correspondence.

Moles: Turgenev starts the simile in 1868, and runs it again in 1871: "We shall live for a while like moles hiding in their holes." Later, he compares Flaubert's tireless labours to those of the ant. Flaubert replies, variously, that he is "like an old toad in his old damp hole"; that he is "an old post-horse, worn out but courageous"; that he works like an ox; that he lives like an oyster. Turgenev raises the bidding stakes in sentimental melancholia by enlarging this last comparison: *he* is "an old oyster that doesn't even open in the sun." Flaubert wishes that the two of them could, like snakes, slough off their skins and start all over again. This gloomy psychic zoo only acquires a cheerful inhabitant in the very last letter Turgenev sent to his French comrade, when he suddenly and uncharacteristically declares, "I am well and darting about like a squirrel in a cage." Ironically, this is the one animal Flaubert doesn't get to hear about: by the time the letter arrives, he is a dead bear in a wooden box.

From the very beginning this is a correspondence between old friends. They admire one another's work, without smugness, but also without the extensive comment later readers might hope for; they agree about younger chaps like Zola and Tolstoy; they agree about the lamentable condition of old age which can only be relieved by work—poetry, writes Turgenev, is "the bodkin in our backs." Flaubert makes gifts of cider and cheese, Turgenev replies with salmon and caviare (which Flaubert eats "almost without bread, like jam"). Both lament the decline of France, and share a loud chuckle when the Comte de Germiny, son of a former governor of the Bank of France, is arrested for buggery in a public lavatory on the Champs-Elysées.

Flaubert is more inclined to rage and complaint, Turgenev to calming good sense and practical help; though each at times sounds like the other. "As for the state of my *soul*—you can get a very accurate idea by lifting up the lid of a cesspool and looking in": this sounds like Flaubert but isn't. Turgenev offers occasional advice about writing: for instance, that *L'Education sentimentale* is a bad, or rather, inappropriate title (correct), or that *Bouvard et Pécuchet* should be treated *presto*, in the manner of Swift or Voltaire (incorrect—or rather, possible for them, but not for Flaubert). The Frenchman doesn't take offence, but neither does he take most of the advice. One of the few things they constantly disagree upon is where, when, and whether they shall meet. Flaubert is constantly pining and whining, almost childish in his attempts to manipulate or bully "my Muscovite" into visiting him at Croisset. His requests are countered by elaborate yet doubtless genuine letters of prevarication and regret from Turgenev: gout is the main plea, but also business, the demands of the Viardot family, trouble in Russia, and partridge-shooting in England. There is some quiet irony here, given Flaubert's letters to Louise Colet: he spent gallons of ink trying to stop her coming down to Croisset; now he begs, and is often disappointed.

Dr. Johnson thought that "the reciprocal civility of authors is one of the most risible scenes in the farce of life." This is probably as true today as it was then. Authors frequently conceal their natural (and cultivated) envy, spite, and malice behind public displays of affability and mutual praise. But in the case of Flaubert and Turgenev, the "reciprocal civility" was genuine, and their correspondence represents rare proof of two great writers taking each other to their hearts.

(13)

Consolation v. Desolation

George Sand, by Nadar

Flaubert's exchanges with Turgenev are full of equality—not to say crusty back-patting—but largely empty of difference. His exchanges with Louise Colet, vivid with difference, lack any useful equality: not just because most of her letters were destroyed, but because of his flamboyant and bullying assertiveness. Only in his great correspondence with George Sand does Flaubert manage to attain both equality and difference.

"Your letters fall upon me," Sand writes with lyrical gratitude, "like a good shower of rain, making all the seeds in the ground start to sprout." But rain cannot alter the nature of the crop; she warns him not to expect her roots "to produce tulips when all they can give you is potatoes." So this is not a correspondence that changes its participants' minds. By the time it starts, with Sand fifty-eight and Flaubert an antiquated forty-one, they are too wise, or set in their ways, for that. Early on, she urges him to criticize one of her novels: "People ought to do this service for one another, as Balzac and I used to do. It doesn't mean you change one another—on the contrary, it usually makes one cling more firmly to one's point of view." Their thirteen-year correspondence exhibits much passionate and at times desperate clinging. On the other hand, this is a correspondence whose two sides make up a whole argument, the argument every writer and reader has with him- or herself, the argument art never ceases to have with itself: Beauty v. Utility, Truthfulness v. Moral Uplift, Happy Few v. Mass Audience, Contemporary Relevance v. Future Durability, Primacy of Form v. Urgency of Message, Style v. Content, The Artist as Controlling Creator v. The Artist as Played-Upon Instrument, and so on. Flaubert, lordly and inflexible, always takes the high aesthetic line: the making of art necessarily entails the partial renunciation of life; the artist can only know humanity, but cannot change it; truth is a sufficient good in itself. Sand's position, to which she is just as committed, is pragmatic and involving: life, and especially love, are more important than art; artists cannot negotiate a detachment from the rest of the human species, since art springs precisely from their intimate, messy commingling with it; art must be useful and moral.

Flaubert told Sand that her work "often set me dreaming in my youth"; and there is corroboration of this in a letter from the seventeen-year-old Flaubert to his school-friend Ernest Chevalier. But most of his references to her before they meet are disparaging. He calls her "that latter-day Dorothée" (after the hormonally confused Mme d'Esterval in Sade's *La Nouvelle Justine*); when her *Histoire de ma vie* comes out, he reports that "Every day I read G. Sand and regularly work myself up into a state of indignation for a good quarter of an hour"; while in 1852, in one of his least gallant similes, he compares her work to leucorrhoea, or vaginal discharge: "everything oozes, and ideas trickle between words as though between slack thighs." Her books put him off; so did her public image as "Mother St. Sand." The two of them were set far apart by age, sex, geography, temperament, politics, aesthetics, and metaphysics.

But Flaubert could be as warm and undogmatic in person as he was stern in matters of art. In 1856, for instance, he had begun his long, touching, and unexpected correspondence with Mlle Leroyer de Chantepie, undeterred by the fact that she was a thoroughgoing Sandian. Shortly afterwards he met Sand herself and was enchanted. This is not surprising. She was by the 1860s a sort of literary monument whom many came to mock but stayed to admire. Her chief characteristics are held to be placidity, dignity, "elephantine gravity" (the Goncourts), stolidity, calm, serenity, platitudinousness, kindness, sweetness, and charm. Male *littérateurs* were reluctantly, even ruefully, won round by her goodness, her honesty, her efficiency, the "frank, cordial simplicity" noted by the young Matthew Arnold back in 1846. Théophile Gautier goes to Nohant, reports it "as amusing as a Moravian monastery," complains of the personnel that "all their fun comes from farting" (not especially monastic, you'd have thought), but ends by admitting that "All in all, she does you very well." Maxime Du Camp writes that she "had the serenity of those ruminants whose peaceful eyes seem to reflect immensity"; but in rather a confused account he is clearly impressed by her honourable nature and awed by her industry. The Goncourts are predictably cattier, but though satirical and prurient, they cannot deny her charm. They record her at her first Magny dinner glancing timidly round the table and murmuring to Flaubert, "You're the only one here with whom I feel at ease"; on another occasion they mock her clothes as being chosen to seduce him. Later, they report an overhearing from Princesse Mathilde's conservatory: amid the habitual *vous* of Flaubert and Sand, a *tu* suddenly escapes Sand's lips, and the Princesse looks meaningfully across at the Goncourts. Was this a theatrical *tu* or a lover's *tu*? In fact, neither: throughout their correspondence Sand regularly addressed Flaubert as *tu*, just as, out of respect for her age and sex, he always addressed her as *vous*. He also called her *chère maître*, the feminizing of the adjective marking a double homage to his friend.

Both were provincials still drawn to Paris; both were established as major writers; both lived in large, comfortable, well-run households making visits agreeable. Nohant is the better documented and mythologized: decades later, Henry James was queasily awed at visiting "the very scene where they pigged so thrillingly together. What a crew, what moeurs, what habits . . . and what an altogether mighty and marvellous George!—not diminished by all the greasiness and smelliness in which she made herself (and *so* many other persons!) at home." Croisset, by contrast, had fewer visitors. Sand found the bearish retreat "comfortable, pretty and well arranged. Good servants; clean; plenty of water; every need thoughtfully *provided for*." Beyond this, their very difference drew them together, and perhaps made them less rivalrous. As Sand wrote to him: "I don't think there can be two workers in the world more different from one another than we are . . . We complete ourselves by identifying every so often with what is not ourselves."

Mutual praise helps friendship; so does sucking-up. Flaubert's behind-the-hand disparagement of Sand did not stop him sending her a dedicated copy of *Madame Bovary ("hommage d'un inconnu")* when the novel appeared in volume form in 1857. She wrote admiringly and defendingly of it in the *Courrier de Paris;* and she was later to praise *Salammbô* in *La Presse* (while privately thinking it "really of interest only to artists and scholars"). In return, Flaubert seems to have tried hard and often succeeded in liking Sand's work. In 1872 Flaubert called on *le père Hugo* and found him "charming! I say it again: *charming*" because "I love to love what I admire." A variant of this is also true: we love to admire what we love. And so Flaubert, won over by Sand's goodness, sympathy, and intelligence, seeks and finds virtue in her writing for the first time since he was seventeen. While remaining intractable in matters of literary principle, he is generous in acknowledging the vivid scene, the plausible character, the flow of plot. He continues occasionally to make an intemperate aside about her work to other correspondents; but this is unexceptional literary behaviour.

The pair of them also cemented their friendship with brief bouts of Old Fartery. They offer, however, an ironic reversal of the classic In-my-day complaint about the sexual morality of the rising generation. In 1866 Sand mentions a young engineer friend of hers, handsome, frequently ogled by women, and yet with a terrible behavioural problem: "He's *in love,* and engaged, and has to wait and work for four years to be in a position to marry, and he's made a *vow*," she records pityingly. "Morality apart, I don't think young people nowadays have the energy to cope with science and debauchery, tarts and fiancées, all at the same time." Flaubert harrumphs back that the engineer's vow is, in his opinion, "Pure foolishness . . . 'In my day' we made no such vows. We made love! And boldly! . . . And if we kept away from 'the Ladies,' as I did, absolutely, for two years (from 21 to 23), *it was out of pride,* as a challenge to oneself, a show of strength . . . We were Romantics, in short—Red Romantics, utterly ridiculous, but in full efflorescence."

Now they are largely retired from the emotional field, and this too is a bond. Sand's well-documented amours lie in the past (though as she Piafly remarked to Maxime Du Camp over dinner in 1868, *"Je ne regrette rien"*). She was established as an active rural grandmother, still swimming in the icy Indre in her mid-sixties, devoted to family and duty, passionate about the education of her granddaughter Aurore. Flaubert was increasingly the book-bound bachelor, letting few into his study and even fewer into his heart. Sand at one point suggests to him that seclusion is "your form of ecstasy"—which he denies with more indignation than conviction.

In addition, they shared an element of gender attenuation, or perhaps gender elision. Sand quotes anatomists to the effect that "there is only one sex," and writes in one of her earliest letters to Flaubert: "Now that I'm no longer a woman I'd become a man if God were just." He addresses her as "You who are of the Third Sex," and after her death recalled "how much femininity there was in that great man." (The Goncourts, who believed genius to be exclusively a male possession, put it with a gloating coarseness: an autopsy on any famous female writer, Mme Sand or Mme de Staël, would reveal a clitoris growing enviously towards the size of a penis.) For his part, Flaubert described himself as a "male hysteric" in 1867, and is delighted seven years later when a certain Dr. Hardy raises the stakes by pronouncing him "a hysterical old woman," an observation he judges "profound."

She post-menopausal, he womb-ridden; both perhaps in the intermediate, sex-free state which is supposedly a writer's ideal. It may have some light significance that both Sand and Flaubert indulged in cross-dressing. In her younger Paris days Sand often wore men's clothes. (There was a restaurateur who once told the Goncourts, "It's a funny thing, but when she's dressed as a man I call her Madame, and when she's dressed as a woman I call her

Monsieur.") As for Flaubert, his only two recorded instances of transvestism both took place at Nohant. On 27 December 1869, he "dressed up as a woman and danced the chachucha with Plauchut. It was grotesque; everyone went wild." (This is not the cha-cha-cha but the *cachucha*, a Spanish dance.) And on Easter Day 1873 Sand reports: "Flaubert put on a skirt and had a shot at the fandango. He was very funny, but gasping for breath after about five minutes."

The correspondence between Flaubert and Sand is unusually and dramatically patterned. What often happens in friendship is that the larger issues and beliefs are elaborated early on, and that the relationship then proceeds in terms of amicable arrangements, news, and gossip. Flaubert and Sand begin by courteously laying out both their difference of ideas and their proximity of heart; but such establishings prove merely preliminary. The correspondence untypically gathers weight as it proceeds, and then bursts into two great argumentative climaxes: the first, about politics, society, and the nature of man, is set off by the events of 1870–1; the second, about the nature and function of art, is surprisingly saved until the very last six months of their friendship.

Flaubert viewed the Prussian invasion of 1870 and the Commune of 1871 as the logical conclusion of a historical cycle begun in 1789. France had wandered off the high road of Voltairean thought and plunged itself into a national stupidity typified by the opposing forces of neo-Catholicism and socialism: "Everything is either the Immaculate Conception or workers' lunches." He is shocked by the fakery of pre-1870 French life, dismayed by French war-lust, indignant at the complacent idiocy of those who govern. George Sand is prepared to agree that "the French no longer have any social or intellectual standards"; after the Lichtenstein crisis of 1867 she writes of a society "paralysed" and "demoralized," wondering metaphorically, "Have we fallen so low we won't eat anything unless we're assured it won't give us indigestion?" But mostly she displays a firm and consistent trust in "the laws of eternal progress," and in the essential virtue of humanity. She believes in mass education, which Flaubert considers a waste of time, leading only to the reading of newspapers (that "school for stultification"). She believes in universal suffrage, whereas he knows "I am worth twenty other Croisset voters," despises the predominance of Number, and proposes government by a Mandarinate. Sand is maternal about human stupidity, regarding it as "a sort of infancy, and all infancy is sacred"; Flaubert regards it as probably ineradicable and certainly inert—"stupidity contains no seed." Finally, essentially, George Sand loves the proletariat "in the classical sense"; she has "dreamed only of its future." Flaubert distrusts and fears the mass viewed simply as a mass: he would grant them liberty but not power.

So the events of 1870–1 were for the two friends more than a foreign invasion and civil war to be answered in terms of nationalism and politics; they were a personal test of their deepest convictions. Flaubert made various military gestures in the face of the Prussian invasion (buying himself a revolver, drilling some men, and taking them on night patrol); but his main response was the protracted howl of one confirmed in his low opinion of humanity. The Prussian victory heralded for him the end of the Latin world and endorsed the historical superiority of Protestant over Catholic; while the Commune was a throwback to medievalism which "seems to me to surpass Dahomey in ferocity and imbecility." (Another objection to the Commune was that it made the French forget to go on hating the Prussians.) And if Flaubert sees himself as grimly vindicated, his predictions for the future are even grimmer. The world, he thought, was now entering its third era: after paganism and Christianity, we had arrived at *Muflisme* (boorishness, yobbery). This would mean "the return of racial wars," so that "Within a century we'll see millions of men kill each other at one go." The future would be "Utilitarian, militaristic, American, and Catholic. Very Catholic!" Predictions of fair accuracy.

For Sand the invasion of 1870 was a moment when humanity took a Pascalian "two steps back." However, she allowed herself to think that "We need these harsh lessons in order to realize our own foolishness"; she continued to insist optimistically that "out of evil comes good," and that soon the world would continue its advance "further than ever." The Commune therefore comes as an unbearable second blow to her: proof that humanity, having learned to take two steps backward, is just longing to take another two. The proletariat, despite being loved in the classical sense, seems no less capable of cruelty, hatred, and blood-lust than its long-term oppressors. Sand is consequently much harder on the Communards than might have been expected: they "have ruined and will continue to ruin the republic, exactly as the priests have ruined Christianity." While Flaubert becomes almost incoherent with rage, Sand falls into a lucid despair. Her sorrow is, as she admits, partly the result of geopolitical solipsism: "I used to judge others by myself. I'd made great progress in schooling my own character: I'd sown my volcanoes with grass and flowers, and they were getting on well. And I imagined that everyone could enlighten and correct and control themselves." But grass was never much defence against volcanoes, and Flaubert offers her typically rough consolation: "Our ignorance of history makes us slander our own time. Things have always been like this." But it would be misleading to see this first climax to the *Correspondance* as an exchange which Flaubert somehow "wins." Sand may be the disillusioned idealist, in a position of classic pain; but Flaubert is the vindicated pessimist, a condition which can produce only a distant and perverted kind of pleasure.

The second great climax comes right at the end of the correspondence, and consists of no more than a dozen letters, begun by Sand's of 18–19 December 1875. She has by now regained that serenity which Flaubert once described as "contagious"—though he himself never contracted it—while he is embarked upon his own violently irascible valedictory phase. In facing old age and death, they remain, as in all things, different. She writes to him with blithe certainty: "Before long you will gradually be entering the happiest and most propitious part of life: old age. It's then that art reveals itself in all its sweetness; in our youth it manifests itself in anguish." Flaubert makes no specific reply to this; but doubtless preferred the more saturnine analysis of his fellow-mole Turgenev: "I have just turned sixty, my dear old fellow . . . This is the start of the tail-end of life. A Spanish proverb says that the tail is the hardest part to flay. At the same time it's the part that gives least pleasure and satisfaction. Life becomes completely self-centred—a defensive struggle with death; and this exaggeration of the personality means that it ceases to be of interest, even to the person in question."

Sand, at ease with use of the word "God," and with a benevolently open mind about the afterlife, moved with comparative calmness towards death. "When I'm no longer useful or agreeable to other people," she had written in 1872, "I'd like to depart peacefully without a sigh, or at least with no more than a sigh over the poor human race: it doesn't amount to much, but I'm a part of it, and perhaps I don't amount to much either." For Flaubert, blackly convinced of final extinction, the last years were a true tail-flaying. He signs his letters with his self-caricatures "Cruchard" and "Polycarpe," the first a wheezing ecclesiastical dotard, the second a (genuine) world-bewailing saint. Melancholy, gouty, and enraged, he turns the old universal charge of stupidity against himself: "I'm becoming too stupid! I bore everybody! In short, your Cruchard has turned into an intolerable old geezer—the result of his own intolerance." He is so insupportable that a servant of ten years' standing and perfect suitability "announced that he no longer wished to work for me, because 'I wasn't nice to him any more.' "

Through this self-lacerating despair George Sand continues to trip—how could she not?—like an aesthetic Florence Nightingale. (Sometimes a literal one, too. When Flaubert, brought low by flu, compares himself to the canon of Poitiers, cited by Montaigne, who reputedly kept to his room for thirty years because he was "incommoded by melancholy," Sand's reply is specific: "There's only one remedy, that's a minimum dose of a demi-centigram of acetate of morphine, taken every evening after you've digested your dinner, for at least eight days.") In that key letter of December 18–19, she bids them both to "get back to the grindstone" and analyses their respective fictional ambitions: "So what shall we be doing? You'll go in for *desolation*, I'll wager, while I go in for *consolation* . . . You make your readers sadder than they were before. I'd like to make them less unhappy." Flaubert's response is especially poignant in the context of this whole correspondence. In one of her earliest letters to him, she signs off with "A kiss on each of the two large diamonds that adorn your *trompette* [nose]." Later the same year, less allusively, she ends with a promise to "kiss you three times on each eye"; while her New Year's greetings for 1868 include further kissing of "your beautiful big eyes." These ocular tendernesses from his old troubadour are perhaps half-remembered when Flaubert replies to her in late December 1875. He doesn't "go in for desolation," at least not "wantonly: please believe me!" The problem, he explains to her, in a tone that is hurt, yet also grand and exact, is this: "I cannot change my eyes!"

These last dozen or so letters are, in personal terms, a tenderly serious exchange between two old friends, one increasingly bossy and the other increasingly irritable. On the professional level they grow to something hauntingly magnificent: a face-off between two artists, each differently aware that they are nearing the end of their creative lives, each committed to radically different principles, fighting for those long-held principles, and also, by extension, fighting for the way they have chosen to live their lives. Flaubert always believed that the production of art necessarily involved some amputation of the life. What if he had been wrong, what if he could have taken a wife, had children to dote on, and discovered that this didn't affect his work? Sand always believed that art was not something separate from life but something that grew out of it and fitted into it, something you did, if you had enough energy (and she had lots), after putting the grandchildren to bed and paying the bills. What if she had been wrong, what if her art were rendered flimsy by its ease and normality of manufacture? And they were arguing about the future as well, about what would happen to their art after their joint deaths. Flaubert claimed to write "not for the reader of today, but for all readers as long as the language exists." Sand replied: "I think *I* shall be completely forgotten, perhaps severely denigrated, in fifty years' time. That's the natural fate of things that are not of the highest order, and I have never thought my work was of the highest order." But like every other writer, she thought her literary principles were of the highest order; and it is the future, as well as the past, of those principles that they argue over in furious friendship. For it is necessary not just to establish the correctness and superiority of your own aesthetic, but also—for the sake of posterity—to kill off your friend's.

Over the previous few years Sand has become increasingly prone to giving Flaubert increasingly basic advice. She has told him to get married (which causes him to complain to the Princesse Mathilde that his friend's "perpetual pious optimism . . . sometimes sets my teeth on edge"); she has told him not to be grumpy; told him to eat properly, take walks, and do some gym—"All your trouble comes from lack of exercise"; told him, after the humiliating failure of his play *Le Candidat,* to " 'Have another go and do better!' as the peasants say." At times her consoling words resemble those of a syndicated astrologist: "Many a man has overcome adversity by his own efforts. Be sure that better days will come . . . So . . . brighten up, write us a good successful novel, and think of those who love you."

Perhaps Sand's exasperating belief that life is a soluble problem gives an extra harsh verve to Flaubert's replies; in any case he now rises once more to a lordly and particular *"deffence et illustration"* of his art. And perhaps Flaubert's increasing crabbiness and gloom make Sand more trenchant in her criticism of his work than she has previously been. Withdrawing one's "soul" from one's books is a "morbid fancy"—"supreme impartiality is anti-human"; he should give up his obsession with form and concentrate on emotion. She wants a return to "true reality, which is made up of a mixture of good and evil, bright and dull"; but she is also afraid that the "unsophisticated reader" will be "saddened and frightened" unless good is shown—and, moreover, shown to triumph. Some of Sand's assault comes from mere aesthetic difference; some from misreading; and some—the part that has a friend's anguish in it— from a despairing sympathy allied to a Romantic view of art as the direct, unfiltered expression of the artist's personality.

What constantly puzzles her, what she can't understand about his books, is why she cannot find in them the good chap she has known for so many years: where is the "affection, protection of others, graceful and simple kindness" she has observed? In this respect Flaubert always escapes Sand. Though both assert their old-Romantic buddiness, she is a moralizing humanitarian, a product of Christian civilization; while he is something assembled from both before and after—pre-Christian in his lofty, austere contemplation of the world, yet modern in his artistic response to that contemplation. He loves to quote his friend Littré's terse summary of the human condition: "Man is an unstable compound and the Earth is a decidedly inferior planet."

Sand is considerably exercised by *L'Education sentimentale,* thinking it would have been improved and made more popular— concepts not far apart for her—by the addition of some authorial statement of intent: "It needed either a short preface, or some expression of disapproval, if only a significant word here or there, to condemn evil, call weakness by its right name, and draw attention to endeavour." (This recalls the suggestion that a "health warning" affixed to Rushdie's *The Satanic Verses* would solve that particular problem.) Flaubert doesn't reply to this, any more than when Sand applauds *Madame Bovary* obtusely, for being a moral book, "a severe and striking judgement on a woman faithless and without conscience; a rebuke to vanity, ambition and folly." Furthermore, "It would have been plainer—plain to *all*—if you'd deigned to show what you thought, and what should be thought, about the woman, her husband and her lovers."

He does, however, restate his aesthetic one final, forceful time. At Nohant they had playfully named a ram after him—the two

M. Gustaves had been introduced to each other in 1869—and even in his last tormented years he can still put his head down and charge. Art is not a vomitorium where one relieves one's personal feelings; the artist must be hidden in the work as God is in Nature; a novel should imply, not state, its moral; form and content are interdependent; the truth of an observation or description is a good in itself; style is not a question of surface gloss—on the contrary, good writing implies good thinking. Of course, he does not convince Sand, any more than she does him: tulips are not going to flower in the potato fields at this late stage.

Is it merely that the two novelists are intellectually loyal to an aesthetic creed each developed early, or is it something more: that the aesthetic creed is itself an emanation of the personality, and that this argument over ideas is really just a clash of chromosomes? One of Sand's charges, for instance, is that Flaubert's celebrated refusal to allow his own personal attitudes to enter his work may not be part of some objective artistic credo but merely a subjective indicator that as a human being he lacks convictions. This may and should strike us as a trifle bizarre: his letters, after all, thunder with convictions, none more so than those George Sand has been receiving over the years.

But Sand could have made the point differently: for instance, Flaubert's insistence on the creator's invisibility in the work does fit with his extreme distaste for journalistic intrusion into his life (and with his distaste for being photographed), just as Sand's easygoing here-I-am moralism accords with her earlier life as a "fast," high-profile public figure. And he is aware of this: he tells her that whereas she instinctively "leaps upward," he remains "glued to the earth, as though the soles of my shoes were made of lead . . . If I tried to assume your way of looking at the world I'd become a mere laughing stock. For no matter what you preach to me, I can have no temperament other than my own. Nor any aesthetic other than the one that proceeds from it."

So perhaps our sense of witnessing some gigantic Franco-Prussian war of ideas is both deeply true and slightly fallacious. A present-day reader will probably find Flaubert's view of the world more truthful than George Sand's because since their deaths the world has itself turned out more to confirm his vision than hers: the return of racial wars, millions of men killed in a single go, and a century which is utilitarian, militaristic, American, and a fair bit Catholic. We also nowadays prefer his art to hers. In her preface to *La Mare au diable* Sand laid down as opposing, irreconcilable forces in art the search for *"la vérité idéale"* and the study of *"la réalité positive"*; these polarities were exemplified for her by *The Vicar of Wakefield* on the one side and *Les Liaisons dangereuses* on the other. In our own century we prefer Laclos to Goldsmith, but what is that the result of? Intellectual argument, the proven nature of the world, changing literary taste? Perhaps the comparative victory of Flaubert's aesthetic over Sand's is mainly a matter of the reader's temperament, or the accumulated mass of readers' temperaments. In which case, Flaubert will have had an ironic triumph, attributable to the hated principle of the predominance of Number.

In his very last letter to his old troubadour, Flaubert's intransigence suddenly appears less granitic. He tells her that he is "not as obstinate as you think," and predicts that she will recognize her "direct influence" on the story he is currently writing, *Un Coeur simple:* "I believe you will like the moral tendency, or rather the underlying humanity, of this little work." After her death he wrote to Maurice Sand: "I began *Un Coeur simple* exclusively for her, solely to please her. She died when I was in the middle of my work. Thus it is with all our dreams." It is a fine and famous literary compliment, though we should allow for Flaubert's innate gallantry: he once claimed that he wrote *L'Education sentimentale* "to please Sainte-Beuve." Nor does the *Correspondance* provide any further corroboration of Sand's supposed influence.

We also need to check the author's amicable declarations against the work itself. It is true that a Sandian reading is loosely possible if you half-close your eyes: here is a tale of ordinary, near-contemporary life about a simple, good-hearted woman who serves others and believes in God. Remove this deliberate soft focus, however, and you see one of the grimmest and most relentless stories ever written, about a downtrodden, ignorant, exploited servant who is ruthlessly stripped of every single person, living thing, or object to which she becomes attached. Her existence is a Calvary of loss, and ends with a deathbed scene whose potential Sandian poignancy is weather-clouded by the Flaubertian grotesque—the monumental, cruel grotesque, as a stuffed parrot, reanimated and gigantized, does service for the Holy Ghost. Unless you believe (and the story does not invite you to) that Félicité's sufferings will be rewarded in Heaven, or that they are somehow a good in themselves, the "moral tendency" of *Un Coeur simple* is unsparingly bleak. The work it lies closest to, in its tone and its machine-like unrolling, is *Madame Bovary*. Truly, its author could not change his eyes.

Flaubert's and Sand's *Correspondance* begins with a small misunderstanding. Sand has received a pressed plant in an envelope with no name on the back, and wonders if the handwriting might be Flaubert's. No, he replies, though curiously enough at about the same time someone had sent him an equally anonymous leaf. (The identity of the horticultural donor or donors remains unsolved.) Three years later, when Sand visits Croisset for the first time, she intends to take away as a souvenir some leaves from a tulip tree— "I need them for arcane purposes"—but forgets them. He brings the leaves up to Paris a few days later, but fails to find her in. Later that year, when the Seine floods, she enquires after the health of the tree. She mentions it again in her diary in 1868, in a letter of 1869, and for the last time ("Tell me whether the tulip tree suffered from the frost this winter") in April 1871.

The tree, like the house at Croisset, has long since disappeared, but arboreal antiquarians who visit George Sand's grave at Nohant can still stand under the yew tree which was growing there when Flaubert helped bury his old friend on 10 June 1876. A fine rain was falling and the mud was ankle-deep. Flaubert wrote to Turgenev, who was in Russia, that Sand's funeral "was like a chapter in one of her books." He reported that he had wept like a calf ("twice," he specified, with unnerving if characteristic precision). To Sand's son Maurice, Flaubert wrote, in the fraternity of grief, that he felt as if "I was burying my mother a second time." The two women had, after all, offered him a similar rebuke. In one of her last letters Sand, defending the eighteenth-century comic dramatist Sedaine, complained to Flaubert that "you look only for the well-turned phrase." Twenty-one years previously, when he was still struggling with *Madame Bovary,* his mother had told him that "your mania for sentences has dried up your heart." Flaubert, good-naturedly, considered her remark "sublime."

(14)

Tail-Flaying

A bad sight for Flaubert: Prussians in the
studio of a Rouen photographer, 1871

In the late autumn of 1875, Flaubert spent six weeks at Concarneau with the naturalist Georges Pouchet. While his friend dissected fish and molluscs, Flaubert took daily sea-baths, gorged himself on lobster, eavesdropped on the table talk of a sardiners' club— confirming yet again the "bottomlessness of human stupidity"— and wrote to his friends. His morale is extremely low, his financial state parlous, his health poor, his brain worn out. He has put aside *Bouvard et Pécuchet* as being too difficult. "The good days are over," he writes to Turgenev. "The end of my life is no joke," he tells Edma Roger des Genettes. He likens himself, in a letter to his niece Caroline, to a piece of dead seaweed, torn from its moorings and blown aimlessly about. Caroline urges a more stoical seaside comparison upon him: he must be like a rock. It is unwise to bandy metaphors with Flaubert; she should know, he tells her in reply, that old granite often breaks down into layers of clay. Even more candidly, he tells Edmond de Goncourt that he awaits the first sign of some mortal illness with impatience. Goncourt knows him well enough, he adds, to realize that "This is not a pose!"

The fourth volume of the Pléiade *Correspondance* covers the period 1869–75, seven years that are the great wailing hinge of Flaubert's existence. There is a cruel structure and movement to this penultimate volume of the novel of his life. It opens with Flaubert, publicly and privately, the mature, successful, industrious, and social being he frequently proclaims he isn't. He is completing *L'Education sentimentale*, and just beginning, he thinks, to understand what a novel could be; he is assiduous at Princesse Mathilde's salon, rather preening himself on his insider status; he is also engaged on one of those pieces of socio-political scheming—to get Caroline's husband, Ernest Commanville, named Prussian vice-consul in Dieppe—which he has considerable taste for, and imagines himself good at. (The record is incomplete, but it somehow seems typical that if this was what Flaubert was manoeuvring for, Commanville ended up as vice-consul for Turkey instead.) Apart from the regular vast irritants to a man of his sensibility—critics, newspapers, politics, progressives, Parisians, provincials, Nature—the world is as satisfying a place as it might be. "1869," he predicts to the Princesse in June of that year, "will have been a good year for me."

The novelist should have known about dramatic irony: 1869 was precisely the starting-point of a catastrophic decade filled with deaths, illness, financial ruin, precipitate old age, and thunderously intrusive History. Less than five weeks after his blithe prediction, he was writing again to Princesse Mathilde to report the death of Louis Bouilhet, the friend he variously described as half his brain, his literary compass, and his left testicle. The mixed reception given to *L'Education sentimentale* later that year hinted that Flaubert would never again repeat the success of *Madame Bovary* or *Salammbô*. The Franco-Prussian War tore at his view of France (and Prussia). Jules Duplan, his closest friend after Bouilhet, died in 1870, followed by Sainte-Beuve (his most important critical supporter), Jules de Goncourt (whose death reduced to three the original seven Magny diners), Gautier, and Ernest Feydeau. His mother died in 1872. Finally, the collapse of European timber prices ruined Commanville and with him, effectively, Flaubert.

After such battering, his health, always fragile, cracks; in these pages he suffers from rheumatism, angina, eczema, swollen glands, dysentery, gout, and the continuing effects of syphilis. Looking back, he judges that he was always afraid of life; he envies other professions, other ways of living; he suffers child-regret. His existence has been arid, "laborious and austere." But a man is not master of his destiny: life just pushes you along, until one day you find yourself in a hole, with nothing to be done about it, and you stay there, all alone, waiting for "the definitive hole."

"Since happiness is impossible in this world," he tells Elisa Schlesinger in 1872, "we must strive for serenity." This is one of the insistent themes of the years 1869–75. But striving for serenity has the same internal contradiction as practising spontaneity. Nevertheless, Flaubert does his best—that best naturally consisting largely of words, of assurances to himself and to others. "I must be philosophical," he repeatedly declares; yet he never had the temperament of a philosopher. "I pass from exasperation to prostration, then I rise from annihilation to rage, so that my mean emotional temperature is a state of annoyance."

George Sand was surely right in suspecting that his irritation was, increasingly, "necessary to his organization." (Flaubert himself tells Goncourt that indignation is the stick which holds up the doll: "If I weren't indignant, I would fall down flat.") But its tonality is not unmitigatedly splenetic or valetudinary. Flaubert's trip to Switzerland in 1874, for instance, is one long, exhilarating display of comic rage. It's serious, too, which makes it the more comic. Like his stay at Concarneau—and one with Caroline at Bagnères-de-Luchon—this had both a medical and a morale-boosting aim. "The theory," he writes sceptically, "is that the lower barometric pressure will relieve my congestion by driving the blood into the lower organs."

His three weeks on Mount Righi make up probably the least calming rest cure any human being has ever taken. For a start, he can't understand a country which doesn't have any real history. Then there is the omnipresence of Nature, which crushes him without inspiring thought. Then there is the problem of boredom, which he assaults by eating, drinking, and smoking a lot. But these activities depend upon the presence of waiters, who here are dressed in black even from early morning, so that they look like guests at your own funeral. "Eight days here," he cries, "are like three centuries." Then there are the other people, the dreadful Germans and the dreadful English, who make him want to hug a

cow for some human contact. His unimpressable eye falls on jaunty
tourists wielding sticks branded with the names of sites they have
visited; a woman who plays Chopin on the hotel piano "in such a
way as to make all the cows of Switzerland flee"; and the cre-
tin installed at the telescope on the hotel balcony, with his arse
pushed out and his hat on the back of his head, uttering imbecilities about the view. Switzerland, he concludes, is only any good for
"botanists, geologists and honeymooners"—into none of which
categories he falls. Sand rebukes him for his disobliging observations: "You're not a man of nature. So much the worse for you . . .
We are nature, we're in nature, made by nature, made for nature."
But Turgenev can be relied upon for support in most things, and
agrees about the Swiss. Despite living among such sublimities,
they are "the most deeply boring and the least gifted people I have
ever met. Whence cometh such an anomaly, as the philosopher
might ask? Or is it perhaps not an anomaly at all? What would
Bouvard and Pécuchet say about the matter?"

Flaubert's signatorial nicknames during this period give evidence of his mood. He still remains *"Ton Géant"* (though on
one occasion *"GEANT Aplati"*—"Flattened GIANT"), but is
increasingly *"Ton Vieux."* When between these moods he is *"Ton
Excessif."* One characteristic way of being Excessive was in a
competitiveness about sensibility and experience, a trait which
becomes more apparent in these painful years. He has, he tells
Caroline, "an exasperated sensibility and a deplorable imagination." "What merely scratches others," he tells Sand, "rips my
flesh." Hence his constitution is more adapted for pain than for
pleasure. And hence his pain is greater than that of others.
Throughout the events of 1870–1, he constantly assures correspondents that he is suffering more than anyone else in France.
"Others are more to be pitied," he writes, "but no one suffers as
much." It seems plodding to point out that a person of lesser sen-
sitivity might suffer more if the damage inflicted upon them were
greater. Neither Flaubert nor any of his family saw action or had
anyone close to them killed. Nor did the writer suffer significantly

from the invasion; the Prussians, he admits, "respected my study," when they occupied Croisset, even if they did commit the Teutonic solecism of leaving their helmets on his bed.

It is the same when his mother dies; he tells Léonie Brainne that since he has the nerves of a flayed man, the loss has caused him more suffering than it would anybody else. He even tells George Sand—of all people—that he has "loved more than anyone" (though he does immediately add that the phrase is pretentious). It is hard to know what to make of this trait. Genuine conviction, raw competitiveness, poetic fallacy (when it comes to taking the suffering of France upon himself), or failure of imaginative sympathy? All four at the same time? Goncourt in his Journal noted Flaubert's "craziness" in imagining that he had done and suffered more than others, and characteristically recorded two of its more risible manifestations. The first has Flaubert getting into a fight with the sculptor Jacquemart over which of them had been host to more lice in Egypt—which of them, as Goncourt cattily put it, was "superior in vermin." On another occasion, laddish talk in the smoking-room at Princesse Mathilde's turned to the lectoral sex-aids of their youth. Many cited *Amours du chevalier de Faublas,* an erotic tale of the late 1780s, as the text which invariably did the trick. Flaubert declared that he personally had never been able to finish it; for him, the key volume had been Meursius's *Aloysiae* (that is to say, *Aloysiae Sygeai satira sotadica de arcanis Amoris et Veneris* of 1658). "How superior, how special," an irritated Goncourt comments. "Only something in Latin could make *him* hard." In Flaubert's defence, he was not always so scholarly. While he was staying in Concarneau, Léonie Brainne sent him her portrait; he told her in reply that, lying in bed one morning and contemplating her image, he had become aware that he was still a man.

Solitary, melancholic, hypersensitive, high-minded, competitive, exasperated, impractical: how should such a temperament best be managed? The forty-seven-year-old bachelor of the start of this volume, living at home with his mother and servants, and lacking most financial restraints, can exist with as much contentment as such a personality might allow; the fifty-year-old whose mother has just died, precariously inhabiting a house now belonging to his niece, and with his finances tied to those of the Commanvilles, finds yet another form of suffering thrust upon him: domestication. Even Flaubert was not competitive about his homemaking skills. The solution was self-evident, especially to women, especially to George Sand: Flaubert should marry. The recalcitrant bachelor regards this as not just a hopeful, but a fantastical misreading of his character. Flaubert has long observed the state of matrimony: his married (male) friends, he writes, do nothing but work, hunt, and play whist; none will read poetry with him. A quarter of a century previously, Flaubert had regarded the marriage of his childhood friend Alfred Le Poittevin as a personal and artistic betrayal; over the years his opinion has scarcely changed. Besides, he is too old now; besides, he can't afford it; besides, he is "too scrupulous to inflict myself upon another in perpetuity."

This last is also the argument of Larkin's "Love" ("My life is for me. / As well ignore gravity"). Marriage? Flaubert's friend Edmond Laporte has the better suggestion: get a dog. Enter Julio, a greyhound on whom Flaubert dotes, even when the dog's unstriven-for serenity makes him envious. Julio lies on Flaubert's famous bearskin rug, sleeps in his bed, gives him fleas. "Send me immediately by the *Union* [the Rouen–La Bouille steamer, which stopped at Croisset] some of that magic *saponaire*." This is one of the unlikeliest sentences to find in Flaubert's handwriting. The soap (is it a plant or a commercial product?) arrives; he washes his dog. The artist as reluctant homemaker: he also, in the course of these pages, finds himself dealing with locksmith, tinsmith, roofer, and builder; he considers wallpaper and the rival virtues of carpet versus plaster on the floor; he asks Caroline to buy curtains in Paris because they're cheaper than in Rouen; he shops for a meat safe; he buys dusters and socks; he loses and finds the sugar-bowl; he worries about the size of the jam bill; he buys a pair of iron fire-dogs. "Household duties bore me to death," he complains. His stance is one of theatrical ruefulness. "I bought a hat. That's all the news."

Writing to Caroline, he begins with a high-toned quotation— "Macbeth hath murdered sleep"—before getting down to his pressing, underlined concern: "My cider bill appals me." Lacking an income of his own, he is constantly applying to the Commanvilles for money, in tones which are variously baffled, peremptory, and piteous. Since Caroline subsequently destroyed all but one of her letters to her uncle, along with most of those from his women friends, we can only guess at her replies. But his constant reminders and demands make it more understandable that she and her husband gave Flaubert the one nickname with which he never signed himself: The Consumer.

There is an element of household duty about many of Flaubert's literary activities at this time: especially in his theatrical ventures and the exploitation of Bouilhet's estate. He displays a dogged, at times fanatical, devotion to projects which mostly fail. There is the posthumous staging of Bouilhet's *Mademoiselle Aïsse* (which, after a successful première, played to empty houses); Flaubert's own *Le Candidat* (taken off after four performances when the male lead came off stage with tears in his eyes); *Le Sexe faible* (Bouilhet's prose comedy, finished by Flaubert), which after interminable negotiations, and talismanic repetition by Flaubert of a producer's careless phrase ("un grand succès d'argent"), was withdrawn at the last minute; the planned publication of Bouilhet's *Dernières chansons* (a commercial disaster, provoking Flaubert's acrimonious break with Lévy) and of a collected Bouilhet (which finally appeared in 1880, the year of Flaubert's death). There is also Flaubert's long campaign to have a memorial statue to his dead friend erected on the streets of Rouen, which provokes him to counter-productive pamphleteering against the municipal authorities.*

Flaubert's failure as a dramatist, understandable enough from

---

*Ford Madox Ford, writing to Conrad from a military hospital in Rouen in 1916, mentions that he had spotted "the whole monument of Bouilhet thro' the tail of the ambulance that brought me here, in the Rue Thiers."

reading the actual plays (which are either too literal and novelistic, or else too whimsical), becomes more so, given the condescending attitude to the theatre revealed here. He doesn't enjoy the medium in itself (calling himself "heroic" for seeing two plays in a single week); it is, he decides, a "false" art, in which it is impossible to say anything "complete." He seems not to understand that "completeness" is different in the theatre—just as the novel, for its part, has its own necessary "falseness." His way of dealing with theatrical managers was probably misconceived (Sand was characteristically more phlegmatic about the overheated optimism and frequent reversals of this world), although there's no denying his assiduity. In countless letters, he badgers and cajoles, bullies and flatters, while fine-tuning the production of plays we now see as of only moderate merit. This all ought to be fairly boring, except to the theatrical historian; and on the surface it is. But each letter he writes about Bouilhet's plays, crammed with forgettable instructions and proposals, can also be read and felt as an act of love and mourning for his dead friend; also, an act of duty and responsibility towards Bouilhet's adopted son, Philippe Leparfait (who doesn't seem especially appreciative).

This is the advantage of letters over biography: letters exist in real time. We read them at about the speed at which they were written. Biography gives us the crane-shot, the time-elision, the astute selectivity. A biographer might tell you that on the night Flaubert's mother died, 6 April 1872, her son immediately wrote five letters (or five which have survived), two timed "the night of," one timed at 12:30 a.m. and two timed at 1 a.m. Since they inevitably contain similar information and sentiments, the biographer might reasonably name the recipients and briefly quote. To read them all, however, one after the other, five in a row (plus a sixth dated the following day, and then replies from friends which imply others sent) is to feel more fully the dull repetitiousness of grief and its expression; also, to experience the very time that passes as Flaubert writes.

So letters may draw strength and truth from what elsewhere

might prove tedious repetition. Here, in this primary form, we can observe the working out and perfecting of a phrase or idea; we learn to recognize an intellectual or emotional trope, a proof of stubbornness, confirmation of obsession, habit of courtesy. When Flaubert tells George Sand, on 3 June 1874, that he has read her book in one go, like downing *"un bon verre de vin,"* we note a friendly if possibly evasive compliment; when, in his very next letter, written on the same day, he tells Zola that he has just read his latest novel in one go, downing it like *"un bon verre de vin,"* we suspect a handy formula.* Repetition implies approval. So, for instance, we can tell how pleased he is with his identification of the three great stages of human development—Paganism, Christianity, *Muflisme*—by the fact that he parades it four times between 11 March and 20 April 1871. After this six weeks' use, however, he loses interest in the triplet, while keeping *Muflisme* in his vocabulary, enlarging it fourteen months later into *Panmuflisme*.

Then there is his chosen self-image as a writer over the period 1871–3. He floats this first to Princesse Mathilde in April 1871. Amid the strife and stupidity of the world, he tells her, he carries on turning out his phrases as before; it is an activity as innocent and useful as that of turning out napkin rings on a lathe. This is a reference back fifteen years to Binet, the tax-collector in *Madame Bovary*, the drone of whose lathe breaks the village silence on Sundays. (Binet, we recall, works away "with the jealousy of an artist and the egoism of a bourgeois": a provocative reversal of epithets.) Pleased with this heroically unheroic comparison Flaubert repeats it in September of that year to George Sand, in May 1872 to Edma Roger des Genettes, in January 1873 to Marie Regnier,

*Writers' excuses and evasions usually remain in character. Here is Mallarmé thanking the Irish poet William Bonaparte-Wyse for his latest: "I haven't yet read it, but I've leafed through it and deflowered it by eye. You know the charm and greed the mind feels in wanting to be initiated into a text before reading it. And from several remarkable pages I *kidnapped* what one might call airy couches, of great intimacy, formed of colour and music which make me dream of water-colours and pianos at the very moment I write to you . . ."

and finally the next month to Mme Roger des Genettes again. The image drones in his ear as persistently as the lathe; and its domestic nature inclines him (unless there are uses I have missed) to employ it only with female correspondents.

Equally, we can follow the exact construction of a famous declaration (or at least seem to do so: letters are inclined to make us forget that writers also go around talking a lot of the time). Thus in November 1872, Flaubert writes to Turgenev, "I have always tried to live in an ivory tower, but a tide of shit is beating at its walls, threatening to undermine it." This appears to come, very precisely, from two previous letters. The first to Princesse Mathilde in September 1871, where he says that now, more than ever, he needs to live in an ivory tower above the mire in which humanity paddles; and the second to Caroline in October 1872, where he reports that the spectacle of the Rouen bourgeoisie, combined with his memory of Gautier's artistic sacrifices, makes him feel as if he is drowning in *"une marée d'immondices"* (a tide of filth). The following month, he combines the two ideas, with the genteeler *"marée d'immondices"* giving way to *"une marée de merde"* in his letter to Turgenev.

The full, fully expressed, and insistent presence of Flaubert, our closeness to the ground, our closeness to the hand that holds the quill pen (he despised the newfangled steel nib) makes us forget that there might be other views of Flaubert than his own. If diaries often alert us to the fact that they might be written at the same time of day and in the same mood—if they confess their partiality—the normal variety of a correspondence, the stylistic heliotropism as different friends are addressed differently, half-assure us that we have been shown the full extent of the writer's character. So it comes as a genuine narrative shock, after a thousand pages of Flaubert's thrilling intellectual company, to read a ten-page appendix of entries from the Goncourt Journal covering the same period. Flaubert's letters to Edmond de Goncourt have throughout 1869–75 been unanimously bonhomous; while in writing to other correspondents, his only criticism of Goncourt has been an aesthetic one—of his simplistic way with reality. Goncourt's diary entries about Flaubert are relentlessly caustic and patronizing. Flaubert is portrayed as a boastful, vulgar provincial, full of false exaggeration; he claims to be a passionate man, yet women count for little in his life, just as he claims to be a spendthrift, yet sudden fancies make no hole in his pocket; as for his work, it relies on intelligent appropriation rather than any act of originality; he chooses exotic locations, yet exhibits a profoundly conventional view of humanity; and how strange, by the way, that such a famous man should have so few friends. Can this, we wonder, possibly be the fellow whose arm we have linked over so many pages and years? Was he putting it all on? Have we been so blind?

Some part of Goncourt's hostility seems properly attributable to metropolitan snobbery and professional envy; other criticisms are less ignorable. There was a boastful side to Flaubert (Goncourt judged him as much a Gascon as a Norman) and at times a foolish one-upmanship. There may also be some truth in Goncourt's claim that Flaubert had "scorn for the qualities he lacked"; although Flaubert was probably bourgeois enough not to show his tender side in the smoking-room; and this volume is increasingly filled with self-doubt, with envy of the normal, non-artistic life. Arguing with Goncourt is like arguing with any consistent misanthrope or cynic; after a while, their refusal to ascribe virtue becomes corrosive. When Flaubert wrote to Goncourt with morbid openness from Concarneau, he was confident his friend would realize that "This is not a pose!" But Goncourt *did* think Flaubert was a poseur. "Though perfectly frank by nature," the Journal records elsewhere, "he is never wholly sincere in what he says he feels or suffers or thinks."

The antidote to Goncourt's malice is to turn back a few pages and reread the last exchange in this volume between Flaubert and Sand. It is December 1875; both of them have been ill and discouraged; both are slowly getting back to work. Instead of New Year's cards, they exchange their serious, long-meditated, and deeply opposed *professions de foi*. Flaubert's letter is wise, desolate, and magnificent. It is also a rebuttal which contains not the slightest element of disparagement for the person rebutted. He ends by warmly embracing his *"chère bon maître adorable"* and expressing the wish that 1876 should be carefree *("léger")* for her and her family.

He still hadn't learnt about dramatic irony; 1876 was the year in which George Sand was to die.

(15)

The Cost of Conscientious
Literature

Caroline Commanville,
Flaubert's niece

These are the leavings of Flaubert's life: six published books (one unfinished); 4,000 or so letters; about 20,000 pages of manuscript; some dud plays; a house which was knocked down shortly after his death; a few paltry possessions (surprisingly few for a writer of his stature); a library, some of which can be seen at the Mairie de Croisset; half a dozen images of him captured by the "untrue" and "mechanical" technique of photography; a body in the Cimetière Monumental at Rouen.

So what he left behind mainly was paper bearing his thoughts; which is as he would have wanted. He despised personal publicity, and scorned those writers who put their photographs on their books. As he wrote to Feydeau in 1859, "I . . . believe that a writer should leave behind him nothing but his works." This position derives equally from temperament and from the highest literary ambition. While exhibiting the normal desire for his books to do well and the normal over-sensitivity when critics attacked them, Flaubert never felt that his contract was with his contemporary readers—or at any rate, no more with them than with their descendants. The notion of "contract," indeed, especially in an economic sense, irritated him. Does the model of the manual worker exchanging services for money extend also to the intellectual worker? Is it a straightforward transaction in which the reader buys the pleasure manufactured by the novelist in his prose? It may seem so to the reader, but Flaubert puts up a "Not for Sale" notice: he writes not for his purchasing coevals but "for all readers in times to come." He concludes a notebook entry of December 1872 with this denial: "What I produce cannot be consumed and my services are neither to be defined nor bought."

Has this strategy (or temperamental inclination) worked over the century since his death? Up to a point. Few nineteenth-century writers could have predicted the mania for biography which has overtaken the twentieth century, and how satisfactory a substitute this has proved for the harder task of actually reading the writers being biographed. Flaubert's example of the bootboy and customs officer wanting to know—and perhaps being told—whether or not he plays the harmonica strikes us as a folksy, innocent fear. Nowadays it seems unremarkable that a professor of nineteenth-century French literature at the University of Nantes should publish *La Vie érotique de Flaubert,* accounting for what he did when and with whom. But on the whole Flaubert has survived better than most the psycho-scrabblings and genial reductivism.

In 1852, when he had written much but published nothing, he told Louise Colet that all he wanted was for his manuscripts to last as long as he did: "It's a pity I'd need too big a tomb, because I'd like to have them buried with me, as a savage is buried with his horse—after all, it's those poor pages which have sustained me while crossing the long plain." This is no doubt a bit disingenuous in its romantic-valetudinarian tone, and we'd be right to suspect that Flaubert had not abandoned hope of publication; but the manner in which he represents things—the writer, the work, the tomb, eternity—has the arid grandeur which he maintained after he became celebrated. In an update of the burial scenario, revised to account for success, the writer would be now alone in his tomb, his known personality fading into insignificance, with readers no longer caring whether he had a taste for drink or skill with the harmonica; while the work would continue into eternity. "Work," of course, meant work in its finished, final form, as perfect as Flaubert could make it. This rage to eliminate fault continued long after initial publication: for the 1879 edition of *L'Education sentimentale* he suppressed 125 examples of *mais,* thirty-nine *alors,* thirty-two *et,* thirty-one *puis,* twenty-three *cependant,* and so on.

But posterity can never be relied upon, the concept of "work" changes, as does what is deemed suitable for posthumous publication. Had Flaubert been able to see a hundred years ahead he might well have been tempted to bear away with him to his tomb every manuscript he possessed. First came publication of his letters, then travel diaries, juvenilia, and the first *L'Education sentimentale;* now—not just to the posthumous astonishment of Flaubert, but no doubt to that of most Flaubertians of the first half-century after his death—we have Pierre-Marc de Biasi's definitive edition of the *Carnets de travail.* These have been known about, and occasionally raided for some succulent source or quotation, for a while. They have also been raided in a more obvious sense: several of the Notebooks (most notably those covering the period 1851–9 when Flaubert wrote *Madame Bovary* and the start of *Salammbô*) have gone missing, either through covert sale or, more probably, straightforward pilfering.

After Flaubert's death his manuscripts passed to his niece, Caroline Commanville, later Franklin-Grout, who treated them rather as she had treated her uncle in life: with a mixture of affection and greed, loyalty and irritation. She guarded the family name while tidying up all around it, censoring Flaubert's letters for publication and making him as respectable as possible; she tended the flame while discreetly selling off some of the firewood which fuelled it. She is usually cast as a prim semi-vandal who failed to treat her uncle and his leavings with the same tender solicitude which those criticizing her would have done in her place; but both her moral disapproving and her literary ethics were those of her period and milieu. Moreover, if Caroline looked back over her life and in particular at the lost years of a first marriage into which her uncle encouraged her, she would have been unnatural not to feel a grudge. The case for Caroline has not yet been fully made. After his death she made up for the resented extravagance of "The Consumer" by raising money from his manuscripts.

Among the "manuscripts" the *Carnets* were for many years virtually disregarded. This is partly because of their nature—they consist mainly of travel journals and detailed working notes rather than private diaries (the "private diaries" are his Letters). But they were also disregarded because they didn't really form part of the "work." There was the book itself, as published and fit for study; before that there was the manuscript, of bibliophilic as much as bibliographical interest; and before that some hazy jottings bearing only curiosity value. So the *Carnets* were merely part of Caroline's minor literary estate; unnumbered and unidentified, they were included in a previously arranged legacy to the Musée Carnavalet along with the manuscripts of the first and second versions of *L'Education sentimentale.* However, when Caroline died in 1931, it was found that she had already sold the manuscript of the first *Education*—the consumer had played supplier once again. The curator of the Carnavalet, piqued by Caroline's behaviour, declined the legacy by refusing to pay the meagre transfer tax that accepting it would have involved. It took five years (in the course of which some of the *Carnets* disappeared) and a new curator at the Carnavalet before the legacy was accepted. This incident shows not only how undervalued the *Carnets* were at the mid-point between Flaubert's death and the present (less than undervalued— valued at precisely nothing, not worth having), but also the unpredictable effect of curators on literary legacies.

In 1942 René Dumesnil in his edition of *L'Education sentimentale* quoted a *calepin d'enquête* of (?)1865—one that has disappeared since he transcribed it. Marie-Jeanne Durry transcribed two and a half *Carnets* for her *Flaubert et ses projets inédits* of 1950. In 1973 the Club de L'Honnête Homme edition edited by Maurice Bardèche gave us the first "integral" transcription of the *Carnets.* It was a well-intentioned project, but ended up as a counter-productive botch. Bardèche managed to turn a patchwork of manuscript into a freely running text, as if the *Carnets* were some sort of continuous diary; he omitted part of one *carnet,* and made hundreds of errors of transcription. Flaubert's handwriting is difficult to read, but even so some of the mistakes are impressive. "*Fille du* *pec"* (abbreviation for *pêcheur*) comes out as *"Catholique"; "mira-cles"* comes out as *"morales";* a piece of furniture "style Louis XVI" followed by two inverted commas is up- or downgraded into a piece of furniture of the invented style Louis XVIII; *"telegraphie"* becomes the not yet invented *"dactylographie"; "Liberté de pen-ser: idem"* in the context of Voltaire turns out as *"Liberté de penser: indifférent"*—a creative misreading. At one point Bardèche even manages to insert the words *"foutu embêtement"* (bloody nuisance) into a sentence, drawing the words from thin air. Not for nothing does Pierre-Marc de Biasi, in his combative introduction, treat Bardèche as an "anti-model," a "counter-text." Perhaps the best that can be said for the CHH edition is that it has spurred Biasi to extra-human assiduousness. Flaubert has in recent decades attracted some extremely good editing (perhaps as a reaction to earlier slop-piness; perhaps also because he is the sort of writer whose presence is broodingly felt when you meddle with his texts). Biasi's edition is dauntingly thorough, meticulous in its transcription of every crossing-out, drawing, squiggle, or unreadable word, brilliantly annotated, and introduced with a mixture of bracing aggression and high common sense. It is a superb edition of what will be (until the unearthing of some surprise cache of letters) the last major piece of Flaubert to be published.*

But what is it, exactly? Certainly not, as we might imagine or hope, some *ur-*collection of *pensées* and reflections precisely illu-minating the sources, pulse, and articulation of his novels. The *Carnets de travail* are haphazard and chaotic, accessible only with the help of considerable critical apparatus; they are incomplete, and those parts which survive are numbered in a batty, non-sequential manner (by a "berserk librarian," Biasi suggests). The most obvi-ously readable sections of Caroline's legacy to the Musée Car-navalet, the travel journals, have long since been hived off and

*There may be more to come. Jean Bruneau, editor of the Pléiade *Correspon-dance,* still has serious hopes that Flaubert's letters to Juliet Herbert will turn up.

separately published. What we have left is the rump, the brute beginning thoughts, the stutterings and jottings, the false early certainties of writing. Biasi, without trying to force categorization on to the eighteen notebooks he here transcribes, divides them into *carnet* and *calepin*, into those containing research for particular novels and the more general *grand carnet d'idées* or *grand carnet de projets;* but subjects criss-cross from one notebook to another, and working problems raised on one page may suddenly be treated as if long solved on the next. Writers don't keep notebooks with a view to making things easy for their subsequent editors; they jot on the run, use shorthand, know what they mean when at their most cryptic, cross things out, have second, third, fourth thoughts. Flaubert, moreover, was a writer who never proceeded with bland orderliness from one project to another; his books were long pondered, and ideas relating to any one of several novels may occur side by side. For instance, the main body of notes for *Bouvard et Pécuchet* that have survived are to be found in *Carnets* 18*bis*, 18, 11, and 6 (covering the period 1874–9: it's a sign of how chaotic the numbering system is that the lower numbers refer to later years). However, his preparatory reading-list for the novel (at least 1,500 books, and probably many more, according to Biasi) occurs back in *Carnet* 15 (1869–74), while the first references to *Bouvard et Pécuchet*—originally *Les deux cloportes*—are found in *Carnet* 19 (1862–3). The *Carnets de travail* are both a palimpsest and a cat's cradle.

Writing to George Sand in 1873, Flaubert describes how he is "ruining himself" with his book-purchases for the background reading to *Bouvard et Pécuchet,* and humorously complains about a journey he made in search of a particular piece of countryside for the novel. He goes from Paris to Rambouillet by *chemin de fer,* Rambouillet to Houdan by *calèche,* Houdan to Mantes by *cabriolet,* then *"re-chemin de fer"* to Rouen. Total expenditure 83 francs— "such is the cost of conscientious literature!" This whole volume is evidence of the cost—in the main not monetary, but measured in time, energy, travel, and lection—of making conscientious literature. It could be submitted to the tax authorities as an example of the hidden but undeductible disbursements of a writer's life.

Flaubert is celebrated as a writer dedicated to research. But what we mean by "research" varies greatly from novelist to novelist. At the simple level of the popular novel there are diligent writers who find out everything they can about a subject—banking, say, or airports or the motor industry—and put this into their work, often in barely assimilable chunks, as proof that they know what they're talking about. More sophisticated novelists pile up research like a compost heap, but then leave it alone, let it sink down, acquire heat, and degrade usefully into fertilizing elements. Thus at the moment of note-taking a novelist may often have no idea how useful his scribble might prove. A good example of this is found in *Carnet* 19, where Flaubert makes three successive notes concerning women of flexible virtue. The first is about Mlle X., former chambermaid of a young *lorette* (a *lorette* being a woman half-way between a *grisette* and a *femme entretenue* on the closely calibrated French sexual scale), who set up next door to her former mistress. Gentlemen leaving the *lorette* would routinely call on the ex-*femme-de-chambre* who, after performing her *exercices de fellation,* would enquire humbly, "Was that as good as Madame?" The second story is about an upwardly mobile bar girl in Algeria who celebrates her risen status by equipping herself with some "ancestors"; surrounded by secondhand pictures of fake relatives, she now plays salon hostess and receives officers she formerly pleasured for 10 francs a go. The third, and briefest note, is about a sixteen-year-old girl waiting in a *boudoir* to lose her virginity. She is served dinner, only eats the *confitures,* and then falls asleep on top of a pile of erotic engravings. Of the three, the first is a jolly story, complete in itself, but with something falsely neat about it—often the case in laddish anecdote; the second is a colourful social vignette; the third an unfinished moment (where is the man? did she lose her virginity? what happened to her afterwards?) which could be funny or sad or anything in between depending how it is told. The first two might be called "closed" stories, the third "open"; and it is a version of the third story (initially communicated to him by Suzanne Lagier) that Flaubert used in *L'Education sentimentale*.

"Research," therefore, isn't something finite and clear-cut which a writer does before "getting down to" the book. It's something wider and vaguer than that, a state of mind, a sort of dreaming which the writer goes in for even though to the outsider the research looks very little like dreaming and probably more like "real work" than anything the writer is subsequently seen to do. It comes in various forms. At its simplest, we see Flaubert posing himself straightforward questions for *L'Education sentimentale:* where in the environs of Paris is Wetnurse country? And what are the requirements for a funeral among the wealthy classes? The first question is answered quickly, a couple of pages later (Taverny, Saint-Leu, Pontoise, vallée de Montmorency); the second at more delighted length.

Research means jotting down possibly useful names (he likes the sound of Cahours as a place; Tardival and Vaudichon as surnames; relishes a prostitute who calls herself "Crucifix"). It means tramping the countryside until you find the right cliff for Bouvard and Pécuchet to be terrified by (he enlists Maupassant's help on this quest), and the correct *plateau stupide* on which to site their village. It means reading enormous quantities of books, and even—if we interpret correctly a couple of brief notes—relying on the loathed craft of photography ("which is never what one has actually seen"). It means doing whatever is necessary: when preparing himself to describe the beheading of Iaokanann in *Hérodias,* he writes to his niece, "I need to have a good look at a head that's recently been cut off." There isn't any evidence that he did; but he might have recalled those childhood walks with Oncle Parain and the bloodied cobbles.

Research isn't just "finding something good you can use." Flaubert is grandly dismissive of this approach: "Goncourt," he writes to George Sand in 1875, "is very happy when he picks up in the street a word he can then shove into a book." At the time

Flaubert makes this complaint about light-fingered literalism he is himself researching *Saint Julien L'Hospitalier* and ploughing through medieval cynegetic treatises, finding out what animals you hunt with, how you hunt with them, where such beasts come from, and so on. In the course of listing the birds with which Julien might hunt, Flaubert notes the Tartaret or Barbary Falcon: "*Le tartaret, taller and plumper than the peregrine falcon, comes from Barbary.*" This he knows, this he has established. But when he comes to write his story, he tries out various other provenances for the tartaret. The drafts show that he had it coming from Norway, from Iceland, from Scandinavia, before he decided on *un grand tartaret de Scythie*. In the end, euphony and association are allowed to win over documentary exactitude.

Realism versus Beauty? Realism or Beauty? Beauty attained through Realism? Flaubertians chase these formulae around their skulls. Flaubert, in his letter scorning Goncourt's skip-hunting type of research, states very clearly that "I regard technical and local details—the precise, historical side of things—as very much of secondary importance." If Goncourt found satisfaction in picking up a tasty word, Flaubert found it, by contrast, "when I have written a page which avoids assonance and repetition." This ought to be clear enough, and indeed Flaubert's denials of realistic intent are frequent: he sought only beauty. But writers' declarations of intent and writers' practices don't always match up. The novelist takes delivery of the researcher's *tartaret de Barbarie*, turns it around, tries out some Northern icy habitats for the bird, and comes down for *tartaret de Scythie*. But not *tartaret de Pont-l'Evêque*, after all. The researcher has given the novelist a body of information from which he can take off and glide and display his feathers; but there are limits to the range of manoeuvres possible. And when Flaubert was attacked for getting things wrong in *Salammbô*, first by Sainte-Beuve, and second, more famously, by Guillaume Froehner (assistant curator in the Department of Antiquities at the Louvre, who reviewed the novel in the *Revue Contemporaine*), he did not retreat behind the screen of Beauty. He didn't argue that he had changed things to avoid assonance or increase euphony. Quite the contrary: he defended himself stubbornly, systematically, violently, referring his assailants to all the sources and authorities he had consulted in the course of his researches.

Research for Flaubert is not preliminary but central; not a matter of "checking" but part of the writing process. On location for a bit of countryside he needs in *Bouvard et Pécuchet,* the novelist sometimes refers automatically to *ils:* his two protagonists are already wandering around in his research notes, as if preparing for their fictional life to come. And what of the Flaubert who can be found wandering around in these *Carnets de travail?* What do we learn about him? Biasi makes an audacious but finally convincing claim about the person we encounter here. In the novels, he suggests, we find the writer; in the letters we find the man; here in the *Carnets* we finally discover that famous hybrid, rare as a Scythian tartaret, *l'homme-plume* (the pen-man). It is a strange and reclusive bird, whose tail-feathers are ready-trimmed quills, and whose capacious gizzard grinds everything—life, books, whole countrysides—into literature.

Biasi admits that his edition is a risk (though it sounds more respectable and Pascalian in French: *"Cette édition est un pari"*). The *Carnets* aren't a novel, nor can they be read like an intimate journal; what they amount to is a catalogue of the writer's thought in its roughest, most nascent form. There is no doubt that it makes difficult reading, as we dodge in and out of text and commentary and try to remember the various editorial signs for such categories as "words added but subsequently crossed out." It does present us with a "third" Flaubert alongside the writer of the novels and the man of the letters, but this Number Three is only approachable after a thorough acquaintance with Numbers One and Two. Thus there are many points at which Flaubert is roughing out ideas and phrases not just for his novels but also for his *Correspondance.* For instance, his epigram "Honours dishonour, titles degrade, office-holding ossifies" (which he was clearly proud of, sending it to three different correspondents in the winter of 1878–9) is found here in its earliest form:

> *[Le grade dégrade]*
> *La Fonction [abbêtit] bêtifie-*
> *<Le grade dégrade.>*
> *Le Titre déshonore.*

Those familar with Flauberts One and Two will not find the *Carnets* full of new ideas, though there are some unfamiliar formulations. Flaubert is always savage and sound on the fallacy of Progress, but I hadn't before come across this theory from *Carnet* 15: "The dogma of Progress is a reaction to the dogma of the Fall." Also new was his epigram on Paris, which he tries out in two formulations: "No longer being able to love Paris is a sign of decadence; no longer being able to do without it is a sign of stupidity." Was Flaubert reworking Dr. Johnson?

But despite the occasional in-character surprises—appreciation for Joseph Wright of Derby, a paragraph on gloves, an account of a busy forty-first birthday, some treasured lubricities—the *Carnets de travail* are almost entirely what they sound like: working notes, often of the smallest and most circumstantial detail. (It comes, for instance, as a severe shock when in the middle of notes on the marital state in *L'Education sentimentale,* Flaubert suddenly jots down a Whole Theme: "Show how, since 1830, Sentimentalism has followed Politics and reproduced all its phases.") If this is the case, is the book of the narrowest interest, best left to close-text scholars needing to demonstrate the genesis of some particular phrase or incident in the novels; or is there any wider appeal? What of Biasi's wager?

It is a very long shot, but it does, surprisingly, come off. One of the many examples of ridiculous, patronizing, and pretentious observations that Flaubert gleefully collected for the "Copie" of *Bouvard et Pécuchet* comes from "Marcellus," or Louis-Marie-Auguste de Martin du Tyrac, a deputy under the Restoration, who in 1825 published *Conseils d'un ami à un jeune homme studieux*. This work includes the following advice: "As for the arts, it's a good idea to be familiar with them, to like them, even to cultivate them up to a certain point." How ironically that quote reads in among these *Carnets de travail*, whose page-by-page credo is that you do not cultivate art up to a certain point but way above and beyond that point; you live it, breathe it, inhabit it—the man and the pen become one, superglued together by a hyphen. And the process of research and writing, that back-to-back activity, comes to its closest fraternity, its most intense pitch, in *Bouvard et Pécuchet*, the ultimate work of *l'homme-plume*, his "indescribable posthumous novel," as Henry James termed it.

In *Carnet 2* (1859–78) Flaubert makes a note about Jean Magnon, a friend of Molière, who proposed to write a work in ten volumes—each consisting of 20,000 lines of verse—which would sum up human knowledge, and be so well devised and wrought that libraries would thereafter become mere useless ornaments. Biasi gives no suggested date for this entry, no indication of its possible use, and no annotation; but it seems plausible to suggest that Flaubert's interest in Magnon's project (which came to nothing, the writer being murdered on the Pont-Neuf in 1662) lay not far away in cerebral circuitry from the idea that turned into *Bouvard et Pécuchet*.

He describes this final project of his life in a letter to Mme Brainne in 1872, when he is deep in the study of medical and educational theory, and reckons he has two or three more years of research to go: "All this for the sole purpose of spitting out on my contemporaries the disgust they inspire in me. I shall finally proclaim my way of thinking, exhale my resentment, vomit my hatred, expectorate my bile, ejaculate my anger, sluice out my indignation . . ."

As a motive for a book, this doesn't sound good enough (though simply from the way Flaubert gets carried away with "exhale . . . vomit . . . expectorate . . ." we can imagine him laying it on for effect—just as in his letters about *Madame Bovary* he is contemptuous of Emma to a degree which, if let into the novel, would have been severely destructive). But it does indicate the curious fusion of rage and research, of driven encyclopaedianism, which fuels the novel. The two copyists would seek enlightenment and understanding in everything from gardening to history, and would everywhere be fooled and disappointed. Then they would return to their old trade of copying, but even here would be deceived, for their "Copie" (the never-completed Part Two of the book) would be a transcription of what they took to be the wisdom of the world, but which would appear to the reader as further proof of its folly.

It is a great idea for a novel: but could it ever have been a great novel? It sounds like something by Borges—and indeed, Turgenev told Flaubert to keep it swift and funny ("If you make it too heavy, if you make it too scholarly . . ."). His advice was disregarded; the monstrous project was already under way. There are 4,000 pages of notes and drafts for the book; the background reading-list is immense and immensely various—Comte's *Principes de la philosophie positive* on the same three-monthly roster as Visca's *Du vaginisme* and *Histoire d'un atome de carbone*. Notes originally taken for *Salammbô*, *L'Education sentimentale*, and *La Tentation de Saint-Antoine* are annexed and redeployed. Flaubert scours the countryside; he visits a model farm; he asks Maurice Sand for *souvenirs agronomiques*, especially of mistakes Sand might have made, and the reasons for those mistakes. He is out to prove something—again and again, chapter by chapter.

Nor, with *Bouvard et Pécuchet*, does he stop researching when he starts writing; the book becomes a rhythmic *va-et-vient* as each digested subject is processed into a chapter. What becomes clear in a quite unexpected and poignant way as you read the *Carnets de travail* is how Flaubert in his final novel created an enormous, weighty, complicated machine, which could be operated solely by pedal power. The cockpit only has room for one, the seat is moulded to his rotund form, and there he sits pedalling furiously, sweating profusely, knowing that only he can get the damn thing off the ground. When we read a writer's letters complaining about the tyranny of his work we may sometimes be sceptical (Flaubert often pleads commitment to Emma Bovary as a means of keeping Louise Colet away); but there is something transparently undeceptive and oddly moving as we follow self-inflicted agonies of composition: page after page of seemingly arid notes, lists of books read, idiocies identified and work still to do. By the end of the *Carnets* the daily reality of *l'homme-plume* has become thunderously present, and M. Biasi has won his wager.

Flaubert told Mme Roger des Genettes that he must be mad (*"fou et triplement phrénétique"*) to take on *Bouvard et Pécuchet*. He also said that his secret plan with Part Two of the novel, the "Copie," was to stun the reader into madness: *"ahurir tellement le lecteur qu'il en devienne fou."* The crazy doggedness of the novelist invites, and demands, an answering crazy doggedness in the reader (sometimes the dupes Bouvard and Pécuchet seem the only sane people around). In 1876, writing his *Trois contes* at the rate of fifteen or sixteen hours a day, he told Caroline that he feared one day he would simply explode like a shell and the bits of him would be found scattered over his desk. Four years later, strapped into the fearsome machine of *Bouvard et Pécuchet*, pedalling frantically away, he exploded. Conscientious literature costs money; and sometimes the price is higher still. It cost Flaubert his life.

(16)

Faithful Betrayal

Isabelle Huppert as Emma Bovary, "a victim who
does not behave as a victim"

Claude Chabrol lives in Gennes (twinned with Wincanton), a small town on the southern bank of the Loire, upstream from Angers. The river here is sluggish, and shallow enough for high-summer fishermen merely to punt their boats. A basic box-girder bridge, crossing the flow in two leaps, was the site of a famous rearguard action by cadets of the nearby Saumur military academy against the advancing Germans in 1940. On the other side of the Loire lies La Rosette, whose traditional small-town rivalry with Gennes can take strange forms. A few days before I met Chabrol, a woman from La Rosette decided to drown herself by jumping off the bridge. An emergency call came through to the *sapeurs pompiers* of La Rosette. "None of our business," they replied. "There isn't enough water on our side for her to drown herself." So the caller was obliged to hang up and dial the *pompiers* of Gennes. By the time they arrived the woman was dead.

Provincial France, now trundled through by British caravans rather than German tanks, has always specialized in tragedies of the comic grotesque, their private misery magnified by casual, uncaring public circumstances. Such was the case of Delphine Delamare, second wife of a health officer in the Normandy village of Ry. A pretty woman, by all accounts, with a taste for reading and interior decoration: her double curtains of yellow and black were much remarked upon. Bored and fanciful, she took first lovers and then poison. This down-page *fait divers* from the Véxin is such a natural Chabrol story that it's surprising he has taken so long to film *Madame Bovary;* the more so since the novel forms a key element in his own psychobiography. When his film project was announced to the press, he stated (without reflection) that he must have first encountered Flaubert at the age of fifteen or sixteen. But after shooting began, the fragrantly French truth came back to him. He had been thirteen at the time, growing up in the Creuse:

> I started reading *Madame Bovary* the day before I lost my virginity. It made a very strong impression. I was fascinated. I didn't understand everything, but I was under its spell. And then the next day, I had a rendezvous with the girl I was in love with. We went for a walk in the woods. We were wearing *sabots*. We had our walk, we kissed a lot, and then what had to happen happened . . . By the time I walked her home it was getting dark. We were holding hands, I was kissing her, but at the same time I was in a hurry to get home and carry on with my book. So I walked her back a little more quickly than was necessary, and as soon as I was alone I ran home as fast as I could. I had to go back through the wood, it was dark, and as I ran I lost one of my *sabots*. It was too dark to find it, and I had to hop my way home, with only one thing on my mind: getting back to my book.

This (distinctly filmic) reminiscence suggests a replacement for the dinner-table question of "Where were you when Kennedy / John Lennon / the Pope was shot?" Ask instead, "What were you reading when you lost your virginity?"

Chabrol is now in his early sixties, married to Aurore, scriptgirl on *Madame Bovary* as she had been on *Les Biches* in 1967, when they first met. The star of that film was Chabrol's second wife, Stéphane Audran, whom Aurore with steely persistence refers to simply as *"l'Autre."* "Three wives," she comments with a mocking shake of the head, "and always the same wedding-ring." Her husband lifts his hand and gazes at the gold band with fake mournfulness, as if it were the only reliable chum in the whole puzzling business. He is a humorous and affable man, palissaded behind an oversize pipe and tinted glasses. Stocky and sedentary, he dislikes travel and revels in junk TV. When I arrive at the house in Gennes at four o'clock on a hot afternoon, I am unable to rouse anyone; so I enter by the open kitchen door and prowl the cool and elegant interior like a Chabrol murderer. Finally, I hear conversation, knock, enter, and see two heads swivel from the sofa in a darkened room. "What are you watching?" "Oh, des âneries," replies Aurore happily—"rubbish." Chabrol is addicted to *Family Feud*, and a great fan of *Le Juste prix*, the French version of *The Price Is Right*. This is broadcast late on Sunday mornings, which means, Aurore uncomplainingly explains, that they can only accept lunch invitations within a radius of fifteen or twenty kilometres. The site-specific Chabrol seems benignly content with this arrangement. Between him and the television, on a large and beautiful oak-parquet table, is his smoking equipment, laid out like the kit of a military surgeon on campaign: a dozen or so very fat pipes, all the requisite tobacco, matches, lighters, plus a bottle of *Antésite*, a patent medicine he swigs to counter drying-out of the tubes.

Chabrol freely admits that his output, while prolific and often swift—he made a German TV version of Goethe's *Elective Affinities* in twenty-six days—has been variable in quality. "I think on the whole I prefer the films which I like and which did badly to the films I made which I dislike and which did well." "Are there any," I asked, "which you don't like and which also did badly?" "Oh, that happens. For a long time I thought I had made the worst film in the history of the cinema. *Folies bourgeoises*. Dreadful. But then I saw Joshua Logan's *Fanny*, an American adaptation of Pagnol, with Charles Boyer, Horst Buchholz, Maurice Chevalier, and Leslie Caron. Then I knew I had not made the worst film in the world."

Madame Bovary, of which Chabrol is properly proud, was filmed at Lyons-la-Forêt, a spruce little town in the Eure bristling with antique-dealers and guard-dog notices. There is a certain misconceived rivalry between Lyons-la-Forêt and Ry as to which was the "real" Yonville of Flaubert's novel. Chabrol favoured Lyons, partly on grounds of topographical plausibility (which is contestable) and partly because of the shared *yon* of each name

(though you could make an equal case for *Ry* being the end of
Bovary). "I got myself hated by the people of Ry," he says. "The
only part I kept of Ry was the church." The rivalry seems misconceived for two reasons: first, because the only "real" Yonville is the
one Flaubert put into *Madame Bovary;* and second, given that the
village is portrayed as such a steaming compost-heap of bores,
prudes, hypocrites, charlatans, and know-nothings, why should
anywhere want to claim itself as the original? But they do, Lyons-
la-Forêt rather more smugly and successfully: it declines any overt
boast, while knowing that it has the prettier face, and that its cine-
geneity has landed both Renoir and Chabrol. Ry is more strident in
its claims, not least because they are stronger. It is indeed just the
sort of undistinguished one-street village which Flaubert had
damningly in mind. In the churchyard there is a memorial tablet
from the Fédération Nationale des Ecrivains de France to Delphine Couturier (later Delamare), without whom indeed. As you
descend from the church you are heftily nudged by La Rôtisserie
Bovary, Le Grenier Bovary (antiques), Vidéo Bovary, and Le
Jardin d'Emma (flowers). (There is even a shop with the depress-
ingly whimsical name of Rêve Ry.) The point is thoroughly made
by the time you reach the village's main tourist attraction, the
Museum of Automata, a collection of 500 moving models, 300 of
which, on the ground floor, recreate scenes from *Madame Bovary.*
The figures are a few inches high and oscillate mechanically to
background music. See everyone sway, sway together at Emma's
wedding! See Emma dancing at the ball! See Binet coming out of
his duck-barrel! See Hippolyte having his leg sawn off! See Emma
ripping off her clothes with Léon! It is all innocently naff and dangerously hilarious, perhaps the only sort of "illustration" of his
novel that Flaubert, with a grim twinkle, might have blessed. In the
same exhibition space you can examine a lifesize reconstruction of
Homais's *pharmacie*—in fact, the *Pharmacie Jouanne Fils*—and two
coachlamps which once belonged to Louis Campion, the supposed
original of Rodolphe Boulanger. These souvenirs produce a curious effect. It is one thing to linger over buffed or frayed memora-

bilia once touched by the living hand of a great writer or artist, another to gawp at personalia which have been wrested from their original owners by the power of a work of art. Are these really Louis Campion's coachlamps? Not any more. Genius has effected their legal assignment to Rodolphe Boulanger—or Rodolphe, as his reader-friends know him. And so you stare at a real item that once belonged to an imaginary character.

According to Chabrol, the inhabitants of Lyons-la-Forêt were at first all Norman and mistrustful about the film, but are now not just reconciled but almost grateful. Chabrol's crew "improved" the village square with a fake fountain; liking it, the municipality commissioned a genuine working replica for the long term. Similarly, most people in Lyons were happy to have false fronts attached to their houses and shops. There was only one recusant, an estate agent in the main square. So whenever a wide shot was required, a wagon piled high with hay would be conveniently parked to block out modern commerce. Perhaps the estate agent disapproved of the book. When Stephen Frears was making *Les Liaisons dangereuses* his location scout came across the perfect château on the borders of Brittany and the Vendée. Praise was offered, negotiations entered into, times and prices discussed, agreement reached. At the last minute, the owner enquired the name of the film. The title of Laclos's novel was uttered. *"Pas de ces cochonneries sous mon toit"* ("None of that filth beneath *my* roof"), replied the owner, and chased the money away.

The story of Emma Bovary promises cinemagoers, if not exactly *cochonneries*, at least the life and death of a transgressive woman. MGM advertised their 1949 Vincente Minnelli production with the slogan: "Whatever it is that French women have, Madame Bovary has more of it!" Stars drawn to the role have included Lila Lee, Pola Negri, Jennifer Jones, and now Isabelle Huppert. There have been American, German, Argentinian, Polish, Portuguese, Russian, and Indian Emmas. The first French Emma was Valentine Tessier in Jean Renoir's 1933 version. "Half swan, half goose," was Pauline Kael's unflattering description of her performance.

Certainly she was too old for the part (being in her mid-forties); worse, her style of acting was too old as well, being part Comédie Française and part tie-me-to-the-track silent-screen exaggeration. As Charles, Pierre Renoir (Jean's brother) managed the realist mode more convincingly, but was hampered by being made up to look like Flaubert himself. This produces the eerie effect of an author walking through a transmogrification of his own work, wondering what they've done to it. Apart from Hippolyte's operation and Emma's death, there's a genteel and strangely underpowered feel to the whole enterprise; Milhaud's perky music sounds appropriate, which it shouldn't.

Before the film's release, an hour was hacked from its original three; though you can't imagine a director's cut being necessarily better—merely longer. In *My Life and My Films* Renoir pointedly makes no mention of the final product, choosing instead to describe a game called "lefoutro" (etymology: from *foutre*, to fuck) which director and stars played over convivial dinners at Lyons-la-Forêt:

> A napkin folded in the shape of the male organ was placed in the middle of the dinner-table, and the rule was that it must be studiously ignored. Anyone who showed the slightest sign of being distracted by it was rapped three times over the knuckles with "lefoutro" while the following sentence was pronounced: "I saw you making advances to your neighbour. You insulted Monsieur Lefoutro. You are hereby punished and your fault is pardoned." The guilty person could protest—"How could I have insulted Monsieur Lefoutro when I was busy cutting up my chicken?" In this case a vote was taken and the penalty doubled if the sentence was confirmed. Harmless games of this kind did more to prepare us for the next day's work than tedious discourses.

A decade later, Renoir tried to set up a Hollywood remake. His letter of 8 June 1946 to the producer Robert Hakim at RKO shows a hopeful director traducing the book (and the novelist's intentions) in order to give the project contemporary relevance and morality:

> The refusal to face facts and look at life from the realistic stand-point is quite a common failing among the young girls of today. And in America particularly, if so many women jump from one divorce into another, and end by living an extremely unhappy life, it is really because, like Emma Bovary, they waste their time hunting for an impossible ideal man . . . I want to show . . . that if her [Emma's] life had been built on sounder principles, she would have been perfectly happy with her husband.

Renoir's proposal came to nothing, and it was MGM, three years later, who released the only Hollywood version of the novel. The eighteen-year-old François Truffaut saw it the following year, and pronounced it "MIND-BOGGLING!"—which is unlikely to be a compliment. Truffaut turns out to have been the silent missing link in the chain of descent from Renoir to Chabrol. In 1960, after the success of *Les 400 Coups,* Jeanne Moreau asked him to direct her in a *Madame Bovary* she also intended to produce. Truffaut turned her down. As he wrote to Renoir, "Knowing all your films almost by heart, I would not be able to stop myself from copying entire scenes, even unconsciously." Instead, he explained, "I have another project with Jeanne . . . It's called *Jules et Jim.*" Moreau next approached Chabrol, who also declined; she had, as he tact-fully put it to me, "certain ideas" about the role.

Three decades later, Chabrol found his Emma in Isabelle Hup-pert. She is a long way from Valentine Tessier, and just as far from Jennifer Jones. Where other actresses offer us a sort of pouty bore-dom which yet seeks to flirt with the audience, Huppert presents severity, anger, and an irritation raised to the condition of nausea. She gives Emma a lucid awareness of her own condition: "She is a victim who does not behave like a victim." Huppert has a capacity to empty her face of expression in a way which both alarms and seduces; like Charles, we blunderingly want to make things right for her. And this harshness and frustration are in place most of the way: she has the control and seeming lack of vanity to hold back her moments of beauty to match those rare times (with Rodolphe and Léon, never with Charles) when the catching of happiness seems possible.

I asked Chabrol how he obtained this, and other carefully authentic performances (only Lheureux is a comic cut too far). He is deliberately unmystifying. "First, there is the matter of selection. I choose Flaubertians, so they won't want to change things, so they can express themselves without any *trouvailles de comédien*. I explain that my idea is to be as faithful as possible to Flaubert. They reread the book at the same time as the scenario. Isabelle claims she hadn't read *Madame Bovary* before making the film, but I remember her reading it on the set of *Violette Nozière* . . ." But how does he create their performances with them? "I work with actors I know, so I can feel when they're not happy. I talk to them before—if they go wrong I have dinner with them and then it goes all right the next day." So what sort of things do they discuss? "Well, Isabelle thinks that one of her profiles is better than the other—I never know which. She was worried that fidelity to Flaubert might conflict with her better side. So I let her have her good profile. The thing about actors is that they must be free yet protected. I never understand those who direct in terms of hours and minutes. I only show the actors the general direction, I give them a pointer. Then occasionally I make small but precise suggestions." For instance? "Well, I might tell Isabelle to open the window more slowly."

It sounds a hands-off technique of remarkable tact. It also sounds too good to be true. Jean-François Balmer, who played Charles, gave it a different slant. "He is someone who directs a very great deal, although when you see him on the set he never says a word, either positive or negative. He just lets the actor get on with it, stew in his own juice. But I think that he's very subtle and very controlling, because the way in which he places the camera, the way in which he chooses the focus, obliges you to be his prisoner, to be within the frame he chooses. So in fact you have very little latitude. He catches you in a pincer movement. An agreeable one, but a pincer movement all the same."

Chabrol's film is without argument the most faithful adaptation so far, a work of intense devotion to the text. Paradoxically, this merely emphasizes his disobedience. Every Flaubertiste knows that the novelist forbade illustration of his work; worse, he actively prohibited—from the very first year of publication—any theatrical version of *Madame Bovary*. Greater fidelity therefore presumes greater disloyalty. Chabrol's self-justification goes like this. First, Flaubert had a cinematic way of writing, both in preliminary composition—visualizing scenes in detail before writing them down—and in his annotations of movement: "The director's requirements are already integrated into the text." Second, while the theatre is confined to a fixed point of view—that of the spectator— film operates in "a game between subjectivity and distance"; this is an exact parallel of Flaubert's prose technique, which eases fluidly between objective description and *style indirect libre*. Third, Chabrol is usefully persuaded that had Flaubert lived a century later, he would have wanted to write and direct films; thus Chabrol can consider himself as Flaubert's "technical adviser" on the project. And finally, "There is betrayal only if I invent or depart from the novel."

Chabrol's beat-by-beat fidelity to the novel is probably unprecedented in the history of cinema. For example, he established an inventory of all the noises mentioned by Flaubert—the bird-calls, buzzing wasps, bleats, and baahs—to use as a basis for the sound-track. So there is no noise in his film which is not in the book. I was surprised that the sun always seemed to be shining— Normandy is, after all, one of the most pluviose provinces of France—and wondered if this was simple meteorological luck. Chabrol courteously directed me back to the text: "It rains very little. There is a storm signalled at the moment when Charles and Emma set off for Yonville. The characters often refer to heat, and to morning mist. Perhaps it rained in Flaubert's head." But not in his book, so not in the film. Nor were the reasons partly economic, as I had also suspected: "We could easily have hired the *sapeurs pompiers*." As long as they didn't try getting them from La Rosette.

When I saw the film, I thought I picked up two moments of Chabrolian invention, even if neither seemed much of a betrayal. Isabelle Huppert shows us her tongue on only two occasions—the first time, very early on, when she licks out the bottom of a wineglass as a coarse come-on to Charles, and the second, right at the end, when the tongue is burgundy with blood and she is dying. This subtle linking of eroticism and death was, it turned out, in the novel all along (though more strongly accentuated by being made visual). The other was a tiny moment as Charles and Emma are leaving their wedding feast: Charles, bumbling along beside his bride, manages to drop his hat and then awkwardly pick it up. Apart from being in character, this also seemed to predict the probable maladroitness of the wedding night. Pressed, Chabrol admits to not exactly an invention but rather a *trouvaille*. "We did the scene three or four times. In only one of them Charles dropped his hat. It was the best take. But let's call it a *trouvaille* that comes from Flaubert."

The problem with film is that it must always find, and state, at a basic level; it cannot not be specific. Flaubert builds up Emma's physical presence in the novel with a kind of delicate *fétichisme*, in allusions to her hair, the tips of her fingers, her shoes, touching and tickling her extremities like a boy whipping a top to get it spinning. Chabrol has to show us Huppert complete, from her first appearance. There are also things the writer sees, but forbears to mention. In a letter to Taine a decade after the novel was published, Flaubert explained how he might picture to himself an entire room in which the action was taking place, with all its furnishings, and yet never mention such surroundings in his text. "There are many details that I don't write down; for instance, in my own mind, Homais is lightly marked with smallpox." What do you do about something like that? Chabrol says that you use only what is in the novel, not what is in the extraneous material. (You can also blur matters by giving Homais a beard.)

Even so, Chabrol did go back to Flaubert's original scenarios. These are succinct summaries, often robustly expressed, of key actions or attitudes; they are not unlike a screenwriter's jottings. It was here, for instance, that Chabrol found guidance on the film's sexual tone. The novel makes the point that in Emma's relationship with Léon, he is more her mistress than she his. The scenario puts it more brutally: *"La garce le chevauche"*—the bitch bestrides him—an annotation Chabrol follows literally when the couple get to bed. On the other hand, he understandably jibbed at some of Flaubert's earthier indicators, like the description of Emma after one of her encounters with Rodolphe: "She came back from the garden with her hair full of spunk."

If Chabrol's film marks the high point of fidelity in treating the original text, with Flaubertistes straining to identify this or that minor invention, Vincente Minnelli's 1949 version seems free-associative by comparison. Is there a single line of original dialogue, a single line of authorial prose, which makes it through to the final cut? The film opens with Flaubert's trial: the prosecuting counsel demands a conviction while banging the rail in front of him with a bound copy of *Madame Bovary*. Pedants may immediately mock: there could have been no bound copy of the novel at the trial, since the supposed outrage to public morals had been provoked by serialization in the *Revue de Paris*. James Mason, as Flaubert, then addresses the court in reply—something the novelist was far too canny to do in reality—offering a defence of the book which, while plausible to modern ears, was far from that presented by his advocate in 1857.

Such minor adjustments—and major restructuring—are typical, guiltfree, and, in a way, blameless. A property is homogenized by a production process into an entertainment whose psychology must be plausible to its makers and comprehensible to its customers. Or, to put it in Chabrol's words, "It's a Western." And as such, seriously and properly made. Thus the ball scene is spectacular; Emma is the whirling belle, the cynosure, and Charles the drunken dolt who spoils her fun and gets humiliated; when Emma seems about to faint, servants are sent with chairs to break some windows. The novel's point, of course, is that it was all much more ordinary than this: what glowed in Emma's anticipation, experience, and memory was mere jolly routine to the other party-goers, who scarcely noticed the unimportant doctor's unimportant wife. Similarly, when Rodolphe ducks out of running away with Emma, it looks well and Hollywood to have her standing with packed trunks outside Homais's pharmacy while the coach thunders heartbreakingly past; but Rodolphe's betrayal was never so grand. Like a true, authentic coward, he merely slipped away. Such differences between film and book unwittingly endorse one of the novel's greatest lines. When Emma goes to see *Lucia di Lammermoor* in Rouen, she guilelessly compares opera's emotions and lifestyle with her own. "And now she knew the paltriness of the passions that art exaggerates." Minnelli's film, in this respect, is operatic.

Irritation at such "betrayal" of the book is short-lived and pointless. It's more interesting to compare what Hollywood presents as human motivation with what Flaubert faultlessly observed to be the case. Hollywood generally prefers the cause-and-effect of human behaviour to be a lucid unit: if *a*, then *b*. What provokes Emma's dissatisfaction and boredom? Reading all those Romantic novels; nothing more, nothing less. In this simplification, MGM revealingly puts itself on exactly the same level as Charles and his mother, who both try to stop Emma reading such fiction; the elder Mme Bovary argues that one has the right to alert the police if a bookseller persists in his trade as a poisoner. More creative is the adjustment Minnelli makes with the operation on Hippolyte's clubfoot. The problem is how to retain sympathy for Charles: if, as in the novel, he botches the operation so badly that the little fellow's leg has to come off, won't this terminally disenchant popcorn-munchers who place their faith in the medical profession? The solution is as follows: at the last minute Charles declines to operate on Hippolyte, pleading lack of experience. For this honourable decision he is mocked by the assembled village, peering in at the apothecary's window. Such unfair, public scorn helps us retain sympathy for Charles. However—if *a*, then *b*—because Charles has failed to become a famous (and potentially rich) person by performing the operation, Emma goes off for the first time with Rodolphe. This, in turn, helps retain sympathy for Emma: everyone can understand how you might be driven to a bit on the side if your husband turns out to be a low-achieving wimp. While Flaubert and Chabrol follow the more brutal and complex realities of human behaviour, Hollywood worries about sympathy rather than truth.

But fidelity has a downside too. Once you realize that little is being invented, then (presuming you know the book), you also realize that little, except perhaps the acting, is going to surprise you. Oh, you feel, well if we're here in the novel now, then we've got about five minutes on that bit, ten on the next, then such-and-such happens, and so on. Furthermore, prose narrative and film narrative inevitably pull against one another. One of the novel's climactic moments, still shocking to read, comes when Emma and Léon fuck in the closed cab as it careers around the streets of Rouen. It is a key moment in Emma's degradation, a vortex of lust, desperation, and snobbery ("They do it like this in Paris" is Léon's seducing phrase). The scene lasts a long time in the book, even if it occupies only a page of prose, and its effect is the more powerful because Flaubert never goes inside the cab but lets us deduce events by annotating the vehicle's route, its changing destination and period of hire; also by evidencing, at one point, the remnants of a torn-up letter being thrown from the window. In Chabrol's film— the director admits it—this scene doesn't work (it doesn't work for Renoir either). It can't be long enough, and it somehow can't be shocking ("Oh, now they're doing it in a cab instead of in a bed," you think). And because film always pulls towards the specific, Chabrol feels obliged to show us a tangle of Emma and Léon inside the cab, just to confirm that they aren't playing Scrabble. If there are moments when cinematic specificity enhances—for instance, in the goriness of the doctoring—mainly the effect of the medium is to iron out the book, to flatten its rhythms.

French Flaubertistes generally applauded Chabrol's film; French film critics had their doubts. "Too academic," some said, blaming the very fastidiousness others praised. "They accept fidelity in minor works," Chabrol muses. "Hitchcock was very faithful to *Rebecca*—no one denounced him for his fidelity. Besides, I always believed that cinema and literature were going in the same direction, were companions." This may be true in the widest sense, but Chabrol's film, by its very scrupulousness, forces the question of Book Into Film. What do we want of it, what is it for, whom is it for? Though cinema has been raiding literature high and low for an entire century, there's still unease about the collaboration, or exploitation. A Shakespeare play may become a Verdi opera without disturbing the theatrical or operatic communities (perhaps in part because Shakespeare was himself intensely parasitical on other sources). But cinephiles tend to feel that a book-based film is less authentic, less purely a film, whereas the book-devoted are wary of . . . what? Vulgarization, simplification, loss of subtlety, for a start; loss of control over how you as reader recreate the characters and action; loss of the experience happening inside you, and in your own time of choosing, rather than out there, publicly, for a period of time imposed by someone else. Is the film an easy point of access for those daunted by a Classic Novel, or a way of avoiding it altogether? And for those who know the book, is the film a parallel experience, an extension, or an alternative? I used to suspect filmic infidelity, and would snort at anachronisms, misquotations, non-quotations, hair-colour changes, and so on. The director's principal task, I assumed, was to protect the integrity of the book against the producer's and money-men's instinctive desire to coarsen and banalize. Now I am much less sure. In part, this comes from the experience of having a couple of my own novels turned into films. One was made by the French director Marion Vernoux. I kept away from the process and only met her—appropriately enough, aboard a cross-channel ferry—half an hour after shooting had finished. The first thing I found myself saying was, "I hope you have betrayed me." "Of course," she replied, with a complicit smile. Neither of us exactly meant it, though we knew what we meant—and what the other meant—all the same.

Chabrol maintains that if Flaubert had lived in the age of cinematography, he might well have made films. This is true: he did, after all, write for the theatre. But if so, he wouldn't have made *Madame Bovary*. Not just in the sense that he wouldn't have adapted it from its prose form; but in the wider sense that were he to decide on recounting the story of Delphine Delamare with story-board and lens rather than quill pen, he would from the very start necessarily imagine it differently. He would think about the external eye rather than the internal; he would know that screen dialogue doesn't work like page dialogue; he would imagine the impersonating actor alongside the character; he would think differently about time, and light. So is this what the loyal film maker should do? Are faithful adaptations inherently unfaithful; indeed, the more faithful, the more unfaithful?

At the end of my visit to Chabrol, we sit over breakfast, the scented Anjou air lightly polluted by a miasma of burnt toast. The morning radio is preparing the French for their annual lemming dash to beach, second home, or up-country *pension*. A bland voice reports the findings of a survey into national expectations in the matter of holiday romance. Fifty per cent of French women apparently hope that the amorous encounter will extend beyond the duration of the holiday. By contrast, only fifteen per cent of French men want such affairs to continue after bag-packing time. Chabrol shrugs. "They need a *survey* to tell us that?" Another summer, another heartbreak. Today's Emmas murmuring, "I have a lover." Today's Rodolphes thinking, "She's not bad, the doctor's wife, I think I'll have her." They should read the novel before their holidays. Or at least see one of the films.

Justin: A Small Major Character

J.B. at the tomb of G.F., Rouen, 1983

Imagine you're sitting down to write a novel of village life—a nineteenth-century novel, when villages were more enclosed and self-sufficient. You have your story—an old one you heard some years before, a dramatic, even melodramatic tale of the wife of a health officer, who takes one lover, then a second, who is filled with romantic fantasies, who is extravagant and scandalous, and who finally poisons herself. All this takes place in a village; therefore you have villagers. The heroine is of a certain social standing; therefore she has a servant. Pretty soon you find that mere fidelity to truth has dealt you a deck of inevitable characters: squire, clergyman, groom, shopkeeper, gravedigger, and so on. You have an inn, therefore you have an innkeeper; your characters ride horses, therefore a blacksmith must exist somewhere. You are stuck with most of these characters—or at least, stuck with their theoretical existence, even if you choose to deny them real fictional existence. Some novelists might find the inevitability and the discipline attractive; though imagine having to invent a new innkeeper every time you wrote PAGE ONE at the top of a sheet of paper. In this respect the modern novelist seems to have the advantage. You think you need the present-day equivalent of a blacksmith, that's to say a garage mechanic, in your story? Simple: give your hero or heroine the sort of car that's expected to break down. You don't need a garage mechanic? Give him or her a nice reliable Japanese motor.

So you have your main story, and you have your surrounding minor characters, some pre-dealt, some personally picked. What, then, are these minor characters for? What are they up to? At a basic level, they are facilitators, they are there to make life go more smoothly for the major characters: they run errands, they run shops, they run baths; they steal dogs if you want your heroine to cry, they rescue dogs if you want your heroine to smile. They are there for plausibility, for colour, for decoration, for incidental humour, for a change of tone, for a change of focus.

And beyond this? Beyond this lies a point of divide among novelists. Do you want your minor characters just to "be themselves," or do you want them to bear weight, to be "significant"? Having minor characters who are "significant," emblematic or symbolic, is a high-risk strategy: the risk is that of over-organization, also of giving the reader too close an awareness of the author's guiding hand. Edith Wharton admired and loved Henry James, but even she had difficulty with what she saw as the airlessness and over-planning of the later work. She thought he had become too theoretical, too geometrical, and that in the process he risked losing what she tellingly described in her autobiography as the "irregular and irrelevant movements of life."

Here she identifies one of the novelist's central preoccupations, and one which can often be seen working itself out among the minor characters. Life has its irregular and irrelevant movements, granted. But a novel is not life, or even an equally weighted representation of life. If you reproduced all life's irregular and irrelevant movements, you would have a novel boring and picaresque to the point of unreadability. This is the fundamental battle between structure and vivacity, which novelists settle according to their temperaments and their theories.

In terms of demonstrating the irregularity of life through his minor characters, the archetypal novelist is Dickens: profligate, virtuosic, carefree, careless. Virginia Woolf, writing about *David Copperfield*, described his unmatched ability to conjure up secondary figures almost without thought or effort. "Dickens made his books blaze up not by tightening the plot or sharpening the wit, but by throwing another handful of people on the fire. The interest flags, and he creates Miss Mowcher, completely alive, equipped in every detail as if she were to play a great part in the story, whereas, once the dull stretch of road is passed, by her help, she disappears." This cavalier way with minor characters no doubt sprang mainly from the nature of Dickens's genius; but it must have been accentuated by a technical aspect, the fact that he wrote for serial publication. Imagine that you are on the eighth of twenty monthly episodes; the previous seven are published, unalterable, tyrannical; and however far you plan ahead, the last ten or so episodes are fluid in your mind—in such circumstances even the greatest genius is likely to concentrate on the major characters and use the lesser ones as Polyfilla, as one-offs, or as rather loosely controlled running gags. Imagine a painter being given a large canvas, told to start painting rightwards from the left, and instructed to complete in its final varnished form exactly one-twentieth of the canvas each month, before moving on to the next one-twentieth. We should, I think, be amazed at any formal success the resultant picture might have. Henry James's judgement on the Victorian novel is well known: he called it "a treasure-house of detail but an indifferent whole."

Flaubert stands at the opposite end of the fictional spectrum to Dickens. He never sullied himself with journalism; he never performed his work in public; he never allowed his books to be illustrated; he published comparatively little; and, most importantly in the present context, he never allowed any part of a novel to appear before the whole was complete. The *Revue de Paris,* when it serialized *Madame Bovary,* was not dealing, as the British serializers of Dickens, Thackeray, Trollope, and Eliot were, with an author inventing against the clock. Flaubert's good fortune came partly from just that—a good fortune, or at least a helpful private income; but it mainly came from an artistic obduracy rare at that time. Dickens was a novelist who flung another handful of people on to the fire to make it blaze; Flaubert stacked his kindling with obsessive care so that the main blaze would come from the logs.

Of course, dividing characters into "major" and "minor" is a critical simplification. There are major, minor-major, major-minor, and minor characters (to propose another simplification). And within what we choose to call the minor characters there are quite different grades with quite different functions. There are those like Dr. Larivière who make a single, splendid cameo appearance: three pages of existence as a *deus ex machina* (except that modern gods do not save any more, and cannot even help; they merely judge, and move on). There are those, like Binet, who are as lavishly characterized as Larivière but whose appearances are intermittent and recurrent, and whose function is more indirect and enigmatic; Binet and his lathe are a sort of droning reminder of transgression in the novel, a moral tinnitus in Emma's ear. And then, at the bottom of the heap, both socially and—it seems—novelistically, there is a character like Justin, whose appearances are tiny and fleeting. Unlike Larivière or Binet, Justin is granted no character-description; it is easy for the reader to ignore him, just as his social superiors in Yonville do; he is only what happens to him. Yet what happens to him, in his disregardable moments of fictional existence, is crucial.

Justin is, primarily (and concludingly), the solution to a narrative problem Flaubert must have faced early in the writing of the novel. Emma is going to die at the end of the book: she is to be a suicide by arsenic poisoning. She could, no doubt, have died in other ways, by rope, gun, or knife; she could, given Flaubert's notorious loathing of the railways, have preceded Anna Karenina as an early track victim, had Flaubert not set his story just before the coming of railways. The fact that Emma's predecessor in life, Delphine Delamare, also took poison should make it less, rather than more, likely that Flaubert would choose the same method for doing in his own character.

But there is a particular appropriateness about arsenic poisoning, since it inflicts the worst torments on the body of a woman who has, in the course of the novel, used that body for scandalous and transgressing pleasure. (No authorial judgement is implied here, merely aesthetic balance.) But if Emma is to swallow arsenic, how is she to get it? She could go into Rouen and shop for it: too boring, and perhaps too difficult—there might be a poisons register to sign. Also, too calculated and time-consuming, since the plot at this point must move headlong, just as Emma herself does. Could she bribe, or perhaps blackmail, Homais? Possible, but unlikely given Homais's established character: she'd just end up with a moral earful. Flaubert's solution, and it is a brilliant one since it combines narrative economy with psychological complication, is to use Justin, and to use him in a particular way. When he leads Emma to the arsenic jar, it is the climax to his traditional minor-character function as domestic facilitator; but on the way there, his every act of facilitation turns out to be double-edged, quietly freighted, allusive.

Justin makes no more than a dozen appearances in the novel; he is such a wisp of a character that he only gets to speak on two occasions. He is, nevertheless, one of the novel's key indicators, the canary found with its feet in the air on the floor of the cage. To string his appearances together inevitably has the effect of making Flaubert's use of him seem more obvious and less delicate than it is; though it won't make it seem less brutal. *Madame Bovary* is a novel about corruption—moral, financial, social, sexual, even sartorial (in the dandification of the mourning Charles). Justin's story is one of almost unnoticeable and yet savage corruption: nowadays the social workers might have been called in.

Justin is the pharmacist's assistant, a distant relation of Homais, who takes him in out of charity and thereafter treats him with relentless lack of charity. The boy's age is never given, nor do we know what he looks like. However, we know that he is old enough to have started noticing that the world is divided into two sexes. He hangs about the Bovary household, initially attracted—at least according to Homais—by Emma's servant Félicité. This sentimental or pre-erotic inclination explains his presence on the day Rodolphe brings along one of his workers to be bled. This is the first encounter between Emma and her future lover; and it is also the first time Justin is seen in Emma's presence. He is ordered to hold the bowl while Charles wields the lancet. Blood spurts, the bowl trembles, Justin faints. Whereupon this happens:

> Madame Bovary began to loosen his cravat. There was a knot in the strings of his shirt; her fingers played softly with the boy's neck for a few minutes; then she moistened her batiste handkerchief with vinegar and dabbed his temples, blowing softly as she did so.

All very normal and housewifely, of course; yet Justin (though he is unaware of it) is virtually in Emma's arms, and she is beginning to undress him. The moment seems completely incidental: the main function of the scene is to bring Emma and Rodolphe together, to display Emma as capable and sexually attractive to Rodolphe, and to display Charles as a clumsy doltish fellow who deserves to be cuckolded. Yet Justin is there at this prime moment, and Justin is the one receiving the sub-erotic attention. Homais, who is also there, bawls out his apprentice for fainting. He does this in a manner which, while entirely consistent with his unsubtle nature, is also significantly out of proportion to the event itself. Justin must learn to behave as a man, because one day "you might have to give evidence in court, in a serious case: the magistrate might need your expert opinion." This is pompous hyperbole; at the same time, Homais unwittingly underlines the scene that has just finished. Its subtext could not be clearer: Blood, Sex, Crime.

From this moment, Justin's fate is bound up with that of Emma. At first, his role seems to be as a fleeting witness to transgression: his next appearance, for instance, occurs when Emma goes out riding with Rodolphe—the occasion on which they first become lovers. Justin slips out of the pharmacy to watch them go. Homais comes out after him, and like some pocket Polonius offers redundant advice to the departing riders: "*Un malheur arrive si vite! Prenez garde!* [etc.]." Polonius, we remember, was not always wrong.

By the time of his next appearance, however, Justin has moved from observer to complicit participant: he is Emma and Rodolphe's go-between, carrying letters from one to the other. There is no ponderous setting-up of this fact, no "Justin, I'll give you a couple of sous if you take this note, and I'm sure I can trust you to keep quiet," just the established fact that he is now her servant, and one whose silence can be relied upon. In a sense, of course, nothing has happened: a boy is taking on some extra errands, a boy who is, in any case, still apparently hanging around Félicité, for here he is in the Bovary kitchen watching her do the bleaching and ironing. What could be more innocent, more domestic, more casual? Except that Félicité just happens to be washing Emma's underwear, and so—in a reversal of that first scene—Justin now becomes acquainted with Emma's intimate garments. He gazes at her petticoats and knickers, runs his fingers over her crinoline, touches its fastenings. He asks Félicité what things are for, and she chases him away.

In parenthesis, the servant Félicité has her own story, both inside and outside the novel. Inside it, she suffers the contagious influence of her mistress, corrupted into indolence, sexuality, and crime. Outside it, she provides one of the great rebukes made by real life to imagined literature. Delphine Delamare killed herself in 1848; Emma died (in the first edition, anyway) in 1857; Flaubert himself in 1880. A quarter of a century later, Delphine Delamare's original servant was amazingly still alive and giving interviews. "Félicité," or rather Augustine Ménage, was then 79, and still had—or claimed—vivid recall of the original events. In 1905 she described the real-life poisoning of 1848 in some detail, and told the interviewer in conclusion: "Oh, it was all a great deal sadder than in the book!"

So Justin is already an intimate in Emma's household. He facilitates her adultery; he also helps cover it up, by cleaning the mud from her boots. This is a moment of particular complicity: first, he is destroying the evidence of Emma's early-morning tramps to Rodolphe's house by removing what Flaubert straightforwardly calls "the mud of her assignations"; second, Justin is presumably—though we are not given a description of his shoe-cleaning technique—placing his hands where Emma had placed her feet. Normal enough, of course; but there is a strong, some would say fetishistic element of podophilia in Flaubert, also in the novel, and here Justin is awarded his momentary share.

When Emma's affair with Rodolphe is terminated, she has a nervous collapse. Who is her regular visitor as she recovers? Justin. He comes with the Homais children and stands just inside the door, silently watching the convalescent:

> Often Madame Bovary would start to dress, as if he wasn't there. She would begin by taking out her comb, and shaking her head sharply; and when for the first time he saw the mass of black hair unroll down her back as far as her knees, it was, for the poor boy, like the sudden entry into something new and extraordinary, whose splendour terrified him.

By his constant, faithful attendance Justin suggests that, unlike Rodolphe, he will not forsake Emma; further, he is permitted that most intimate of male sights—of a woman letting down her hair—which would normally have been reserved for husband or lover. Once more, nothing has really happened: Emma does not even notice Justin. But on the other hand, his surrogacy as a lover has almost been achieved, and the prose points us to it with the phrase "sudden entry" *(l'entrée subite).*

With these few, tiny scenes, the sub-plot is primed and cocked, ready for Emma's second affair to fail, for her despair, her ruin, her suicide. Justin, for his part, is as potentially lost as any doomed lover. He is also as sex-crazed as any normal adolescent; Homais discovers him with a dirty book in his pocket. It has the pointed title of *Conjugal Love*. "And with pictures!" as the outraged pharmacist observes. Justin has also, we learn, asked Emma to take him into her service. Again, we are not given Justin's inner life, only a fleeting outer confirmation of what is already in place: a devotion, and a powerful sexual thrall, which sets up Justin's final and fatal participation in the plot. Emma, bent on suicide, demands from Justin the key to the laboratory, lies to him, overrules his protests, hustles him to what she seeks, and swallows a handful of arsenic. Naturally, we have eyes mainly for Emma at this time, so there are two aspects of Justin's story, rather than hers, which we might easily overlook.

The first is that though Emma is desperate, humiliated, ruined, and outcast, "She seemed to him extraordinarily beautiful, and as majestic as an apparition." At this climactic moment Flaubert—for the first and last time—inserts us directly into Justin's head. Briefly, we both see and hear as he does. And what does he hear? Emma speaking in a whisper, "in a gentle, melting voice." This is the *only* occasion in the novel when Emma speaks to Justin. This is a gauge of how brutal Justin's story is: he is in thrall to Emma, she never notices him, and his only use in her eyes is to enable her to kill herself. Imagine having that on your emotional record.

And the second aspect of this fatal scene is that it involves going upstairs. Emma leads, Justin follows, and they go upstairs together. In other words, the seduction is complete—that parallel, metaphorical, extended, unrealized, and often unnoticeable seduction, which reveals the fanatical care with which Flaubert composed his novel.

Justin has fulfilled his function. Will he be punished for his crime of aiding and abetting suicide, will magistrates need his expert opinion, as Homais predicted? It doesn't matter, because the real punishment, the real damage, lie elsewhere, and Flaubert wisely discards this legal side-issue. But he hasn't quite finished with Justin. At the lunch Homais gives for Dr. Larivière, there is a crafty—and crafted—repeat of that early image of Justin with the bowl of blood. This time he is holding a pile of plates. Homais wonders aloud where Emma might have got the arsenic. Justin begins to tremble, as before, and this time he drops the plates.

He is glimpsed three times more as Flaubert gives final shape to his novel. When Emma's funeral procession leaves the church,

Justin appears at the door of the pharmacy: that's to say, he is watching her go on her final journey from the same spot from which he watched her set off to begin her adventure with Rodolphe. Emma is buried; later that night, with the village dark and silent, Flaubert lists those awake and those asleep. Emma's two faithless lovers, Rodolphe and Léon, are both out for the count; her two faithful lovers are still awake—Charles in his bed, Justin at her graveside, his heart "overflowing with a grief that was as tender as the moon and as unfathomable as night." Finally, we learn, as if by afterthought, that Justin has run away from Yonville, run away to Rouen where he has become a grocer's boy. But this is much more than an afterthought: it's a reminder that Justin was a stranger to the village in the first place. He was taken in by Homais out of charity; and charity was the thing he failed to discover in Yonville. He arrives, he suffers, he flees: his time in Yonville is framed into an enclosed and traumatizing period.

One of the great leaps forward in opera was when recitative-and-aria gave way to through-composition. Something similar happened to the novel during the nineteenth century. It's instructive to read *Madame Bovary* side by side with *Middlemarch*. Both are novels of provincial life set back in time, one with the subtitle *Moeurs de province*, the other with the uncannily similar "A Study of Provincial Life." Both are written with the keen sense that, as Eliot tells us on the last page of *Middlemarch*, the heroic age is past; both are works of powerful psychological insight; both are, for want of a better phrase, great novels. But the surprise, looking back from this distance, is that *Madame Bovary* was published in 1856–7 and *Middlemarch* in 1870–1. In terms of fictional technique, Flaubert is far more sophisticated; *Middlemarch* reads like the novel of an earlier generation. Eliot holds our hand and directs our eye, and offers herself as a strong and opinionated authorial presence; Flaubert leaves us alone to find our own bleak way through his constructed universe. Eliot throws down her narrative in great blocks, side by side; Flaubert's narrative is through-composed.

There are many different (and conclusive) answers to the question, Why is *Madame Bovary* the first modern novel? One short way of answering is to say: Look at Justin. His is a tiny and unnoticed story as far as everyone in Yonville is concerned; yet one which, if we notice it, is shaped with as much care as any larger story in the novel. Justin's brief erotic tragedy goes as unnoticed in Yonville as Emma's erotic tragedy goes unnoticed in the wider world. He is an echo of her, that perfectly placed bit of kindling which makes Emma's story blaze the brighter. To change the metaphor: if *Madame Bovary* were a mansion, Justin would be the handle to the back door; but great architects have the design of door-furniture in mind even as they lay out the west wing.

Acknowledgements

Original versions of these pieces appeared as follows:

1 Richard Cobb: *New York Review of Books*, 12 August 1999.
2 Georges Brassens: *Picador 21* (Pan Books), 1993.
3 Truffaut: *New York Review of Books*, 11 October 1990.
4 Elizabeth David: *The New Yorker*, 21 September 1998.
5 Edith Wharton: Preface to *A Motor-Flight Through France* (Picador), 1995.
6 Tour de France: *The New Yorker*, 21/28 August 2000.
7 Simenon: *Literary Review*, April 1992.
8 Baudelaire: *New York Review of Books*, 20 November 1986.
   Courbet: *New York Review of Books*, 22 October 1992.
   Mallarmé: *New York Review of Books*, 9 November 1989.
9 Lottman: *London Review of Books*, 4 May 1989. Vargas Llosa: *New York Times Book Review*, 21 December 1986.
   Sartre: *London Review of Books*, 3/16 June 1982.
10 *Rage and Fire, a Life of Louise Colet*, by Francine du Plessix Gray, *New York Review of Books*, 26 May 1994.
11 Flaubert, *Correspondance III, 1859–1868* (Gallimard), *Times Literary Supplement*, 6 September 1991.
12 *Flaubert and Turgenev, A Friendship in Letters* (Athlone), *London Review of Books*, 23 January 1986.
13 *Flaubert-Sand: The Correspondence* (Knopf), *New York Review of Books*, 10 June 1993.
14 Flaubert, *Correspondance IV, 1869–1875* (Gallimard), *Times Literary Supplement*, 18 December 1998.

15   Flaubert, *Carnets de Travail* (Balland), *Times Literary Supplement*, 7/13 October 1988.
16   Chabrol: *Writers at the Movies,* edited by Jim Shepard, HarperCollins (US), 2000.
17   Justin: "The Process of Art," *Studies Offered to Alan Raitt* (Oxford), 1998.

Index

Greer, Germaine, 169
Guardian, The: joke, 89n
Guérot, Alfred, 50

Hamard, Caroline (later
    Commanville, later Franklin-
    Grout, Flaubert's niece), 155–6;
    and Flaubert's letters, 161–2; 185,
    186, 187; marriage, 188–91; a
    grandmother's betrayal, 189; 221,
    224, 226, 227, 230; attitude to
    Flaubert's manuscripts, 237–8;
    248
Hanem, Kuchuk, 170–1
Henley, W. E.: and French obscenity,
    20n
Herbert, Juliet, 142, 162, 187, 239n
Hodgkin, Howard, 46
Hodgkinson, Terence, 45
Hugo, Victor: "France's National
    Bore," 13; Baudelaire takes him
    for a ride, 107–8; awes Courbet,
    117; the Hugolian smoker, 126;
    hogs the rainbow, 133; supports
    Louise Colet, 163, 167, 172;
    Flaubert on *Les Misérables,* 184;
    192; charms Flaubert, 206
Huppert, Isabelle, 255, 257–60
Huysmans, Joris-Karl, 127–9, 132
Hysteria: cultivated by Baudelaire,
    104; admitted by Flaubert, 186,
    207

Infidelity: Gaullist, 13–14; Belgian,
    23; and journalists' wives, 27;
    cheerful, 28; complicated, 28; with
    actresses, 37; and Simenon, 97, 98;
    and Courbet, 118; and Mallarmé,
    122; and Emma Bovary, 261, 263,
    273–7

Isherwood, Christopher: sympathy
    for Jeanne Duval, 106
Itard, Dr.: Truffaut as, 37; Sartre as,
    151

Jacobs, Alphonse, 181, 193
James, Henry, 4, 59–70; love of
    motoring, 59; the cost of rich
    friends, 61–2; travels with Edith
    Wharton, 61–4; and Nohant, 62,
    76, 205; *A Little Tour in France,*
    63, 64, 67–9; finds the Pont du
    Gard "stupid," 67; boiled eggs,
    67; "glorious grub," 69; doesn't
    get to Croisset, 69; visits
    Meredith, 69–70; 246, 270, 271
Johnson, Samuel, xiv, 200, 245
Jones, Jennifer, 143, 255, 257
Jong, Erica: a contemporary Louise
    Colet?, 165
Jules et Jim, 38, 40, 257
Justin (in *Madame Bovary*), 272–9

Karr, Alphonse: caddish article,
    163–4; stabbed, 164, 173; 186;
    bamboo named after him, 164n;
    link between two great novels,
    164n; retires to grow flowers, 164n
Kavanagh, Pat, 3, 46
Kinsey, Alfred, 54
Koestler, Arthur, 121

Lacan, Jacques, 111
Laporte, Edmond, 162, 177, 226
Larkin, Philip: loses interest in
    people, 106; poem "Love," 226
Le Poittevin, Alfred, 175, 226
Lee, Hermione, xvi
leeks: Sartrean dispute over, 148
lefoutro, 256

Index

Mathilde, Princesse, 182, 185; gift of
 turnip seeds, 185; 188, 192, 205,
 213, 221–2, 225, 229, 230
Maupassant, Guy de, 62, 162;
 mistranslated, 176–8, 242
Mayflower: Triumph, xi–xiii
Melancholy: cure for, 211–12
Ménage, Augustine: life's rebuke to
 literature, 275
Menuhin, Yehudi, 21
Meredith, George, 69
Michelin Guide: quasi-religious
 status, xii; boasted longevity, 59;
 formula for eye-lotion, 62
Mignot, Papa, 156
Minnelli, Vincente, 255, 261–3
Misérables, Les: "infantile," 184; 192
Mistons, Les, 36, 38
mistral, 75
Moine, Claude: changes name, 18
Money: creates an instant film critic,
 42; Simenon's suitcase, 93;
 mocking repayment, 98;
 Baudelaire's winged bag of gold,
 105, 108; its priority in a marriage,
 188; the cost of conscientious
 literature, 240–1
Monroe, Marilyn, 173
Montaigne, 184, 191, 211
Mothers: male writers' implacable
 mothers, Simenon's, 95, 98–9;
 Baudelaire's, 103, 109–10;
 Flaubert's 189, 197, 218
Motoring, xi–xiii, 4, 59–70
Mots, Les, 148–50, 153
Mottet, Charly: clean, 81;
 unfulfilled, 89
Musset, Alfred de, 63, 139, 163; kiss-
 and-tell, 165–7; car named after
 him, 166n; unsafe in a cab, 167;

168, 172; a "sentimental
 hairdresser," 184

National Film Theatre: Godard's daft
 proposal, 42
newspapers: apprehension over
 buying one, xii; British tabloids
 fail to charm, xvii; behaviour of
 journalists' wives, 27; as an escape
 from Belgium, 95; fashion journalists, 129–30, 174; unfair treatment of poets, 130; high rates of
 pay in Russia, 197; "a school for
 stultification," 209; a vast irritant,
 222; Flaubert unsullied, 271
Nike: and Jean-Luc Godard, 42
Nohant, 62–3, 69, 205, 208, 214,
 217–18
nouvelle cuisine, 49, 53
nouvelle vague, 35–6, 38, 49
Nuit américaine, La, 35, 36, 37, 39, 40
nutmeg: an expensive, 55

Oliver, Hermia, 142, 161, 162, 187

Panhard: formidable eccentricity of,
 xiii; features in assassination, 10;
 Edith Wharton's husband buys
 one, 60; Henry James's silent
 presence in, 68
Pantani, Marco, 87, 89n
Paris, xix, 5, 6, 13, 61, 69, 95, 263
Pau: Henry James writes from, 61;
 Edith Wharton examines
 Pyrenees from, 66
Peasant: ultimate, 3–5; penultimate,
 4, 13n; glimpsed, 64; quotable, 76;
 stupid, 118; fake, 130; "wise," 213
pedicurist's: overcrowding at the, 174
Petrarch: climbs Mont Ventoux, 74, 76

washing machines: an excess of, 93

Waugh, Evelyn, 45, 47, 51, 54

Wharton, Edith, 5, 13, 59–70; love of motoring, 59–60, 166n; love of luxury, 161; Vehicle of Passion, 63; "trivial motorist," 64; wise tourist, 64–7; competitive with Henry James, 68; as bird of prey, 69; 75n; on life's irregular movements, 270

Woolf, Virginia: on Dickens, 270–1

Yobbery: third stage of civilisation, 209

Yonville, the "real," 253–4

zebras: les Deux, xix; the usual question, 104

Zola, Emile: double-edged compliment from Mallarmé, 124; initial disappointment with Flaubert, 140; estimates mourners at Flaubert's funeral, 142; 184, 199, 229

A Note on the Type

This book was set in Fournier, a typeface named for Pierre Simon Fournier, a celebrated type designer in eighteenth-century France. Fournier's type is considered transitional in that it drew its inspiration from the old style yet was ingeniously innovational, providing for an elegant yet legible appearance.

Composed by Creative Graphics,
Allentown, Pennsylvania
Printed and bound by R. R. Donnelley & Sons,
Harrisonburg, Virginia
Typography and binding design by
Dorothy S. Baker